Landscapes of
the Ethnic Economy

Landscapes of
the Ethnic Economy

Edited by
David H. Kaplan and Wei Li

ROWMAN & LITTLEFIELD PUBLISHERS, INC.
Lanham • Boulder • New York • Toronto • Plymouth, UK

ROWMAN & LITTLEFIELD PUBLISHERS, INC.

Published in the United States of America
by Rowman & Littlefield Publishers, Inc.
A wholly owned subsidiary of The Rowman & Littlefield Publishing Group, Inc.
4501 Forbes Boulevard, Suite 200, Lanham, Maryland 20706
www.rowmanlittlefield.com

Estover Road, Plymouth PL6 7PY, United Kingdom

British Library Cataloguing in Publication Information Available

Library of Congress Cataloging-in-Publication Data
Landscapes of the ethnic economy / edited by David H. Kaplan and Wei Li.
     p. cm.
   Includes bibliographical references and index.
   ISBN-13: 978-0-7425-2947-2 (cloth : alk. paper)
   ISBN-10: 0-7425-2947-9 (cloth : alk. paper)
   ISBN-13: 978-0-7425-2948-9 (pbk. : alk. paper)
   ISBN-10: 0-7425-2948-7 (pbk. : alk. paper)
   1. Ethnic neighborhoods—Case studies. 2. Ethnic neighborhoods—Economic
aspects—Case studies. 3. Minority business enterprises—Case studies. 4. Urban
geography—Case studies. I. Kaplan, David H., 1960- II. Li, Wei, 1957-
   HT215.L36 2006
   307.3'362—dc22
                                                              2006010648

Printed in the United States of America

♾^{TM} The paper used in this publication meets the minimum requirements of American
National Standard for Information Sciences—Permanence of Paper for Printed Library
Materials, ANSI/NISO Z39.48-1992.

Contents

Figures

Tables

x   *Tables*

Chapter One

Introduction: The Places of Ethnic Economies

David H. Kaplan and Wei Li

We are riding the crest of an immigration wave. For example, in the United States there was a net increase of 4.3 million new immigrants between 2000 and 2004 alone. Immigrants now count for about twelve percent of the total population, the highest in over eighty years (Camarota 2004). There is a greater diversity of immigrants as well, as people arrive from Latin America, all parts of Asia, and Africa, along with renewed immigration from eastern European countries. The impact on American society is profound, ranging from the restructuring of our major cities to the prospect that the United States will soon become a "minority-majority" society where members of various minority groups combine to constitute over half of the country's population. The revival of immigration does not exclusively belong to America, Canada, or Australia—long-time immigrant destinations—but is instead widely shared among many developed societies, some of which were net exporters of people just a few decades before. Western European countries like France, Italy, and Germany now beckon to peoples from Africa, Asia, and the Caribbean. This causes tremendous change in these societies, change that is often focused on the urban centers.

The immigrant effects on cities varies considerably, of course, but it is remarkable that the economic effects have been largely positive. One important reason has to do with the entrepreneurial spirit exhibited by many new immigrants. In the United States, the 1997 Economic Census reported that the number of minority business establishments increased by thirty percent from 1992—four times faster than businesses overall. Much of this activity occurs near locations where immigrant groups settle and also often where rentals are less expensive. This has had a notable effect as once-forlorn inner cities have been transformed into bastions of new economic activity. Observers have witnessed a revitalization led by small businesses owned and operated by recent

1

immigrants and other ethnic minority groups. But inner cities are not the only places to experience dramatic transformations. Many suburban areas have also taken on an entirely different character, as ethnic business enclaves and activities have followed population, capital, and markets into the outer city.

Given the significance of the ethnic economy in urban areas, we consider the factors that help to determine the success of ethnic entrepreneurs as well as the creation and sustenance of an ethnic economy. Much of the literature has examined the effects of financial capital, human capital, and ethnic or social capital (Bankston and M. Zhou 2002; Bates 1994; Bourdieu 1985; Coleman 1988; De-Fillipis 2001; Dymski and W. Li 2004; P. S. Li forthcoming; W. Li et al. 2001, 2002; Portes 1998; Portes and Sensenbrenner 1993; Portes and M. Zhou 1996; Teixeira 1998, 2001; M. Zhou and Logan 1989). Perhaps it is useful to explore the role of spatial capital. Another set of questions involves the impact that ethnic economic activity has on the metropolitan landscape. Ethnic communities spark our imagination partially because of the businesses they contain. When such communities become large enough, they may even be promoted as tourist draws. But ethnic economic imprints go deeper than a few celebrated "towns." With a wider variety of groups occupying a greater selection of metropolitan locales, the landscape of the ethnic economy looks very different today than it did in the past, with implications that go beyond the purely visual.

We have titled this book *Landscapes of the Ethnic Economy* because it is now time to devote an entire book to how geography shapes and is shaped by the ethnic economy. In the city, landscapes are constructed from various geographical processes. A geographical perspective entails examining the role that location plays in helping, hindering, or shaping ethnic economies. It looks at the relationship between ethnic business networks and other geographically identifiable phenomena, such as residential segregation, underserved markets, or institutional distributions, and it assesses the impact of ethnic business activity in shaping the urban landscape. This volume contains a series of case studies that address 1) the significance of geographic factors in the development of ethnic economies and 2) how ethnic economies create special landscapes within the metropolitan area. In this first chapter, we introduce some of the concepts and theories behind ethnic economies, emphasizing the research that has examined the relationship between ethnic economies and spatial context.

OVERVIEW OF ETHNIC ECONOMY:
DEFINITIONAL CONCERNS AND TYPOLOGIES

What is an *ethnic economy*? The term is used fairly loosely and denotes the multifarious ways in which ethnic groups intersect with almost any sort of economic activity. The Chinese laundry, the Italian bakery, the Mexican construction crew, the Asian Indian-owned motel: all of these have some claim to being a part of the ethnic economy, although such use also leads to ambiguity and confusion. Like other social scientific terms used in an informal sense, the concept of an ethnic economy needs to be defined more clearly in order to be scrutinized systematically. At the same time, the exact contours of a definition have been debated. Essentially, the criteria involve several inter-related attributes.

The most basic item has to do with *proprietorship*, the extent to which members of an ethnic group are self-employed. In general, immigrants are more entrepreneurial, often out of necessity, but there also exists tremendous variation between different ethnic groups. A closely related aspect has to do with *co-ethnic employment*. Many ethnic entrepreneurs are small scale, and they are likely to use only family labor, but larger operations that employ more people may find it advantageous to hire within the community (Light 1979; Light and Karageorgis 1994; Light and Rosenstein 1994; Light et al. 1994a; Portes and Jensen 1987).

The next item involves the tendency of ethnic groups to focus disproportionately in a few economic sectors. This *specialization* stems from many factors: the skills that ethnics bring with them, the opportunities available in a particular context, the legacy of longstanding activity in a sector, and the structural barriers set by hosting societies that prevent ethnic minorities from penetrating certain economic sectors. Sectoral specialization can mean that many of the skills required to work or manage a particular kind of business are passed down and that certain businesses may also be bought and sold between co-ethnics. The clientele of these specialized ethnic economic sectors often reaches beyond the particular minority group in question (Light et al. 1994a; Siu 1987).

By themselves, entrepreneurship and specialization make for a dispersed and perhaps unrelated collection of ethnic businesses, but many have yet to cross the threshold into a true economy. One significant aspect to the development of an ethnic economy has to do with its interaction with an *ethnic market*: how well the businesses appeal to co-ethnic customers (P. S. Li and Y. Li 1999; W. Li 1998a). It stands to reason that the more the needs of ethnics can be met by co-ethnic businesses, the larger and more comprehensive the ethnic economy. This is important because it demonstrates a connection between ethnic businesses and ethnic households and neighborhoods, a type of forward linkage. Beyond the ability of ethnic businesses to supply an ethnic market is their ability to supply each other in a series of backward and lateral linkages, in other words, how well *integrated* ethnic businesses are with each other through co-ethnic suppliers and clients. Buying and selling within the ethnic economy allows for money to remain within the group.

Finally, the relationship between ethnic businesses, ethnic residences, and *spatial concentration* bears scrutiny. The residential concentrations of an ethnic group—at various scales—sometimes relates to the clustering of ethnic business activity. Sometimes the relationship between residence and business is weak, as they are separated spatially. Still, spatial concentration of whatever sort continues to be an important consideration and raises the issue of whether a true ethnic economy can exist without some sort of geographic proximity. While several discussions of ethnic economic activity mention the importance of space, the issue has received less consideration, partly because it is difficult to find spatially specific data but also due to a lack of research among geographers until recently (see, for instance, Kaplan 1997, 1998; W. Li 1998a; Waldinger, McEvoy, and Aldrich 1990; Wang 1999; Wood 1997; Y. Zhou 1998a).

The different criteria used to define an ethnic economy lead naturally into a discussion about how ethnic economies can be categorized. Beyond the more generic *ethnic economy*, some different terms have been employed that clarify some of these distinctions (Barrett, Jones, and McEvoy 1996, 2001; Light and Gold 2000; Light and Roach 1996). Clearly, a set of businesses owned and operated by a single ethnic group differs from a fully integrated economic *society* that includes all of the criteria cited above. In the research literature on ethnic economies, a few representative types have informed our current conceptions of the forms an ethnic economy might take. Light's (1972) early work on *ethnic entrepreneurship* looked simply at the differences in self-employment among some American ethnic groups. The idea of a larger ethnic economy did not figure much in this work, but aspects important to ethnic economies, especially entrepreneurship and ethnic capital, were introduced.

A related concept introduced even earlier, that of the *middleman minority*, focused on the role played by members of an ethnic group situated between a "dominant" ethnic group (sometimes colonialists) and a "subordinate" ethnic population (sometimes the colonized) (Bonacich 1973, 1987; Bonacich and Modell 1980). The middlemen would foster their own trading society that sold goods to members of both dominant and subordinate groups, although mostly focusing on the latter. Such instances abound in the world from Asian Indians in colonial East Africa to Korean merchants in modern American urban ghettoes. The middleman minority concept suggests a degree of internal cohesion, often intensified through a pariah status.

Another related category of ethnic economy is an *ethnic-controlled* economy in which ethnic networks channel minorities or immigrants to particular mainstream economic sectors. The consequence of an ethnic-controlled economy is reflected in the sectoral concentration of ethnic economies. Such sec-

toral concentration can stem from either higher self-employment and entrepreneurship of a particular group (ethnic ownership) or access to existing
mainstream jobs by ethnic networks (ethnic control). In either case, sectoral
concentration forms an ethnic niche economy (Gold and Light 2000;
Kesteloot and Mistiaen 1997; W. Li and Dymski forthcoming; M. Zhou
2004).

The typologies of ethnic economies introduced in the 1980s and 1990s
concern factors of separation/integration and scale. There has been a long
running debate over the extent that some ethnic groups are able to construct
a parallel economy, less dependent on the mainstream economy, that offers
opportunities and rewards to members of a particular ethnic group. This type
of economy, defined as an *ethnic enclave economy*, exists in only a few instances, if it truly exists at all. However, we might be able to view this as the
end point of a continuum that begins with a few ethnically defined businesses
(whether through ownership, management, employment, or customer base)
and ends with a situation in which the ethnic economy somewhat parallels but
also integrates into the mainstream. In essence, an *ethnic enclave economy* or
an *enclave economy* is a special case within the general framework of ethnic
economy. Such enclave economies are defined as possessing a sizeable entrepreneurial class with diverse economic activities, and co-ethnicity between
owners and workers and, to a lesser extent, consumers. But most importantly,
they must evince a geographic concentration of ethnic economic activities
within an ethnically identifiable neighborhood with a minimum level of institutional completeness (Light and Karageorgis 1994; Light et al. 1994b;
Portes and Bach 1985; Portes and Jensen 1987; Portes and Manning 1986;
Sanders and Nee 1987; Wilson and Portes 1980; M. Zhou 2004).

Our understanding of ethnic economies, described above, is largely based
on five primary criteria for identifying an ethnic economy: ethnic ownership,
employment, customer base, sectoral specialization, and spatial concentration.
Yet it is important to note that most ethnic economies resemble more of a
mixed economy (Nee, Sanders, and Sernau 1994; Kloosterman and Rath 2001;
M. Zhou 2004) or *integrated economy* (Li and Dymski forthcoming), especially prevalent as the result of increasing economic globalization and domestic economic restructuring. Despite possessing one or more components of
ethnic economies, such as ethnic ownership and/or employment, these mixed
economies are also an integrated and indispensable part of the mainstream
economy. They include, for instance, ethnically owned firms in Silicon Valley
(Saxenian 1999) and garment industries in large metropolitan areas whose
ownership, operation, labor supply, and consumers traverse various ethnic
group boundaries. Even one of the traditional forms of ethnic economy, import
and export trade, changes its scope and intensity due to international trade

agreements such as NAFTA and WTO. Today, this sector involves transnational finance, manufacturing, transportation and distribution goods, and cross-national brokerage by ethnic groups based on both origin and destination countries of migrants. The small-scale mom-and-pop inner city stores usually associated with the ethnic economy have increasingly given way to firms and sectors that are transnational in nature, large in scale, and a vital part of the global network of goods, finance, and information (Chin, Yoon, and Smith 1996; W. Li et al. 2001; Lo and Shuguang forthcoming; Lo this volume; Portes, Haller, and Guarnizo 2002).

The type of ethnic economy determines the opportunities that it provides to its participants. In general, immigrant groups are more likely to engage in entrepreneurial activity, which suggests that there must be some sort of reward involved. These rewards need not be only monetary; they could include status rewards, the opportunity to employ family and friends, and a chance to build up the ethnic community. Yet initial opportunities provided by the ethnic community can turn into hindrances further on, as particular ethnic groups are left to scramble within a secondary economy that offers little mobility and far lower monetary rewards. It is important to understand, therefore, the levels at which ethnic economies operate, their capacity for growth, and whether they are a result of discrimination or choice. Clearly the cases run from those that may represent vibrant alternative economies, such as in some of the volume's chapters, to some which principally serve poor, protected markets.

THE GEOGRAPHIC CONTRIBUTION:
HOW SPACE OPERATES AS A RESOURCE

This book is dedicated to exploring the ethnic economy from a particular vantage point: that of the spatial aspect. As a discipline, geographers would appear naturally attracted to the study of ethnic economies, inasmuch as there is usually a strong geographical component. The criterion of spatial concentration has long formed a major part of the attributes that make up ethnic economies, but what that means is not always understood. Despite the central argument that an ethnic enclave economy is geographical by nature, there is a paucity of geographic research that systematically examines whether and how space can be used as a resource and can be categorized as a form of capital (Kaplan 1998). Are we talking about residential segregation, where members of a particular ethnic group are separated from other groups? Or is it a concentration of ethnic businesses, often in a defined district but removed from patterns of ethnic residential location? Any sort of spatial concentration must also be examined through the aspect of scale. Tightly bound, clearly defined ethnic districts still exist, but ethnic groups in an automotive culture may concentrate over several square miles. Yet space can still play an important role. The question is, what kind of role?

The first set of chapters examines how spatial concentration (at whatever scale) can operate as a resource and the different roles space plays. Many ethnic economy studies have focused on the financial, social, and human capital resources that particular groups can bring into a particular context. The value of ethnic resources—special avenues toward acquiring credit, the significance of trust and self-enforcement mechanism, passing on of particular businesses within a group—has long been documented (Bankston and M. Zhou 2002; Portes and Sensenbrenner 1993; W. Li et al. 2002). We can speculate on peculiar benefits that accrue from spatial location.

In some instances, proximity offers particular advantages. If members of an ethnic group are less mobile, then they are also more spatially confined. In that instance, geographical proximity can help to create *protected markets* (Hum 2000). Without the ability to travel long distances, customers may patronize ethnically owned stores. In some cases, this could lead to exploitation, whereby prices charged are far in excess of what would be available in mainstream markets. But it can also have the positive effect of making specialty goods available, provided by someone from within the ethnic community—an important asset for many members of an ethnic group. An analog to protected markets among customers would also be the *opportunities for nearby employment* for co-ethnics in search of a job (W. Li 1998b). These jobs may be (and usually are) low wage, but the ethnic connection can make them easier to obtain, with fewer credentialing demands, than jobs within the mainstream economy. There are also big advantages to the business owner, who may feel a greater sense of trust regarding employees from within the same ethnic community.

Within this volume, Airriess (chapter 2) takes two instances of a Vietnamese ethnic economy within New Orleans and demonstrates the differences between them. One is far more inward looking and more spatially focused, while the other operates as more of an ethnic central place for a larger community. Alberts (chapter 3) examines how different types of ethnic economies fulfill different functions and have different spatial orientations, marked by an inner and an outer boundary. Teixeira (chapter 4) speaks to the strong sense of institutional completeness enjoyed by the Portuguese community of Toronto and their high levels of spatial concentration. Kaplan and House-Soremekun (chapter 5) note the importance of spatial context in shaping the experiences of ethnic entrepreneurs, as African American entrepreneurs in Cleveland evince a stronger perception of crime. Lo (chapter 6) shows how the Chinese community in Toronto utilizes space variously, with a mix between an enclave and a non-enclave component. For Hillmann (chapter 7), spatial differences occur on the basis of gender. Female Turkish entrepreneurs in Berlin are less likely to locate in Turkish areas, to employ Turks, to have Turks as customers, and to feel as if they belong to the Turkish ethnic economy.

The clustering of ethnic businesses within an area can help to create a special dynamic that assists other businesses seeking to become established. Ethnic groups often have a wide range of demands that are best accommodated with several stores and services. These stores and services have a better potential to attract customers who see them from the sidewalk or the street. The growth of ethnically defined malls, as discussed in several chapters in this book, testifies to the power of *agglomeration*. Such ethnic business agglomerations often provide co-ethnics with opportunities for one-stop shopping, entertaining, and services that are similar to but often beyond functions provided by mainstream shopping malls. Businesses that would not possibly be able to make it in a non-ethnic milieu can thrive where they feed off of the traffic for other shops (W. Li 1998a; Lo and Shuguang forthcoming; Loukaitou-Sideris 2002; McLaughlin and Jesilow 1998; Preston and Lo 2000).

These spatial factors can be key to the development of ethnic economic structure, and their effects will vary depending on several things. Group characteristics play a role, since we would expect more financially successful groups to utilize space in a different way than those with fewer financial resources. The context itself matters—the question being whether the metropolitan structure rewards spatial proximity and how these rewards might vary. Clearly ethnic groups within a more sprawling metropolis will utilize space in a manner distinct from groups within a denser urban landscape. It is important, too, to consider the developmental stage of the ethnic economy. As an ethnic economy expands and matures, it may have less need for traditional concentration although, alternatively, it may seek to build ethnic spaces on its own terms, like shopping malls. Finally, we must consider the types of businesses involved. Retail and service-based businesses have different markets than manufacturing businesses—they are likely to have different locational demands and so use space in a different way (Lo, this volume; Y. Zhou 1998b).

THE GEOGRAPHIC CONTRIBUTION:
THE DEVELOPMENT OF ETHNIC LANDSCAPES

Past and present ethnic economies have gone a long way toward creating identifiable neighborhoods, from Chinatown in San Francisco to Little Havana in Miami, because of the variety of goods and services they provide. We all know of the ethnic places that figure so prominently in our cultural imagination and often form a major component of a city's marketing emphasis. These types of spaces continue to flourish, but under the guise of diverse groups and in unexpected locales. Ethnic economic activity now stems from ethnic groups that originate from around the world, that may continue to foster transnational ties, and that are very often located at the suburban fringe of the city rather than near its core. The landscape of the ethnic economy looks very different today than it did in the past, with implications that go beyond the purely visual. The emerging landscapes also speak to changes in the way that neighborhoods in the city are structured and organized (Buzelli 2001).

The second set of chapters looks at the impact that ethnic economic activity has on the metropolitan landscape. The idea of an ethnically defined landscape bears some elaboration. Landscape research provides an important topical focus in geography and other social sciences. Long associated with art history, landscape has come to mean the ordinary, visible surroundings that are imbued with multiple layers of meaning (Muir 1999). Ethnic groups have the ability to imprint landscapes with their own meaning in ways both evident and subtle. These might be architecturally distinct buildings, particular institutions, statuary, or other markers. This in turn has an effect on ethnic identity.

Within this volume, several contributors note the transformation of a community's space with the influence of ethnic economic activity. One item to note is the expansion of ethnic economic landscapes into suburban regions. Li et al. (chapter 8) show that the Chinese presence in the San Gabriel Valley and throughout suburban Los Angeles has been bolstered by the role of Chinese banks. Banks play such an incredible role in community building because they provide the capital that allows other ethnic businesses to flourish and point the way to a more mature ethnic economy. Collins (chapter 9) demonstrates the ethnic presence in several neighborhoods within Sydney, Australia. This creates a series of ethnic precincts, from Chinatown to Little Italy to the pan-Asian community of Cabramatta. Many of these precincts are found in the outer suburbs and are no longer simply inner-city phenomena. Oberle (chapter 10) focuses on the Latino presence in metropolitan Phoenix, specifically Mexican *carnicerías*, as he shows that while traditionally found in the urban core, this presence is found more and more in the suburbs.

Another set of chapters examines the transformation of smaller-scale spaces, mostly within the inner city. That this is an international phenomenon is attested by the ethnic character of some neighborhoods within Rome. Italy has long been considered a country of emigration, but Mudu (chapter 11) shows how immigrants (particularly Chinese and Bengalis) are reshaping two neighborhoods. Some social conflict has erupted as a result, as some Italians mourn the loss of "exquisitely Roman traits." Smith (chapter 12) discusses the well-defined and bounded Japanese ethnic enclave known as Little Tokyo in Los Angeles. While long marked as an ethnic enclave, the character and landscape geography of Little Tokyo has been altered over the years by spatial processes operating at a variety of scales. For Barrett and McEvoy (chapter 13), the development of a Curry Mile within Manchester, UK, has been a consequence of a proliferation of restaurants. This has become a major marketing point for the city and has sparked competition from other British cities. The development of ethnically defined places carries a great deal of importance in the development of ethnic economies. The effect is synergistic. Ethnically owned and operated businesses provide for neighborhood definition in a direct way through signage, language, and specialty goods. In that regard, ethnic businesses make and mark ethnic places. These ethnically defined places, as in the case of ethnic enclave economies, in turn become magnets for co-ethnics seeking to obtain goods and services, for established institutions looking for a good location, and perhaps even for political activity. The interconnections of ethnic economies, ethnic neighborhoods, and ethnic institutions mark such places as ethnic communities at their most complete form. Such neighborhoods may also draw outsiders who crave an ethnic experience and some of the accoutrements that go with it. The place-making quality of ethnic economies stamps an ethnic identity onto a district and creates a special landscape.

THE STRUCTURE OF OUR BOOK

The title of this volume is intended to evoke the ways in which landscapes shape and are shaped by ethnic economies. In particular, we center the book around two themes of 1) how spatial location and configuration can help to condition the activities and opportunities of the ethnic economy and 2) how ethnic economies help shape the landscape and perhaps in so doing affect ethnic identity. These questions are critical to an understanding of the interplay between ethnic economies, contexts, landscapes, and ethnic identity.

We believe that the best answers come from detailed case studies. Here we present case studies that examine the intersection of ethnic economic activity and geography. The authors have each examined a particular group in a particular context—only a tiny fraction of all possible combinations—but with enough variation to note many differences in the ways ethnic economies operate and what they mean for the metropolitan landscape. The cases run from quite successful ethnic economies to those that are largely poor and undercapitalized but still have a major impact on the community. Half of our cases come from the United States, whereas the other half includes examples from Canada, Australia, Britain, Italy, and Germany. The inclusion of these attest to the worldwide importance of the ethnic economy and the ways it manifests itself in different geographical milieus.

REFERENCES

Bankston, C. L., III, and M. Zhou. 2002. Social capital as process: The meanings and problems of a theoretical metaphor. *Sociological Inquiry* 72 (2): 287–322.

Barrett, G. A., T. P. Jones, and D. McEvoy. 1996. Ethnic minority business: Theoretical discourse in Britain and North America. *Urban Studies* 33 (4–5): 783–809.

———. 2001. Socio-economic and policy dimensions of the mixed embeddedness of ethnic minority business in Britain. *Journal of Ethnic and Migration Studies* 27 (2): 241–58.

Bates, T. 1994. An analysis of Korean-immigrant owned small business startups with comparison to African American and non-minority owned firms. *Urban Affairs Quarterly* 30 (2): 227–48.

Bonacich, E. 1973. A theory of middleman minorities. *American Sociological Review* 38: 538–94.

———. 1987. "Making it" in America: A social evaluation of the ethics of immigrant entrepreneurship. *Sociological Perspectives* 30 (4): 446–66.

Bonacich, E., and J. Modell. 1980. *The economic basis of ethnic solidarity*. Berkeley: University of California Press.

Bourdieu, P. 1985. The forms of capital. In *Handbook of theory and research of the sociology of education*, ed. J. G. Richardson, 241–58. New York: Greenwood.

Buzelli, M. 2001. From Little Britain to Little Italy: An urban ethnic landscape study in Toronto. *Journal of Historical Geography* 27 (4): 573–87.

Camarota, S. 2004. *Economy slowed but immigration didn't: The foreign-born population 2000–2004*. Washington, DC: Center for Immigration Studies.

Chin, K.-S., I.-J. Yoon, and D. Smith. 1996. Immigrant small business and international economic linkage: A case of the Korean wig business on Los Angeles. *International Migration Review* 30 (2): 485–510.

Coleman, J. S. 1988. Social capital in the creation of human capital. *American Journal of Sociology* 94: S95–S120.

DeFillipis, J. 2001. The myth of social capital in community development. *Housing Policy Debate* 12 (4): 781–806.

Dymski, G., and W. Li. 2004. Financial globalization and cross-border co-movements of money and population: Foreign bank offices in Los Angeles. *Environment and Planning A* 36 (2): 213–40.

Gold, S. J., and I. Light. 2000. Ethnic economies and social policy. *Research in Social Movement, Conflict, and Change* 22:165–91.

Hum, T. 2000. A protected niche: Immigrant ethnic economics and labor market segmentation. In *Prismatic metropolis: Inequality in Los Angeles*, ed. L. D. Bobo,

M. L. Oliver, J. H. Johnson, and A. Valenzula Jr., 279–314. New York: Russell Sage Foundation Press.

Kaplan, D. H. 1997. The creation of an ethnic economy: Indochinese business expansion in Saint Paul. *Economic Geography* 73:214–33.

———. 1998. The spatial structure of ethnic economies. *Urban Geography* 19:489–501.

Kesteloot, C., and P. Mistiaen. 1997. From ethnic minority niche to assimilation: Turkish restaurants in Brussels. *Area* 29:325–34.

Kloosterman, R., and J. Rath. 2001. Immigrant entrepreneurs in advanced economies: Mixed embeddedness further explored. *Journal of Ethnic and Migration Studies* 27 (2): 189–201.

Li, P. S. Forthcoming. Social capital and economic outcomes for immigrants and ethnic minorities. *Journal of International Migration and Integration*.

Li, P. S., and Y. Li. 1999. The consumer market of the enclave economy: A study of advertisement in a Chinese daily newspaper in Toronto. *Canadian Ethnic Studies* 31 (2): 43–60.

Li, W. 1998a. Los Angeles' Chinese *ethnoburb*: From ethnic service center to global economy outpost. *Urban Geography* 19 (6): 502–17.

———. 1998b. Anatomy of a new ethnic settlement: The Chinese *ethnoburb* in Los Angeles. *Urban Studies* 35 (3): 479–501.

Li, W., and G. Dymski. Forthcoming. Globally connected and locally embedded financial institutions: Analyzing the ethnic Chinese banking sector. In *Chinese ethnic economy: Global and local perspectives*, ed. E. Fong. Philadelphia: Temple University Press.

Li, W., G. Dymski, Y. Zhou, M. Chee, and C. Aldana. 2002. Chinese American banking and community development in Los Angeles County. *Annals of Association of American Geographers* 92 (4): 777–96.

Li, W., Y. Zhou, G. Dymski, and M. Chee. 2001. Banking on social capital in the era of globalization: Chinese ethnobanks in Los Angeles. *Environment and Planning A* 33 (4): 1923–48.

Light, I. 1972. *Ethnic enterprise in America: Business and welfare among Chinese, Japanese, and Blacks*. Berkeley: University of California Press.

———. 1979. Disadvantaged minorities in self-employment. *International Journal of Comparative Sociology* 20:31–45.

Light, I., and S. J. Gold. 2000. *Ethnic economies*. San Diego: Academic Press.

Light, I., and S. Karageorgis. 1994. The ethnic economy. In *The handbook of economic sociology*, ed. N. J. Smelser and R. Swedberg, 647–69. New York: Russell Sage Foundation Press.

Light, I., and E. Roach. 1996. Self-employment: Mobility ladder or economic lifeboat? In *Ethnic Los Angeles*, ed. R. Waldinger and M. Bozorgmehr, 193–213. New York: Russell Sage Foundation Press.

Light, I., and C. Rosenstein. 1994. Why entrepreneurs still matter. In *Race, ethnicity, and entrepreneurship in urban America*, ed. I. Light and C. Rosenstein, 1–29. New York: Aldine de Gruyter.

Light, I., G. Sabagh, M. Bozorgmehr, and C. Der-Martirosian. 1994a. The four Iranian ethnic economies in Los Angeles. In *Immigration and absorption: Issues in a multicultural perspective*, ed. L. Isralowitz and I. Light, 109–32. Beer-Sheva, Isr.: Ben-Gurion University of the Negev.

———. 1994b. Beyond the ethnic enclave economy. *Social Problems* 41:65–80.

Lo, L., and W. S. Shuguang. Forthcoming. The new Chinese business sector in Toronto: A spatial and structural anatomy of medium- and large-sized firms. In *Chinese ethnic economy: Global and local perspectives*, ed. E. Fong and C. Luk. Philadelphia: Temple University Press.

Loukaitou-Sideris, A. 2002. Regeneration of urban commercial strips: Ethnicity and space in three Los Angeles neighborhoods. *Journal of Architectural and Planning Research* 19 (4): 335–50.

McLaughlin, C. M., and P. Jesilow. 1998. Conveying a sense of community along Bolsa Avenue: Little Saigon as a model of ethnic commercial belts. *International Migration* 36 (1): 49–63.

Muir, R. 1999. *Approaches to landscape*. Lanham, MD: Rowman and Littlefield.

Nee, V., J. Sanders, and S. Sernau. 1994. Job transitions in an immigrant metropolis: Ethnic boundaries and the mixed economy. *American Sociological Review* 59:849–72.

Portes, A. 1998. Social capital: Its origins and applications in modern sociology. *Annual Review of Sociology* 24:1–24.

Portes, A., and R. L. Bach. 1985. *The Latin journey: Cuban and Mexican immigrants in the United States*. Berkeley: University of California Press.

Portes, A., W. J. Haller, and L. E. Guarnizo. 2002. Transnational entrepreneurs: An alternative form of immigrant economic adaptation. *American Sociological Review* 67 (2): 278–98.

Portes, A., and L. Jensen. 1987. What's an ethnic enclave? The case for conceptual clarity. *American Sociological Review* 52:768–71.

Portes, A., and R. D. Manning. 1986. The immigrant enclave: Theory and empirical examples. In *Competitive ethnic relations*, ed. S. Olzak and J. Nagel, 47–68. Orlando, FL: Academic Press.

Portes, A., and J. Sensenbrenner. 1993. Embeddedness and immigration: Notes on the social determinants of economic action. *American Journal of Sociology* 98:1320–50.

Portes, A., and M. Zhou. 1996. Self-employment and the earnings of immigrants. *American Sociological Review* 61:219–30.

Preston, V., and L. Lo. 2000. "Asian theme" malls in suburban Toronto: Land use conflicts in Richmond Hill. *The Canadian Geographer* 44:182–90.

Sanders, J., and V. Nee. 1987. Limits of ethnic solidarity in the enclave economy. *American Sociological Review* 52:745–73.

Saxnenian, A. 1999. *Silicon Valley's new immigrant entrepreneurs*. San Francisco: Public Policy Institute of California.

Siu, P. C. P. 1987. *The Chinese laundryman: A study of social isolation*. New York: New York University Press.

Teixeira, C. 1998. Cultural resources and ethnic entrepreneurship: A case study of the Portuguese in real estate industries in Toronto. *The Canadian Geographer* 42:267–81.

――――. 2001. Community resources and opportunities in ethnic economies: A case study of Portuguese and Black entrepreneurs in Toronto. *Urban Studies* 38 (11): 2055–78.

Waldinger, R., D. McEvoy, and H. Aldrich. 1990. Spatial dimensions of opportunity structures. In *Ethnic entrepreneurs: Immigrant business in industrial societies*, ed. R. Waldinger, H. Aldrich, and R. Ward, 106–30. Newbury Park, CA: Sage Publications.

Wang, S. 1999. Chinese commercial activity in the Toronto CMA: New development patterns and impacts. *The Canadian Geographer* 43:19–35.

Wilson, K., and A. Portes. 1980. Immigrant enclaves: An analysis of the labor market experience of Cubans in Miami. *American Journal of Sociology* 86:295–319.

Wood, J. 1997. Vietnamese-American place making in northern Virginia. *Geographical Review* 87 (1): 58–72.

Zhou, M. 2004. The enclave economy and community building: Chinatown and Koreatown in Los Angeles. Paper presented at the Pacific Rim Research Conference, Hong Kong.

Zhou, M., and J. R. Logan. 1989. Returns of human capital in ethnic enclaves: New York's Chinatown. *American Sociological Review* 54:809–20.

Zhou, Y. 1998a. How do places matter? A comparative study of Chinese ethnic economies in Los Angeles and New York City. *Urban Geography* 19:531–53.

――――. 1998b. Beyond ethnic enclaves: Location strategies of Chinese producer service firms in Los Angeles. *Economic Geography* 74 (3): 228–51.

Part One

HOW GEOGRAPHY SHAPES THE ETHNIC ECONOMY

Chapter Two

Scaling Central Place of an Ethnic-Vietnamese Commercial Enclave in New Orleans, Louisiana

Christopher Airriess

Ethnic-Vietnamese comprise a significant slice of the post-1965 "new wave" of Asian immigrants to the United States; approximately 1,122,530 ethnic-Vietnamese accounted for nine percent of the total Asian-American population in 2000. Unlike most immigrants who leave their source regions voluntarily for primarily economic reasons, most ethnic-Vietnamese adults arrived as political refugees from the 1975 installed Vietnamese Communist government and comprise the largest refugee resettlement program in American history (Airriess and Clawson 2000; Rumbaut 1996). Despite their large numbers, little research has been conducted specifically on the geographical aspects of commercial enclaves or on the ethnic economy of ethnic-Vietnamese or other Mainland Southeast Asian refugee populations (Kaplan 1997; Wood 1997). Nongeographers have also examined Vietnamese commercial enclaves, but this research is exclusively limited to California, particularly the business community of Westminster in Orange County, California, the largest of its kind in the United States (Loukaitou-Sideris 2002; Mazumdar, Docuyanan, and McLaughlin 2000; McLaughlin and Jesilow 1998; Gold 1994).

This chapter focuses on a relatively small ethnic-Vietnamese commercial enclave in New Orleans, Louisiana. The enclave is what Aldrich and Waldinger (1990, 123) might characterize as a "local ethnic market," in which a specialized business economy serves an adjacent and spatially concentrated co-ethnic residential population (Waldinger, McEvoy, and Aldrich 1990, 124–25). Nevertheless, some business owners have begun to broaden their scales of commercial exchange to include a more distant co-ethnic and majority population customer base. Because the socioeconomic context is critical to understanding the nature of locality and commercial exchange in this specific case study, the first part of this chapter provides the demographic profile of the

17

residential cluster, followed by a description of the spatio-structural evolution of the commercial enclave. Next, an analysis of the diversity of business sectors and the contours of human capital, business tenure, and ownership are offered to provide evidence of the enclave's local ethnic market character. Equally important, however, is that these economic attributes are geographically or locationally differentiated within the commercial enclave and also influence the nature of enclaves' central place function. This research then harnesses Kaplan's (1998) typology of how the spatially concentrated nature of ethnic entrepreneurs assists in several spatial forms of economic exchange. In this sense, space is conceptualized as a defined resource and is especially important in explaining the business enclave as an ethnic central place attracting nonlocal co-ethnics. Critical here is the recognition that individual businesses possess their own central place characteristics based on relative location within the enclave as well as specific business strategies. As a conclusion, this research briefly compares the geographical nature of business activity in the enclave with another concentration of ethnic-Vietnamese business activity in the West Bank communities of New Orleans.

Business establishments included as part of the ethnic commercial enclave are those owned by ethnic-Vietnamese whether their customer base is exclusively co-ethnic or not. The research methodology includes a combination of both quantitative as well as qualitative information-gathering strategies. Of the 93 businesses that comprise the ethnic business enclave, 49 percent of business owners/managers were contacted by telephone and asked 23 short and close-ended questions by a Vietnamese-speaking research assistant. Of the 46 business owners/managers interviewed by phone, 50 percent were interviewed personally by the author to elicit more detailed answers of a qualitative nature concerning specific questions from the telephone interview. Additional qualitative interviews were also held with a handful of community leaders to extract information concerning nonbusiness owners' perception of the ethnic business enclave.[1]

THE SOCIOECONOMIC CONTEXT

While dwarfed in size by the ethnic-Vietnamese populations in much larger MSAs (Metropolitan Statistical Areas), the 14,868 ethnic-Vietnamese of the New Orleans MSA ranked sixteenth largest in the country in 2000. The population has almost doubled since 1980. Ethnic-Vietnamese in the MSA are spatially concentrated into either the Versailles community of Orleans Parish that is the focus of this chapter or a handful of spatially contiguous West Bank communities in Jefferson Parish (figure 2.1).

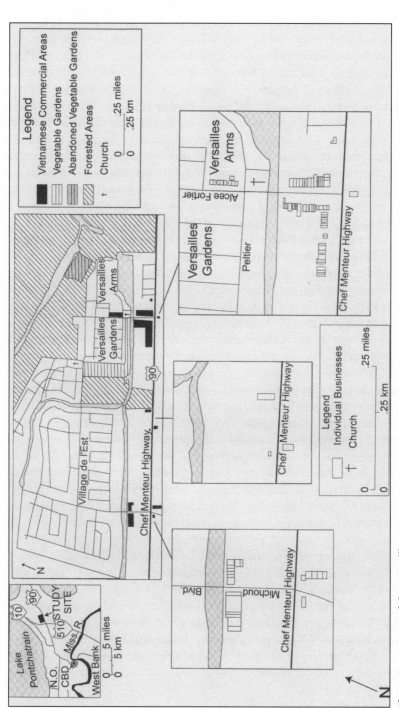

Figure 2.1. Map of the Versailles Area

Both concentrations account for 58 percent of the total ethnic-Vietnamese population in the New Orleans MSA. Using the ethnic-Vietnamese population of the respective parishes (counties) as surrogates, the Orleans Parish population as a share of the New Orleans MSA decreased from 64 percent (5,030) in 1980 to 47 percent (7,118) in 2000, while the Jefferson Parish population as a share increased from only 8 percent (672) in 1980 to 44 percent (6,601) in 2000. In-migration of ethnic-Vietnamese into the MSA has overwhelmingly favored the West Bank communities of Jefferson Parish. Although functioning as the original core of ethnic-Vietnamese settlement in the MSA, the Versailles settlement cluster has thus lost its ethnic prominence in terms of population and economic centrality within the larger MSA context.

The cultural and historical experience of an immigrant group is critical to understanding economic adaptation in their destination country, and this is certainly true of the distinct migration and settlement history of Versailles' ethnic-Vietnamese population (Airriess 2002). In the early 1990s, sixty percent of the adult population originated in just two Roman Catholic dioceses in northern Vietnam, but fled to the south following the Geneva Agreement in 1954. In addition, approximately sixty percent of the adult population in the early 1990s were "first wave" (1975–1977) refugee cohorts, but unlike most first wave refugees elsewhere in the United States who were urban residents and relatively well educated, the Versailles refugees were primarily rural fisherfolk. While there exists a tendency to romanticize the ethnic homogeneity and solidarity of an ethnic settlement cluster by not recognizing community segmentation based upon class, gender, and generation (Mitchell 2003), the role of shared ethnic loyalties as valuable to building an enclave customer base must be considered in this particular context.

The urban context in which immigrants are embedded is equally as important (Dijst and van Kempen 1991), particularly with reference to the impact of ethnic residential clustering on an adjacent business enclave (Logan, Alba, and McNulty 1994). The Versailles ethnic-Vietnamese community is concentrated in the three contiguous residential developments of Versailles Arms, Versailles Gardens, and Village de l'Est located at the most eastern suburban edge of metropolitan New Orleans (figure 2.1). In the process of neighborhood succession, ethnic-Vietnamese have replaced many white and black residents since their arrival in 1975. In census tract 17.42, which covers all the territory east of Michoud Boulevard and 90 percent of the ethnic-Vietnamese population within the study area, the 4,063 ethnic Vietnamese comprise 45 percent of the population and African Americans account for 48 percent of the total. African Americans numerically dominate the Versailles Arms apartment complex and residential space on the periphery of the census tract.

Within the larger urban context, New Orleans is a poor city and the Versailles community even more so. In terms of poverty status, a substantially high 31 percent of the ethnic-Vietnamese population possesses incomes below the poverty level, compared to 18 percent of the MSA as a whole and 14 percent of Vietnamese Americans nationally. Only 45 percent of ethnic-Vietnamese owned their own homes in 1999, compared to 60 percent nationally. Reflecting their rural and refugee backgrounds, educational attainment is also relatively low. In 2000, only 7 percent of individuals 25 years or older possessed a college degree, compared to 24 percent for the MSA and 28 percent for Vietnamese Americans nationally. As a result, many working adults are forced to enter the low pay service sector or non-unionized manufacturing workforce. The relative poverty of Versailles residents, due in part to the low levels of human capital of the refugee population, partially explains the absence of a diverse business mix as well as higher value services characteristic of a local ethnic market.

SPATIAL EVOLUTION OF THE COMMERCIAL ENCLAVE

The earliest commercial development, and indeed the persistent core of the ethnic commercial enclave, arose from open fields at the junction of Chef Menteur Highway and Alcee Fortier (figure 2.1). The west side of Alcee Fortier emerged in the late 1970s and development was complete by the early 1980s. Individual land plots were purchased by business owners from an American owner. The land comprising the entire east side of the commercial strip was bought outright from an American by the first grocery store owner in the enclave in 1984, and most plots were sold individually to prospective co-ethnic entrepreneurs. Although not a classic example of an "immigrant entrepreneur" (Light 2002) because this individual did not attract ethnic businesses from elsewhere, he did create permissive conditions for the establishment of such economic activity. A portion of this land not sold to individual co-ethnic business owners was then sold to his cousin, who as a landlord built commercial space. By 1987, the entire west side of Alcee Fortier was filled with businesses (figure 2.2).

Aside from two restaurants and a bakery along Chef Menteur established in the late 1970s and early 1980s, the balance of the business enclave was developed throughout the 1990s, but in ways different from the older core businesses at the Chef-Alcee Fortier intersection. Those structures along Chef Menteur stretching contiguously from Alcee Fortier westward were almost exclusively new builds by store owners (figure 2.3). On the northwest and southeast sides of the Chef Menteur and Michoud Boulevard intersection,

Figure 2.2.   Alcee Fortier Businesses

Figure 2.3.   MC Center along Chef Menteur Highway

businesses opened in derelict commercial space while residential apartment space was rezoned commercial on the northeast corner of the intersection and on the corner of Alcee Fortier and Peltier. The reoccupation of derelict commercial space and the conversions from residential to commercial space are examples of what Loukaitou-Sideris (2002, 335) refers to as "ethnic gentrification" resulting from a reterritorialization of space to meet the various economic and cultural needs of the new ethnic-Vietnamese community. The relatively quick pace of reterritorialization was afforded by the localized "opportunity structures" (Aldrich and Waldinger 1990) that favored ethnic-Vietnamese entrepreneurs. The absence of African American businesses, despite a substantial co-ethnic residential population, meant little competition for commercial space that is common in the process of "occupational succession."

CONTOURS OF BUSINESS OWNERSHIP

The diversity of business sectors in terms of the range of goods and services is relatively narrow, reflecting the "local ethnic market" or first stage of ethnic business patterns (Waldinger, McEvoy, and Aldrich 1990). Of the 93 businesses, the largest business sector in terms of number of establishments is food/grocery. Numbering fourteen establishments that range from one supermarket-sized establishment to smaller businesses, all sell a wide range of goods except for two fresh meat markets, one seafood market, and one bakery. The second largest business sector is restaurants and cafes; the eleven establishments range from large formal restaurants to small coffee shops. In descending order of frequency are ten medical service establishments comprising six doctor's offices and four pharmacies, nine beauty salons, nine legal/financial businesses, five jewelry stores, five video rental stores, four auto-related businesses, four travel agencies, and three non-profit services, entertainment, and clothing apparel businesses each. The remaining businesses total thirteen and include mostly service-based businesses such as floral design, tailors, laundromats, and retail and wholesale cosmetics. Two attorney's offices specifically catering to ethnic-Vietnamese were not enumerated because of their majority population ownership.

With few exceptions, the small scale nature of businesses in terms of physical space and number of employees is a reflection of the relative absence of human capital and the financial capabilities of both entrepreneurs and their customer base. Of the 46 businesses surveyed, only 25 percent had business experience in Vietnam, and 45 percent possessed no business experience because they were either too young when they left Vietnam or were born in the

United States. Of those 34 businesses owners who did not possess business experience in Vietnam, however, 43 percent did possess business experience in the local business community before establishing their present business. These figures point to three observations. First, there exists a relative absence of entrepreneurial talent external to the local ethnic market economy. Second, there exists a recirculation of business experience in the community, perhaps based on skills acquired while working at an existing business (Light et al. 1994). Third, the second generation appears to be entering the small business sector and thus regenerating the commercial enclave.

It is this second generation that deserves some quick attention here based on a single theoretical justification. Gold (1992) makes a convincing argument that economic independence from the larger majority population economy plays an important role in explaining self-employment. For example, two insurance agents once worked as agents of a national insurance firm but decided to become independent agents in the community because of the freedom it afforded. One medical doctor who worked for a downtown hospital for three years after receiving his medical degree decided that a private practice serving Vietnamese patients was more desirable. A young women with a college degree in business studies used her experiences working as a hairstylist at a local J. C. Penney's to open her own hair salon. One pharmacist, who opened his business directly out of pharmacy school rather than working for a national chain, perhaps captures the feeling of second generation entrepreneurs by offering the following Vietnamese proverb as a philosophical basis for self-employment: *lấy công làm lời* meaning "profits or products are the fruit of their own labor."

The small scale and local market nature of the commercial enclave is evidenced by the contours of employment patterns. Of the 46 businesses interviewed, only 17 percent possessed exclusively non-family employees, while 68 percent are characterized by only family members as a labor resource. Those businesses employing non-relatives are almost exclusively beauty salons and the three larger scale restaurants possessing a substantial non-local population customer base. The small scale nature of most businesses, however, allow for a simple husband-wife partnership; of the businesses that rely exclusively on family members, 44 percent are comanaged by a husband and wife who are the only employees. The husband-and-wife businesses are not concentrated in any one business sector.

Business establishments averaged 7.8 years of operation. Approximately 25 percent of the businesses date to 1990 and before; the oldest establishments are the two large scale Chinese-Vietnamese restaurants (1979 and 1983) on Chef Menteur catering in part to non-co-ethnics, and four of the six jewelry stores possess a collective average tenure of 18 years. Approximately

25 percent of business establishments are three years old or younger. Reflecting ease of entry because of low start-up costs, beauty salons, restaurants, and grocery stores account for 66 percent of these youngest businesses. Likewise, these are the types of businesses that also experience the highest failure rates. The vacancy rate for the enclave as a whole is not high; only five percent of available commercial space stands empty.

Ownership of commercial space is not equally distributed structurally or geographically. Of the 46 business spaces surveyed, 71 percent are rented from a landlord and 28 percent are owned by the business owner. Similar patterns of ownership are characteristic for the Bolsa Avenue commercial strip of Little Saigon in Orange County, California (Loukaitou-Sideris 2002). When examining the nature of landlord ownership, however, the concentration of commercial space ownership points to the degree to which commercial property development is an important part of the growth of the business community.

Based on data gathered from a few of the more knowledgeable 23 interviewees concerning ownership of all commercial property, approximately 52 percent of commercial units were owned by nine individuals. Four of the nine landlords are enclave business owners who possess between two to five properties each. One, an ethnic-Chinese Vietnamese, or *Viet Hoa,* who arrived in the enclave in 1993 from Orange County, California, is the owner of two large commercial blocks on Chef Menteur occupied by five businesses. The remaining five landlords are not enclave business owners. The most important single landlord is responsible for refurbishing Michoud Plaza, which houses eleven business. The largest owners of commercial space owners tend to be located along Chef Menteur and the Michoud-Chef Menteur intersection, where single owners were able to purchase existing blocks of derelict commercial space or rezoned blocks of residential space.

The place of residence of business owners provides an additional perspective on the nature of the business enclave based on the assumption that as the commercial enclave evolves and matures, more entrepreneurs choose to live outside the community (Tseng 1994). Indicative of the local ethnic market character of the enclave, only 36 percent of business owners reside outside the community. There exists, however, a positive correlation between living inside or outside the community and store location. Of those operating stores in the core of the commercial enclave along Alcee Fortier and Peltier, 70 percent reside in the community. In contrast, 42 percent of store owners along the more auto-oriented Chef Menteur and the Michoud-Chef Menteur intersection live in the local community. Second generation entrepreneurs who dominate the professional services tend to live outside the residential enclave. For example, seven of the eight store owners who reside outside the community and own businesses in the enclave's core are second generation entrepreneurs who have only been in business for an average of five years. Ownership of commercial space is also positively correlated with residence because four of the five owners of commercial space with five or more properties reside outside the residential enclave.

SCALING ETHNIC CENTRAL PLACE

The relatively narrow range of business sectors, the small-scale nature of business activity, an almost complete reliance on family labor, and a primarily local customer base point to the enclave's classification as a "local ethnic market" (Waldinger, McEvoy, and Aldrich 1990). While such a classification of an ethnic-business community is useful based on evolutionary process, it is deterministic and provides only a starting point for a more complex understanding of the spatial dimensions of economic exchange. While the ethnic business enclave generally functions as a central place for enclave residents, it also possesses central place functions for co-ethnics who reside in distant suburbs and regional urban places. Because for the most part, specific businesses function as central places, we are then able to conceptualize the business enclave as a spatial concentration of many small businesses that each function as a commercial central place based on distance and a variety of demographic variables that characterize its customer base. Thus, the concept of central place requires the geographical scaling of commercial exchange because the maturation of an ethnic economy produces more complex spatial patterns of exchange. These different spatial geometries of commercial exchange between ethnic customers and ethnic businesses as outlined by Kaplan (1998) anchor this analysis.

The most simple exchange is between ethnic businesses and the local pool of co-ethnic customers. Ecological relationships are critical to this "protected market" in that the residential clustering of the ethnic population as consumers allows easy physical access to the commercial enclave (Light 1972). The continued movement of refugees into the community allows the residential community to reproduce itself and thus assists in sustaining, if not expanding, opportunities for businesses serving co-ethnics. At the same time, however, business owners become captives as well because the relative poverty of the enclave's residents reduces the demand for a greater diversity of potential business activities (Waldinger, McEvoy, and Aldrich 1990).

Of the 46 businesses surveyed, 41 percent indicated that 80 percent or more of their customer base is local and co-ethnic in nature. When the local customer base threshold is reduced to 60 percent, approximately 70 percent of businesses are what Tambs-Lyche (1980) refers to as "internal shopkeepers." Only three of the 46 businesses sampled rely solely on a local, co-ethnic customer base: a "fisherman's" café, an herbal medicinal store, and a video store. These businesses aside, the business sectors most dependent on a captive customer base are beauty salons, jewelry stores, and non-profit services as they all provide goods and services that are culturally specific to the community. Five of the seven beauty salons possess a local co-ethnic clientele of 80 percent or more because as one salon owner claimed "only Vietnamese stylists know Vietnamese hair." The gold and jade–based jewelry stores sell goods with a deep significance in Vietnamese material culture. The non-profit business services include a Head Start–like program, a refugee/immigrant resettlement office that has branches nationwide, and a Vietnamese-American Fisherman's Union office serving a substantial number of commercial shrimpers.

Physical proximity to enclave businesses is especially important for two specific groups. The first are elderly Vietnamese Americans who possess strong social relationships with particular business owners and often walk to the enclave core along Alcee Fortier because they do not possess auto transport. The second group is comprised of local African Americans who generally patronize only grocery and medical service establishments. Of the nine grocery businesses surveyed, all but one rely on African American customers for at least ten percent of their business, one of the grocery stores is one hundred percent reliant on African American business, and another fifty percent. Medical services are equally reliant on the local African American customer base; one pharmacist's African American customer base is fifty percent and one doctor's office is twenty percent.

While spatial proximity initiates economic exchange between entrepreneurs and customers, so do linkages between co-ethnic businesses. For example, medical doctors write prescriptions that are often filled at enclave pharmacies; one doctor estimated that 85 percent of his patients requiring prescription medicines use local pharmacies. Another example is the purchase of restaurant food supplies from local grocery stores, particularly with reference to perishable products such as fresh green vegetables. Although less common today, producer linkages existed between a number of elderly vegetable gardeners who supplied fresh greens to restaurants and grocery stores (Airriess and Clawson 1994). Similarly, fishermen and shrimpers supply fresh seafood to grocery stores.

Space as a specific resource to increase enclave commercial exchange becomes more complex when the geographical scale includes a more distant customer base. Increasing the spatial reach or geographical scale of commercial exchange is critically important because for the most part, those successful ethnic-owned businesses over the long term are those that are able to secure a non-ethnic customer base (Waldinger, McEvoy, and Aldrich 1990). While businesses in the enclave have yet to develop a substantial non-ethnic clientele, most are dependent on co-ethnics from elsewhere in the MSA and the Mississippi Gulf Coast. Located on the eastern edge of the MSA and tied to the Mississippi Gulf Coast by Interstate 10, the 4,204 ethnic-Vietnamese populating the Long Beach-Gulfport-Biloxi corridor possess easy access to the commercial enclave. In this case of non-local but co-ethnic commercial exchange, space becomes a resource based on agglomerative economies of an ethnic central place in which visitors are able to efficiently patronize a variety of business establishments in a single visit. Weekends are especially popular for distant co-ethnic visits; the Saturday morning wet market provides an important draw, and Sundays are the busiest business days, when customers can combine visits with family and friends and mass at the Mary Queen of Vietnam Church with commercial exchange. This notion of space as a defined resource whereby economic exchange is supported by sociocultural relationships prompts Chacko (2003) to refer to ethnic commercial enclaves as "ethnic sociocommerscapes."

Restaurants are often the first business sector to reach beyond their co-ethnic or local geographical base (Kaplan 1998). The local and co-ethnic restaurant clientele base, for example, ranges between 25 and 80 percent, but those establishments with the highest non-local customer base possess a highway location. The two restaurants that possess the highest non-local co-ethnic and majority population customer base (75 and 40 percent) are both ethnic-Chinese owned and are the oldest surviving restaurants in the enclave. The enclave's only bakery, owned by a relative of one of these restaurant owners, possesses the highest non-ethnic customer base (15 percent) of any business establishment; the location adjacent to the restaurant provides substantial agglomeration-based business. The owners of two additional and newer restaurants with a high non-local co-ethnic and majority population customer base (30 percent) indicate that their business strategy is to build up a majority population customer base. One of these restaurants is owned by a family that moved from Orange County, California, and opened two restaurants in the metropolitan area and one in Biloxi with the same name. This example is instructive because, as Gold (1992) observes, success in attracting non-ethnic business is often dependent upon past business experiences servicing a majority population clientele.

Grocery stores have developed a substantial non-local customer base as well. Of the eight grocery stores surveyed, five possessed a local, co-ethnic customer base of 60 percent or greater, but three specific grocery stores have developed a more distant customer base. The largest establishment occupies an abandoned Winn-Dixie supermarket and relies heavily on co-ethnics from the greater metropolitan area (20 percent), co-ethnics from other smaller regional urban places (20 percent), and non-ethnic customers (10 percent) in search of "Asian" food supplies. Another grocery store is characterized by a customer base similar to the first, but with a smaller percentage of non-ethnic customers (5 percent). This second grocery store, combined with a fresh meat market, is especially attractive to Mississippi Gulf Coast co-ethnic grocery store owners as a source of provisions when they visit on Saturday mornings. Because these co-ethnic stores along the Mississippi Gulf Coast do not generate sufficient business to warrant visits by delivery trucks from the major Asian foods distribution center of Houston, Texas, Versailles grocery stores function as a central place for these lower order retail businesses. The third grocery store has a reasonably strong non-local base (25 percent) in part because it is the store adjacent to the Saturday morning wet market. Being a sidewalk seller of fresh vegetables before opening the store in 1991, the store owner was able to convince the sellers of wet market produce through local ethnic networking to relocate to a courtyard adjacent to her store. The resulting business spillover based on agglomerative economies at the microscale is substantial among non-local co-ethnics and the majority population customers alike.

The desire to cultivate a non-local customer base expresses itself in several ways. One way is the geographical location of business establishments; those based on auto traffic (instead of foot traffic) require sufficient parking space. Indeed, those businesses located in the densely compacted establishments located along Alcee Fortier are perceived by business owners to be lacking in parking space and less likely to attract non-local customers. The types of businesses and the physical scale of specific businesses located outside the core are also reflective of this desire to attract a non-local customer base. These include both of the ethnic-Chinese restaurants as well as the two largest, newest, and airy restaurants; in fact, of the nine restaurants, only four are found in the core and these are the café-like restaurants relying on local co-ethnic traffic. Also included in this outside group are the two nail supply businesses, the supermarket, an electronics store, a shoe store, and a wedding reception hall. Another indication of the desire to increase a non-local and perhaps non-ethnic customer base is in part afforded by reading the language, or semiotic landscape, of business signs located inside versus outside the core. While 44 percent of those more auto accessible and post-1990 businesses outside the core possess store signs that are entirely in the English language, only 17 percent of stores comprising the pre-1990 core establishments are exclusively in the English language.

CONCLUSION

The socioeconomic and locational attributes of the Versailles commercial enclave might be better understood if we compare this business community to that of the ethnic-Vietnamese business enclave on the West Bank of New Orleans. When compared to the West Bank business community, the Versailles commercial enclave is perceived by even local co-ethnics as being inward looking and conservative. Indeed, a number of business owners interviewed referred to the original core as the "village." One reason is the poor and rural origin of its nearby residential customer base whose still very influential elderly members value frugality which in turn does not allow for product and service diversification. In fact, two business owners located outside of the original core referred to the core businesses in a derogatory manner by claiming that they cater to fisherman and do not possess progressive business practices.

The West Bank business community is quite different, perceived by those in Versailles as being more modern or progressive. First, business owners and their co-ethnic customers do not possess rural backgrounds as in Versailles; they were urban, educated, and Buddhist in Vietnam. In addition, the West Bank population possesses experiences that are more diverse in the United States before engaging in secondary migration to New Orleans during the 1990s. Indeed, compared to Versailles, the West Bank has a co-ethnic customer base that possesses significantly higher educational attainment and income levels. Unlike the spatially concentrated Versailles commercial enclave, businesses are geographically dispersed across the West Bank communities and far more oriented to a non-co-ethnic customer base. This pattern resembles the more prosperous ethnic-Vietnamese in northern Virginia (Wood 1997) characterized by "heterolocalism" (Zelinsky and Lee 1998) of both residential and commercial space. One business leader claims that unlike in the West Bank, business owners in Versailles either live near or above their businesses and learn little about the "American way of doing business." Being far more centrally situated within the New Orleans MSA, West Bank businesses, particularly restaurants, attract many more non-co-ethnic customers such as ethnic-Chinese, Koreans, and Filipinos. While Versailles possesses convenient interstate access, it is located in the most distant eastern suburb, thus inconvenient for potential non-ethnic customers. In fact, Interstate 10 has usurped east-west traffic from Chef Menteur Highway, resulting in just a trickle of local traffic passing the enclave.

Perhaps one observation that captures the essential difference between the two business communities are the names of co-ethnic, locally financed shopping centers being planned for each location. The shopping center planned for the West Bank is called Hong Kong Plaza, named after the primary ethnic-Vietnamese shopping center in Houston. The name *Hong Kong* attached to any shopping complex is common throughout the Pacific Rim and in a sense is a brand name with cache. Possessing fewer external or globalized connections, the name of the planned shopping center in Versailles is simply Saigon Plaza. These semiotic clues tell much about the differing scales of their respective worldviews.

While the New Orleans East community shares with the ethnic-Chinese ethnoburbs of the Los Angeles Basin the characteristics of suburban location, medium density settlement, and multiethnicity (Li 1998), in most other respects the community has more in common structurally with older ethnic enclaves near downtown. Unlike the Bolsa Avenue commercial strip of Orange County, California, lined by some 2,000 ethnic-Vietnamese businesses (McLaughlin and Jesilow 1998), Versailles, especially the commercial core, exhibits physical decay, which like all undesirable zones of transition make potential non-co-ethnic customers wary or cautious. Also, unlike ethnoburbs whose origins are traced to dynamic global economic restructuring and inhabited by a relatively affluent and well-educated population, the Versailles community is a byproduct of the Cold War conflict, has experienced the process of neighborhood "invasion and succession" and is characterized by relatively high rates of poverty perhaps more characteristic of smaller ethnic-Vietnamese settlement and business concentrations elsewhere in urban America.

NOTE

1. The author gratefully acknowledges the important role played by Cyndi Nguyen and Lan Hoang in the research process.

REFERENCES

Airriess, C. A. 2002. Creating landscapes and place in New Orleans. In *Geographical identities of ethnic America: Race, space, and place*, ed. K. A. Berry and M. L. Henderson, 228–54. Reno: University of Nevada Press.

Airriess, C. A., and D. L. Clawson. 1994. Vietnamese market gardens in New Orleans. *Geographical Review* 84 (1): 16–31.

———. 2000. Mainland Southeast Asian refugees: Migration, settlement, and adaptation. In *Ethnicity on contemporary America: A geographical perspective,* ed. J. O. McKee, 311–46. Lanham, MD: Rowman and Littlefield.

Aldrich, H. E., and R. Waldinger. 1990. Ethnicity and entrepreneurship. *Annual Review of Sociology* 16:111–36.

Chacko, E. 2003. Ethiopian ethos and the making of ethnic places in the Washington metropolitan area. *Journal of Cultural Geography* 20 (2): 21–42.

Dijst, M. J., and R. van Kempen. 1991. Minority business and the hidden dimension: The influence of urban contexts on the development of ethnic enterprise. *Tijdschrift voor Economische en Sociale Geografie* 82 (2): 128–38.

Gold, S. J. 1992. *Refugee communities: A comparative field study*. Newbury Park, CA: Sage Publications.

———. 1994. Chinese-Vietnamese entrepreneurs in California. In *The new Asian immigration in Los Angeles and global restructuring*, ed. P. Ong, E. Bonacich, and L. Cheng, 196–226. Philadelphia: Temple University Press.

Kaplan, D. H. 1997. The creation of an ethnic economy: Indochinese business expansion in Saint Paul. *Economic Geography* 73 (2): 214–33.

———. 1998. The spatial structure of urban ethnic economies. *Urban Geography* 19 (6): 489–501.

Li, W. 1998. Los Angeles' Chinese ethnoburb: From ethnic service center to global economy outpost. *Urban Geography* 19 (6): 502–18.

Light, I. 1972. *Ethnic enterprise in America*. Berkeley: University of California Press.

———. 2002. Immigrant place entrepreneurs in Los Angeles 1970–99. *International Journal of Urban and Regional Research* 26 (2): 215–28.

Light, I., G. Sabagh, M. Bozorgmehr, and C. Der-Martirosian. 1994. Beyond the ethnic enclave economy. *Social Problems* 41:65–80.

Logan, J. R., R. D. Alba, and T. L. McNulty. 1994. Ethnic economies in metropolitan regions: Miami and beyond. *Social Forces* 72 (3): 691–724.

Loukaitou-Sideris, A. 2002. Regeneration of urban commercial strips: Ethnicity and space in three Los Angeles neighborhoods. *Journal of Architectural and Planning Research* 19 (4): 335–50.

Mazumdar, S., F. Docuyanan, and C. M. McLaughlin. 2002. Creating a sense of place: The Vietnamese-Americans and Little Saigon. *Journal of Environmental Psychology* 20 (4): 319–33.

McLaughlin, C. M., and P. Jesilow. 1998. Conveying a sense of community along Bolsa Avenue: Little Saigon as a model of ethnic commercial belts. *International Migration* 36 (1): 49–63.

Mitchell, K. 2003. Networks of ethnicity. In *A companion to economic geography*, ed. E. Sheppard and R. J. Barnes, 392–407. Malden, MA: Blackwell Publishing.

Rumbaut, R. G. 1996. A legacy of war: Refugees from Vietnam, Laos and Cambodia. In *Origins and destinies: Immigration, race, and ethnicity in America*, ed. S. Pedraza and R. G. Rumbaut, 315–33. Belmont, CA: Wadsworth Publishing.

Tambs-Lyche, H. 1980. *London Patidars: A case study in urban ethnicity*. London: Routledge and Kegan.

Tseng, Y.-F. 1994. Chinese ethnic economy: San Gabriel Valley, Los Angeles County. *Journal of Urban Affairs* 16 (2): 169–89.

Waldinger, R., D. McEvoy, and H. Aldrich. 1990. Spatial dimensions of opportunity structures. In *Ethnic entrepreneurs: Immigrant business in industrial societies*, ed. R. Waldinger, H. Aldrich, and R. Ward, 106–30. Newbury Park, CA: Sage Publications.

Wood, J. 1997. Vietnamese American place making in northern Virginia. *Geographical Review* 87 (1): 58–72.

Zelinsky, W., and B. A. Lee. 1998. Heterolocalism: An alternative model of the sociospatial behaviour of immigrant ethnic communities. *International Journal of Population Geography* 4 (4): 281–98.

Chapter Three

Geographic Boundaries of the Cuban Enclave Economy in Miami

Heike Alberts

Since the early 1980s, academics and journalists alike have published enthusiastic reports about the Cuban enclave economy in Miami. Some celebrate it for the upward mobility it provides to Cuban immigrants. Others credit it with Miami's ascent to the "Capital of Latin America" or the "Gateway to the Americas" (Rieff 1999; Stepick 1994). While observers agree that the Cuban enclave economy provides the Cuban community with ethnic goods and services and functions as a hub for U.S. trade with Latin America, they disagree about how it operates and what its exact boundaries are.

Over the years, researchers have proposed a number of different explanations for the development of ethnic entrepreneurship and ethnic enclave economies. Some of these center on the characteristics of the immigrant group including previous business experience, a willingness to work long hours, and most prominently the close-knit nature of ethnic communities that allows immigrants to mobilize ethnic resources (Boissevain et al. 1990; Bun and Hui 1995; Light, Bhachu, and Karageorgis 1993; Light and Rosenstein 1995; Portes and Bach 1985; Waldinger 1993; Wilson and Portes 1980). Others emphasize the importance of external factors such as the structure of the economy, discrimination against immigrants, and government policies toward ethnic entrepreneurs (Bonacich 1973; Bonacich and Modell 1980; Light and Bonacich 1988). Despite some attempts to combine these different factors in a single framework (most notably Waldinger, Aldrich, and Ward 1990a), the way ethnic groups' cultural, social, and occupational characteristics interact with the urban and economic environments to form ethnic enclave economies remains understudied. Additionally, while numerous researchers have defined ethnic enclave economies (e.g. Light et al. 1993; Light and Karageorgis 1994; Logan, Alba, and McNulty 1994), there is still no consensus among scholars about what exactly

constitutes an ethnic enclave economy and how its boundaries can be de-
lineated (Kaplan 1997; Portes and Jensen 1987; Sanders and Nee 1987,
1989).

I believe that the classic theory about ethnic enclave economies has to be
revised in several different ways. First, since the theory was developed in the
1980s, both the Cuban community and the city of Miami have undergone rad-
ical changes, making it necessary to investigate whether the contemporary
concentration of Cuban businesses in Miami still meets the criteria established twenty years ago. Second, the geographic contexts in which ethnic
economies are embedded have only recently attracted the attention of geographers (see Chin, Yoon, and Smith 1996; Dijst and van Kempen 1991; Kaplan 1998; Kloosterman, van der Leun, and Rath 1999; Kloosterman and Rath
2001; Ram et al. 2002; Schnell, Benenson, and Sofer 1999; Zhou 1998).
These studies show variations in the development of ethnic economies in different metropolitan areas but do not examine boundaries within an ethnic
economy in a certain metropolitan area. I argue that the interaction of the
characteristics of Miami neighborhoods with the changing characteristics of
the Cuban immigrants themselves have over time resulted in the creation of
several specialized Cuban enclave economies rather than a single unified one.

REEXAMINING THE CLASSIC CONCEPT
OF THE ETHNIC ENCLAVE ECONOMY

When Wilson and Portes (1980) first developed the concept of the ethnic enclave economy based on a large survey they conducted with Cubans in Miami in the 1970s, they defined its participants as Cubans who had Cuban employers, independent from where the businesses were located. If the shared
ethnicity of the employers and employees is what distinguishes the Cuban enclave economy from the general labor market, we should see differences between Cubans employed by other Cubans and those with employers of other
ethnicities. To test this hypothesis, I conducted my own survey of 150 Cuban
workers in contemporary Miami and then cross-tabulated the ethnicity of
their employers with a wide range of social and work-related variables. Of the
more than fifty variables cross-tabulated, only two showed statistically significant differences (table 3.1). In my sample, Cubans working in Cuban businesses usually have predominantly Cuban coworkers and are much more
likely to work in Little Havana, the original core of the Cuban community just
west of downtown Miami, than in other neighborhoods.

The absence of any other significant differences shows that in contemporary Miami the ethnicity of one's employer does not have a major influence

Table 3.1.   Place of Work and Ethnicity of Coworkers by Ethnicity of Employer

Ethnicity of Employer	Place of Work						Ethnicity of Coworkers			
	Little Havana		Coral Gables		Hialeah		Cuban		Other	
	N	%	N	%	N	%	N	%	N	%
Cuban Employer	41	60	11	16	16	24	53	65	29	35
Non-Cuban Employer	5	28	9	50	4	22	3	13	20	87

on one's work experiences, calling into question whether this variable is a valid criterion for establishing the external boundaries of the Cuban enclave economy. Rather, the results support the claims by Sanders and Nee (1987, 1989) that the enclave economy should be defined as an area of concentration of Cuban businesses. This definition acknowledges that there are other factors rather than a special relationship between employers and employees that define a Cuban's work experiences. Ethnic solidarity, for example, may not be so important on the level of individual workplaces but may play a vital role on the community level.

Researchers believe that ethnic solidarity is crucial in the early stages of business development, as it allows entrepreneurs to raise capital through ethnic networks and gives them access to business information as well as a cheap and loyal ethnic labor force (Boissevain et al. 1990; Light and Karageorgis 1994). In most existing studies, the presence of ethnic solidarity is taken for granted and portrayed as a factor that does not change (Menjivar 2000). This static perspective on ethnic solidarity in the research on ethnic economies is somewhat surprising, since scholars studying social relations in immigrant groups have emphasized that ethnic networks change over time (see, for example, Boyd 1989; Hagan 1998; Mahler 1995; Menjivar 2000). If ethnic solidarity, including the strength of ethnic networks, changes over time, the ability to mobilize ethnic resources in ethnic economies should also be temporally variable.

My survey and interview research shows that ethnic solidarity in the Cuban community has decreased over time. Most of the Cubans who came to the United States in the 1960s had known each other in Cuba, migrated for the same reasons and under the same conditions, and felt isolated in Anglo-dominated Miami. Therefore, they quickly reestablished the social ties they had in their homeland. Community solidarity remained strong throughout the 1960s and 1970s, when more Cuban migrants arrived aboard the Freedom Flights. Many of the Cuban newcomers were relatives of those already in the United States and shared a similar social and economic background.

However, the Mariel Boatlift in 1980 drove a wedge into the Cuban com-munity. The newcomers differed from the more established Cubans in their socioeconomic characteristics, work ethics, and values. As opposed to the two earlier Cuban refugee waves, the Marielitos and later arrivals had lived most of their lives under the Castro regime. While the earlier arrivals strongly believed in hard work as a way to success, in their opinion the newcomers were "not used to work. . . . In Cuba there are no incentives to work because you won't get anywhere no matter if you work or not" (Roberto, interview, December 2000). Additionally, they had developed high expectations of life in the United States. According to a woman who had migrated to Miami in the 1950s and witnessed the arrival of all subsequent migration waves, "The Marielitos did not want to work; they wanted everything handed to them. . . . I know that they have gone through a period of not having, but you cannot al-ways be 'I want. I want'" (Teresa, interview, January 2001).

These differences in attitudes, and the impression that the new arrivals de-stroyed the Cubans' model minority image in the United States, created a deep rift in the Cuban community. In fact, several of my Cuban interviewees from different migration waves stated that ethnic solidarity no longer exists in the contemporary Cuban community: "Cuban solidarity is a lie. It's just propaganda. That's what you say aloud, but there is no solidarity" (Juan, in-terview, January 2001). The weakening of ethnic ties translates into a de-crease in the use of ethnic resources in Cuban businesses (compare Yoon 1991). For example, the vast majority of my respondents relied on their im-mediate family, rather than on the Cuban community as a whole, for support.

These findings show that any definition of an ethnic enclave economy based on a shared ethnicity alone is problematic. In contemporary Miami, the experiences of Cubans with Cuban employers do not significantly differ from those of Cubans employed by people of another ethnicity. Ethnic solidarity is also no longer a major factor setting the Cuban enclave economy apart from the mainstream economy. Defining the Cuban enclave economy as a concen-tration of Cuban businesses, by contrast, allows for a role for ethnicity but ac-knowledges that there are other important determinants of how it functions. Furthermore, a spatial definition can distinguish between different ethnic en-clave economies in the same metropolitan area.

INTERNAL BOUNDARIES OF THE
CUBAN ENCLAVE ECONOMY

By now scholars acknowledge that ethnic economies are embedded in a wide range of different contexts that influence their development (Kloosterman

and Rath 2001). The wider economic context, in particular, constrains or fa-
cilitates immigrants' economic opportunities. The immigrants themselves
also play an active role in shaping their own opportunities.

When the first large wave of Cubans arrived in Miami in the 1960s, the city
was an important center of winter tourism but was not otherwise well developed. This worked to the advantage of the Cuban newcomers. They did not
have to insert themselves into an existing economic structure but could develop their own businesses in the once deteriorating neighborhood later
known as Little Havana (Boswell and Curtis 1982). Since the 1970s, however, wider shifts in the economy opened further opportunities for Cubans.
First, an economic downturn forced larger Anglo firms to downsize, creating
opportunities for smaller, more flexible businesses. This trend accelerated
with the expansion of informal employment in the 1980s (Sassen-Koob
1989). Second, increasing U.S. investment in Latin America created a demand for a well-trained, bilingual labor force in the headquarters of multinational companies (Arboleya 1996; Stepick and Grenier 1993), opening new
prospects for Cubans in Miami. These economic changes provided Cubans
with opportunities both within and outside the ethnic enclave economy.

While scholars acknowledge that different metropolitan economic and urban contexts result in differences among ethnic enclave economies (Kaplan
1998; Schnell, Benenson, and Sofer 1999; Zhou 1998), there are only few examinations of intrametropolitan differences (e.g., Kwong 1987; Lin 1998).
The wider economic changes outlined above, for example, had differing effects on individual neighborhoods in Miami (figure 3.1). Coral Gables benefited the most from the increasing trade connections with Latin America as
multinational corporations moved their headquarters to this upper-class area.
Hialeah, by contrast, evolved into a significant manufacturing center as
sweatshops proliferated in the 1980s. Despite these substantive differences,
most researchers describe the entire Miami metropolitan area as the Cuban
enclave economy rather than considering separate Cuban enclave *economies*.
Furthermore, they ignore that Cubans who migrated at different points in time
and who have different educational and occupational backgrounds dominate
these neighborhoods. A systematic discussion of the development and functioning of ethnic enclave economies must therefore combine an analysis of
the characteristics of the places and the people who live and work in them.

Little Havana

The area now called Little Havana was a declining Anglo neighborhood in the
late 1950s. It attracted the Cuban exiles since it offered cheap housing, was
close to jobs downtown, and had adequate business space. Immediately after

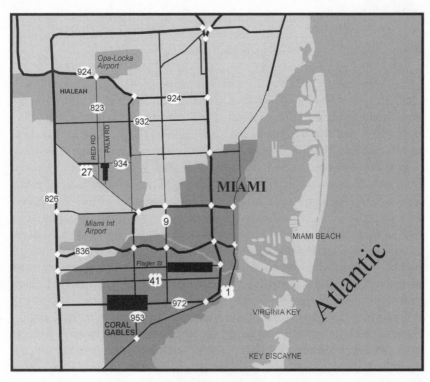

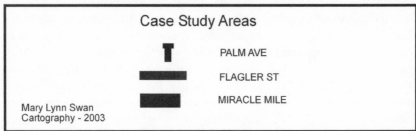

Figure 3.1.   Case Study Areas of Cubans in Miami

their arrival, Cubans started improving existing housing and opening businesses, transforming the area into a vibrant neighborhood (Boswell and Curtis 1982). Little Havana served not only as the cultural nucleus of the Cuban
community, but also as the port of entry for subsequent refugee waves. Many
newcomers first lived and worked in Little Havana before moving to better
neighborhoods once they experienced upward mobility. This trend of out-
migration accelerated in the 1980s, when refugees from Central America
flooded the neighborhood. To this day, Little Havana remains important as a

point of reception for new immigrants, as indicated by the large number of immigrant aid associations in the neighborhood. It also continues to be the cultural core of the Cuban community and home to a large number of Cuban monuments, restaurants, and cultural institutions.

Many of the Cuban businesses started in the early 1960s as small family operations and have expanded continuously since then. The Caraballo family, for example, had owned a locksmith business in Cuba. Upon arriving in Miami, they served the neighborhood from a small van. Eventually, they were able to rent a small business in the back of their current location in Little Havana before moving to the front business in the 1980s. Caraballo Locksmith now has several employees and continues to expand (figure 3.2).

Cubans run most of the businesses in Little Havana. Today this area has the most diverse economic base of all Cuban neighborhoods, with Cuban businesses ranging from informal fruit stands to medical centers, from small cafés serving Cuban coffee to large supermarkets. Businesses in Little Havana employ Cubans and other Latin Americans in manual, service, and professional functions. Many companies cater to the wider Miami community, but the percentage of businesses serving mostly Hispanics is much higher in Little Havana than in the other two neighborhoods considered in this study (table 3.2), confirming its role as the main cultural hub.

Figure 3.2.   Fourth Generation Business in Little Havana

Table 3.2.   Market Served by Place of Work

	Market Served			
Place of Work	*Hispanic Market*		*General Market*	
	N	%	N	%
Little Havana	17	30	40	70
Coral Gables	1	4	25	96
Hialeah	5	18	23	82

Coral Gables

Coral Gables is a planned residential community with tree-lined avenues and Spanish-style houses. Today, about thirty percent of its population is Cuban. While most of the Cubans I surveyed migrated directly to Little Havana and Hialeah, Coral Gables is clearly dominated by Cubans who migrated to the United States before the 1980s and moved to Coral Gables once they had regained their upper-middle- or upper-class status.

In the 1960s, the city's main thoroughfare, later called Miracle Mile, developed into a commercial center with expensive boutiques, bridal stores, and other upscale specialty stores. The vast majority of the customers are non-Latinos and most of the goods and services offered are non-ethnic. Therefore, Coral Gables offers few employment opportunities for recent arrivals who do not yet speak English. Coral Gables has virtually no businesses that could be classified ethnic businesses.

In the 1970s, multinational companies increasingly moved their headquarters to Coral Gables (figure 3.3). In fact, Coral Gables evolved into the "Corporate Capital of the Americas," with the highest concentration of multinational corporations per capita of any city in the United States (Coral Gables Chamber of Commerce 2000). Due to their trade relationships with Latin America, many of the multinational corporations needed a highly skilled bilingual workforce, attracting more established Cubans. However, they do not form part of the classic Cuban enclave economy.

Hialeah

Hialeah developed in the early twentieth century in the Everglades. It was insignificant until it became a manufacturing center after the Second World War. It is by now Florida's most extensive manufacturing complex, with a wide range of factories producing garments, electronics, and other labor-intensive goods. It also houses a large number of construction firms, car repair shops, and other companies relying heavily on manual labor. Hialeah at-

Figure 3.3.   Multinational Company on the Miracle Mile

tracts large numbers of recent immigrants since rents are cheap and jobs plentiful. Cubans alone account for over sixty percent of its residents (Hialeah-Dade Development n.d.), and almost all other residents are immigrants from Latin America.

This recent influx of Cubans into Hialeah is clearly visible in my survey. While 75 percent of the Cubans I surveyed in Coral Gables and 59 percent in Little Havana are naturalized citizens, only 18 percent in Hialeah have taken American citizenship. Another indicator of their recent arrival is their use of and proficiency in English. The Cubans surveyed in Hialeah rarely speak English at home or consider themselves proficient in English. They are also more likely to use Spanish both at home and at work, while a significant percentage in Little Havana and Coral Gables are bilingual.

While some commercial establishments in Hialeah could be classified ethnic businesses, most of the factories and other larger companies are run by Anglos or more established immigrants who want to take advantage of the cheap immigrant labor force. The vast majority of the Cubans I surveyed in Hialeah work in manual jobs, while those in Little Havana and Coral Gables are more likely to be part of the service and professional sectors. Furthermore, Hialeah's workers rarely receive insurance or benefits. Many of the goods produced in Hialeah's factories are shipped to department stores and other distributors, so they serve a non-ethnic clientele. However, the services offered in Hialeah cater almost exclusively to Hispanic residents. While it is an important port of entry for new immigrants, Hialeah is not nearly as institutionally complete as Little Havana. It has a few immigrant aid agencies but lacks Cuban cultural institutions.

As these brief sketches show, Little Havana, Coral Gables, and Hialeah vary widely in their development, the social characteristics of their population, the sectoral composition and size of businesses, economic development over time, goods produced, and customer base. They fulfill different functions for Miami's overall economy. They are also influenced in different ways by wider economic developments. In short, they are three very different places. I therefore propose that these three clusters of Cuban businesses should be seen as three separate ethnic enclave economies rather than one single, unified Cuban enclave economy.

These three ethnic enclave economies do not exist in isolation, however; their development is interconnected. Little Havana was the first Cuban enclave economy to develop. As several researchers described, it started out with only a few small Cuban family businesses. In the absence of other resources, the mobilization of ethnic resources was probably crucial in the development of these businesses. The unified Cuban enclave economy at that time served a relatively homogeneous and close-knit Cuban community.

This classic enclave economy soon changed in response to developments both within the Cuban community and in the wider contexts in which it is embedded. In the 1970s and 1980s, the Miami area was affected by wider economic shifts that strongly influenced the trajectory of the Cuban community. Both of these changes—though very different in nature—offered Cubans opportunities outside Little Havana. First, the arrival of multinational companies in Coral Gables provided good jobs for Cubans who were by now fluent in English. As a result, a new cluster of Cubans working in different professions emerged in Coral Gables. Second, the increase in factory work in Hialeah transformed the area into a new Cuban port of entry. Since a cultural center of the Cuban community already existed, it did not become as institutionally complete as Little Havana. The three neighborhoods have evolved into different ethnic enclave economies, and the nature of their businesses has changed. They rely less on ethnic resources than before, only few are run by families, and the vast majority serve a non-ethnic clientele.

CONCLUSION

As this investigation shows, the Cuban enclave economy in Miami has evolved since it first emerged in the 1960s. Instead of emphasizing the role of ethnicity in determining the boundaries of the contemporary Cuban enclave economy and explaining the way it functions, I believe that it is important to pay attention to the interaction of external and internal factors in influencing its development. External contexts, such as the general urban and economic development of the city of Miami, shape the opportunities available to Cuban entrepreneurs. Just as these contexts change, so do the geographic boundaries of the Cuban enclave economy. For example, the original Cuban enclave economy was more or less limited to Little Havana. As multinational corporations moved to Coral Gables and the manufacturing industry in Hialeah boomed, opportunities for Cubans developed in different neighborhoods, expanding the geographic boundaries of the Cuban enclave economy. Because of the different characteristics of these places, the unified ethnic enclave economy splintered into more specialized clusters of Cuban businesses. Each of these concentrations is connected to the mainstream economy in different ways and is integrated with it to varying degrees.

At the same time, internal changes also have an influence on how the ethnic enclave economy functions. The decreasing strength of ethnic solidarity and the associated decline in the Cuban community's ability to mobilize ethnic resources no longer clearly distinguishes the Cuban enclave economy from Miami's overall economy. Changes in the markets served and the sectoral composition of the businesses are other indicators of this increasing integration. It is important to determine whether the outlined development of the Cuban enclave economy in Miami parallels that in different cities and among other ethnic groups and whether ethnic enclave economies eventually lose all their special traits and become completely undistinguishable from the mainstream economy.

REFERENCES

Alberts, H. 2003. Rethinking the ethnic enclave economy: Cubans in Miami. PhD diss., University of Minnesota.

Arboleya, J. 1996. *Havana-Miami: The US-Cuba migration conflict.* Melbourne: Ocean Press.

Boissevain, J., J. Blaschke, H. Grotenberg, and I. Joseph. 1990. Ethnic entrepreneurs and ethnic strategies. In *Ethnic entrepreneurs: Immigrant business in industrial societies,* ed. R. Waldinger, H. Aldrich, and R. Ward, 131–56. Newbury Park, CA: Sage Publications.

Bonacich, E. 1973. A theory of middleman minorities. *American Sociological Review* 38:583–94.

———. 1993. The other side of entrepreneurship: A dialogue with Roger Waldinger. *International Migration Review* 28 (3): 685–92.

Bonacich, E., and J. Modell. 1980. *The economic basis of ethnic solidarity: Small business in the Japanese American community*. Berkeley: University of California Press.

Boswell, T. D., and J. R. Curtis. 1982. *The Cuban-American experience: Culture, images and perspectives*. Totowa, NJ: Rowman and Allenheld.

Boyd, M. 1989. Family and personal networks in international migration: Recent developments and new agendas. *International Migration Review* 23 (3): 638–70.

Bun, C. K., and O. J. Hui. 1995. The many faces of immigrant entrepreneurship. In *The Cambridge survey of world migration*, ed. R. Cohen, 523–32. Cambridge: Cambridge University Press.

Chin, K.-S., I.-J. Yoon, and D. Smith. 1996. Immigrant small business and international economic linkage: A case of the Korean wig business in Los Angeles. *International Migration Review* 30 (2): 485–510.

Coral Gables Chamber of Commerce. 2000. *The city beautiful: The Coral Gables Chamber of Commerce official community guide*. Coral Gables, FL: Coral Gables Chamber of Commerce.

Dijst, M., and R. van Kempen. 1991. Minority business and the hidden dimension: The influence of urban contexts on the development of ethnic enterprise. *Tijdschrift voor Economische and Sociale Geografie* 82 (2): 128–38.

Hagan, J. M. 1998. Social networks, gender, and immigrant incorporation: Resources and constraints. *American Sociological Review* 63:55–67.

Hialeah-Dade Development. n.d. *Profile of the city of Hialeah*. Hialeah, FL: Hialeah-Dade Development.

Kaplan, D. 1997. The creation of an ethnic economy: Indochinese business expansion in Saint Paul. *Economic Geography* 73 (2): 214–33.

———. 1998. The spatial structure of urban ethnic economies. *Urban Geography* 19 (6): 489–501.

Kloosterman, R., and J. Rath. 2001. Immigrant entrepreneurs in advanced economies: Mixed embeddedness further explored. *Journal of Ethnic and Migration Studies* 27 (2): 189–201.

Kloosterman, R., J. van der Leun, and J. Rath. 1999. Mixed embeddedness: (In)formal economic activities and immigrant business in the Netherlands. *International Journal of Urban and Regional Research* 23 (2): 252–66.

Kwong, P. 1987. *The new Chinatown*. New York: Hill and Wang.

Light, I., P. Bhachu, and S. Karageorgis. 1993. Migration networks and immigrant entrepreneurship. In *Immigration and entrepreneurship: Culture, capital and ethnic networks*, ed. I. Light and P. Bhachu, 25–50. New Brunswick, NJ: Transaction Publishers.

Light, I., and E. Bonacich. 1988. *Immigrant entrepreneurs: Koreans in Los Angeles 1965–1982*. Berkeley: University of California Press.

Light, I., and S. Karageorgis. 1994. The ethnic economy. In *The handbook of economic sociology*, ed. N. J. Smelser and R. Swedberg, 647–71. New York: Russell Sage Foundation.

Light, I., and C. Rosenstein. 1995. *Race, ethnicity, and entrepreneurship in urban America*. New York: Aldine de Gruyter.

Light, I., G. Sabagh, M. Bozorgmehr, and C. Der-Martirosian. 1993. Internal ethnicity in the ethnic economy. *Ethnic and Racial Studies* 16 (4): 581–97.

Lin, J. 1998. *Reconstructing Chinatown: Ethnic enclave, global change.* Minneapolis: University of Minnesota Press.

Logan, J. R., R. Alba, and T. L. McNulty. 1994. Ethnic economies in metropolitan regions: Miami and beyond. *Social Forces* 72 (3): 691–724.

Mahler, S. 1995. *American dreaming: Immigrant life on the margins.* Princeton, NJ: Princeton University Press.

Menjivar, C. 2000. *Fragmented ties: Salvadoran immigrant networks in America.* Berkeley: University of California Press.

Portes, A., and R. L. Bach. 1985. *Latin journey: Cuban and Mexican immigrants in the United States.* Berkeley: University of California Press.

Portes, A., and L. Jensen. 1987. What's an ethnic enclave? The case for conceptual clarity. *American Sociological Review* 52:768–71.

Ram, M., T. Jones, T. Abbas, and B. Sanghera. 2002. Ethnic minority enterprise in its urban context: South Asian restaurants in Birmingham. *International Journal of Urban and Regional Research* 26 (1): 24–40.

Rieff, D. 1999. *Going to Miami: Exiles, tourists and refugees in the New America.* Gainesville: University Press of Florida.

Sanders, J., and V. Nee. 1987. Limits of ethnic solidarity in the enclave economy. *American Sociological Review* 52:745–67.

———. 1989. Problems in resolving the enclave economy debate. *American Sociological Review* 54:415–18.

Sassen-Koob, S. 1989. New York City's informal economy. In *The informal economy: Studies in advanced and less developed economies*, ed. A. Portes, M. Castells, and L. A. Benton, 60–77. Baltimore: Johns Hopkins University Press.

Schnell, I., I. Benenson, and M. Sofer. 1999. The spatial patterns of Arab industrial markets in Israel. *Annals of the Association of American Geographers* 89 (2): 312–37.

Stepick, A. 1994. Miami: Capital of Latin America. In *Newcomers in the workplace: Immigrants and the restructuring of the U.S. economy*, ed. L. Lamphere, A. Stepick, and G. Grenier, 129–144. Philadelphia: Temple University Press.

Stepick, A., and G. Grenier. 1993. Cubans in Miami. In *In the barrio: Latinos and the underclass*, ed. J. Moore and R. Pinderhughes, 79–100. New York: Russell Sage Foundation.

Waldinger, R. 1993. The two sides of ethnic entrepreneurship: Response to Bonacich. *International Migration Review* 27 (3): 692–700.

Waldinger, R., H. Aldrich, and R. Ward, eds. 1990a. *Ethnic entrepreneurs: Immigrant business in industrial societies.* Newbury Park, CA: Sage Publications.

———. 1990b. Opportunities, group characteristics, and strategies. In *Ethnic entrepreneurs: Immigrant business in industrial societies*, ed. R. Waldinger, H. Aldrich, and R. Ward, 13–48. Newbury Park, CA: Sage Publications.

Wilson, K. L., and A. Portes. 1980. Immigrant enclaves: An analysis of the labor market experiences of Cubans in Miami. *American Journal of Sociology* 86:295–319.

48 *Heike Alberts*

Yoon, I.-Y. 1991. The changing significance of ethnic and class resources in immigrant businesses: The case of Korean immigrant businesses in Chicago. *International Migration Review* 25 (2): 303–31.

Zhou, Y. 1998. How do places matter? A comparative study of Chinese ethnic economies in Los Angeles and New York City. *Urban Geography* 19 (6): 531–53.

Chapter Four

Residential Segregation and Ethnic Economies in a Multicultural City: The Little Portugal of Toronto

Carlos Teixeira

Toronto, the largest and economically most important city in Canada, has historically been the major receiving area, or port of entry, for immigrants arriving in this country (figure 4.1). Even in an era of emergent globalism, Toronto is remarkable for the degree to which immigration has defined its physical, social, and economic landscapes. Today some 42 percent of Toronto's population are foreign-born, in contrast to 34 percent in Sydney, 31 percent in Los Angeles, and 23 percent in New York (Anisef and Lanphier 2003). In terms of ethnic and racial diversity, the "internationalization" of immigration to Toronto since the Second World War has dramatically altered the sociodemographic profile of its population and neighborhoods (Murdie 1996; Preston and Lo 2000; Ley 2003). In the period between 1945 and the early 1970s, the leading source countries of immigration to Canada were European, initially from Western Europe with later immigrants tending to come from southern Europe, in particular, from Italy, Greece, and Portugal. However, following changes in Canadian immigration policy in the mid-1960s, there was an important increase in immigrants from non-European countries. Since that time, countries in Asia, Latin America, Africa, the Middle East, and the Caribbean have become the most important providers of immigrants (Troper 2003).

These immigrants, coming from a vast range of cultures and social backgrounds, represent a significant supply of human capital whose diverse skill sets contribute positively to Toronto's—and Canada's—economy through participation in both paid and self-employment. Today immigration accounts for approximately fifty percent of Canada's population growth and almost seventy percent of its labor force growth (Lo, Teixeira, and Truelove 2002; Tuck 2003; Jansen and Lam 2003). One of the most significant economic

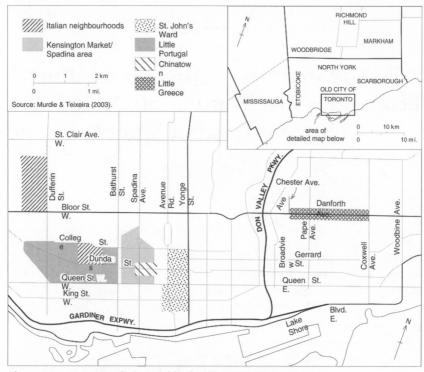

Figure 4.1. Toronto Ethnic Neighborhoods, 1900–1970

changes to impact Toronto during this time has been the increasing role of small business and entrepreneurs in the city's growth and development. In this context, ever-larger numbers of immigrants have turned to the self-employed sector of the economy and today are much more likely to be self-employed (15 percent) than those born in Canada (12 percent) (Lo, Teixeira, and Truelove 2002; Razin and Langlois 1996; Hiebert 1994). This is especially true of new Portuguese immigrants.

THE LITTLE PORTUGAL OF TORONTO

For most of the twentieth century, new immigrant groups to Toronto arrived and settled in inner city immigrant reception areas where they formed institutionally complete ethnic neighborhoods. Here they established businesses and religious and cultural organizations and reproduced many of the characteristics and traditions of the societies that they left behind in their countries of origin. Over time, once these groups became established in Toronto, they gradually moved to the suburbs in search of the "Canadian dream" (e.g., a single family dwelling) in an intra-city migration that usually involved some form of segregated resettlement.

The Portuguese group is representative of this traditional settlement pattern, having occupied an important position in Canada's major urban centers—in particular, in Toronto—since the mid-1960s. According to the 1996 Canadian Census, approximately 58 percent of Portuguese immigrants to Toronto arrived in the period 1966–1975 (Murdie 1996). Extended Portuguese families settled in Toronto through chain migration, a factor that ultimately led to the formation of distinctive residential streets and neighborhoods (e.g., Little Portugal) in downtown Toronto (Teixeira and Murdie 1997; Anderson and Higgs 1976). Establishing roots became a priority for new Portuguese arrivals to Toronto. Beginning in the 1950s with the arrival of the pioneers, Portuguese immigrants to Toronto built a compact community in and around Kensington Market (see "initial area of settlement" in figure 4.2). The Kensington area—centered on Nassau Street—housed the first Portuguese cultural organization in Toronto, and this street was also the location of the first Portuguese-owned business (a restaurant) in the mid-1950s.

From the end of the 1950s to the early 1970s, an infusion of Portuguese businesses revitalized Kensington Market. During this time on Augusta Avenue, Baldwin Street, Kensington Avenue, and Nassau Street, Portuguese businesses such as fruit stores, fish markets, grocery stores, clothing stores, restaurants, barber shops, and bakeries opened in rapid succession. By the mid-1960s Kensington Market was, in effect, a Portuguese market, due not only to the large number of businesses owned by Portuguese entrepreneurs in the area, but also to the population of Portuguese immigrants in the surrounding neighborhoods who went to the market to purchase groceries and other goods. Within a short span of years, Augusta Avenue (Kensington's main commercial street) became known as the *rua dos Portugueses* (street of the Portuguese) (Ribeiro 1990).

From the mid-1950s to the end of the 1960s, Kensington Market and the surrounding neighborhoods was the major port of entry for Portuguese arriving in Toronto (figure 4.2). Portuguese immigrants purchased inexpensive houses that were earlier occupied by Jewish and Italian immigrants and, through renovations and upgrades, rejuvenated run-down neighborhoods. Given that most of these immigrants originated in the rural areas of Portugal, in particular the islands of the Azores, their housing renovations—both in Kensington and later in Little Portugal—reflected the rural aesthetics and

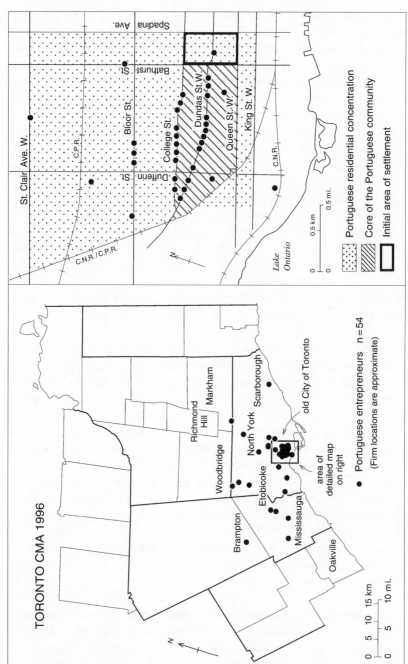

Figure 4.2. Distribution of Portuguese Entrepreneurs in Toronto CMA, 1996

cultural values of their homeland. As an article in the *Toronto Star* at the time noted:

> The Portuguese, like the equally charming Newfoundlanders, like to paint their houses bright colours, scarlet being the favourite. They will even occasionally paint the mortar between the bricks white. They often grow cabbages and other vegetables in their front yards unless the yard contains a shrine to Our Lady of Fatima, in which case flowers are preferred. (Turner 1973, A3)

In the late 1960s, the Portuguese community moved west of Kensington Market along College and Dundas Streets. The businesses, as well as the social, cultural, and religious institutions of the community, followed this residential migration leading to the creation of an area known today as Little Portugal. As an article in the Portuguese media of the time noted:

> For the last two years, that area [Dundas Street, west of Bathurst Street] has suffered such important transformations that in a short period of time it may become the first area of Portuguese businesses concentration in Toronto. Within the boundaries of an area with a high concentration of Portuguese, everything converges to that point. New businesses move to the area, others transfer their businesses from other places [e.g., Kensington Market] to there. (Ribeiro 1970, 5)

In this area the Portuguese created, in a relatively short period of time, one of the most visible ethnic economies and institutionally complete communities in Toronto: Little Portugal (see figure 4.2). By the early 1990s, most of the Portuguese in the city of Toronto (excluding its suburbs) resided in this relatively compact cluster bounded by Bathurst Street (East), College Street West (North), Queen Street West (South), and CNR/CPR (West) (figure 4.2). This residential neighborhood has remained intact and contains most of the community's social, cultural, and religious institutions as well as its two most important commercial strips—Dundas and College Streets. There are about 39,000 Portuguese in this area, the core of the Portuguese community accounting for approximately 86 percent of the total Portuguese population in the city (Teixeira and Murdie 1997).

By the mid-1990s, approximately two-thirds of the 3,500 businesses owned by Portuguese immigrants in the province of Ontario were located in the city of Toronto, especially within Little Portugal and surrounding neighborhoods (see "Portuguese residential concentration" in figure 4.2). Today, this high concentration of Portuguese businesses in a relatively small geographical area is among the most visible and important ethnic economies in the city (Teixeira 2000; Qadeer 2003). The Portuguese have also been among the most segregated groups in Toronto, having the second highest segregation index (0.63) after the Jewish population (0.78) (Dakan 1998). Thus, the Portuguese not only built an institutionally complete community but also an important ethnic economy within a highly spatially-restricted co-ethnic (Portuguese) market. In contrast to other immigrant groups (e.g., Chinese, Italians) who resettled their core businesses in other parts of the city and/or in the suburbs of Toronto, the Portuguese retained a very strong visible presence—both residentially and commercially—in the downtown Little Portugal. This high concentration of the Portuguese in a well-defined neighborhood has effectively transformed the ethnocultural landscape of this part of Toronto.

Despite the suburbanization of many Portuguese, Little Portugal remains healthy and continues attracting many of those who left Toronto. Cultural factors, including a desire to shop for Portuguese goods in a Portuguese environment, seem to have played a role in the business decisions of Portuguese entrepreneurs to remain in important numbers in the downtown core. As one successful Portuguese businessman, who lives in Mississauga but has his businesses in Toronto, notes: "The businessmen who have businesses in Toronto do not need business in Mississauga—some were unfortunate with business initiatives in Mississauga. It's always a risk that is taken. A lot of Portuguese go to Toronto to shop, especially for Portuguese products such as sausage and fish" (Teixeira 2002, 261). Some suburban business leaders criticize this activity because it undermines the economic vitality of their own communities. One businessman observes: "Why not invest here [Mississauga]? Others go to Toronto to shop in Portuguese stores when here we have exactly the same products. We can't depend exclusively anymore on the Portuguese clientele—it's not enough if we want to survive, as businessmen. Only 10 to 15 percent of my clients are Portuguese" (Teixeira 2002, 262).

The residential mobility of the Portuguese community reflects their desire to live in better conditions, preferably in a single family dwelling located in a good neighborhood. This resettlement of the Portuguese in Mississauga (see figure 4.3) followed a series of successful marketing campaigns by Portuguese real estate agents. Another reason for this choice was the existence of public and private transportation networks in the area that facilitate suburban access to downtown ethnic shops. Using these networks, suburbanite Portuguese continue to participate in the institutional life and vitality of the downtown community.

Clearly, the Portuguese in Toronto have constructed a well-defined community with an appreciable number of diverse social and economic organizations and an established business structure. In this context, institutional completeness represents a cultural resource or a structural condition (see Breton 1964). However, questions remain as to how entrepreneurs utilize group resources

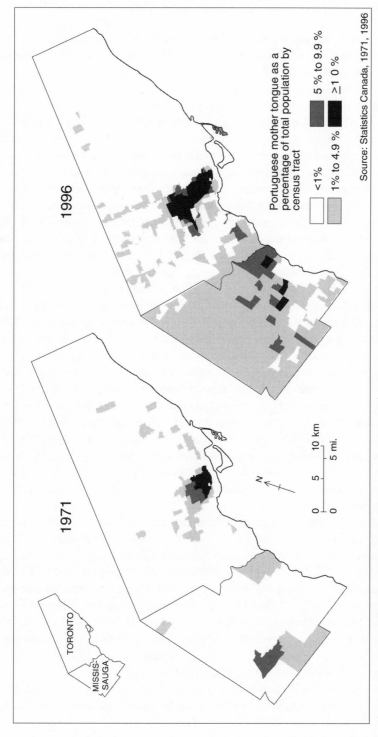

1971

1996

TORONTO

MISSIS-SAUGA

Portuguese mother tongue as a
percentage of total population by
census tract

□ <1%

□ 1% to 4.9 %

■ 5 % to 9.9 %

■ ≥1 0 %

Source: Statistics Canada, 1971, 1996

N

0   5   10 km
0   5 mi.

Figure 4.3.   Portuguese Population in the Cities of Toronto and Mississauga, 1971 and 1996

and how these resources contribute to the formation, maintenance, and success of Portuguese-owned businesses. To answer these questions, we surveyed about fifty Portuguese entrepreneurs.[1]

STARTING A PORTUGUESE BUSINESS IN TORONTO

For first generation Portuguese immigrants in Canada, both homeownership and becoming an entrepreneur on Canadian soil are signs of success and ultimately of social and economic mobility (Teixeira 2000, 2001). Portuguese entrepreneurs—especially the more successful ones—are respected figures in Toronto's Portuguese community, occupying prestigious positions in the community's main social, cultural, and business organizations. Given these multiple consequences of entrepreneurship, we asked Portuguese entrepreneurs what reasons motivated their going into business.

The most common answers to this question were to achieve "control of their own destiny" and to "do better economically." For most of these Portuguese entrepreneurs, being owners of their own business represented the fulfilment of a dream as an immigrant in Canada. Portuguese entrepreneurs have not been pushed into self-employment. In fact, only one out of ten respondents cited "lack of jobs" as a major push factor behind going into business, a finding which suggests that discrimination in the job market is a nonissue for this group of entrepreneurs. Instead, the reasons behind Portuguese entrepreneurship appear to be more of a pull. The responses of some of the participants reflect this conclusion. One person said, "I am a very ambitious person and my dream was always to have my own business . . . to give my family a better life." Another said, "I wanted to have control of my own destiny. . . . During recessions, immigrants are the first ones to be laid off and the last to be called back."

Reinforcing this finding, results indicate that only about one-third of the Portuguese interviewed experienced barriers during the establishment of their businesses. Of those citing barriers, the most important ones were language problems (unfamiliarity with English), lack of information about business practices, and problems obtaining clients. The responses of participants indicate that these main barriers did not occur singly but often reinforced each other: "The first barrier was the language and we also encountered many difficulties, specifically not being able to compete with bigger companies/ stores." Another respondendent listed "Language barriers . . . new Canadian system [of doing business] and lack of contacts."

Compared to the barriers experienced by visible minority entrepreneurs in both the United States and Europe (i.e., institutionalized discrimination), the

Portuguese group in Toronto have operated within a much more favorable business environment for ethnic entrepreneurship (see Waldinger, Aldrich, and Ward 1990; Rath and Kloosterman 2000; Lo, Teixeira, and Truelove 2002). One Portuguese entrepreneur declared, "I encounter the normal difficulties when one starts a business. However, I did not go into business thinking that I was an immigrant." This response illustrates not only the lack of discrimination faced by entrepreneurs from this group but also the business strategy that some Portuguese immigrants adopt in Canada. Portuguese entrepreneurs assume that they will enter business with the same absence of discriminatory barriers faced by other Canadian entrepreneurs.

Co-ethnic and family labor seems to play an important role in the operational life and success of Portuguese businesses. Portuguese businesses tend to be small, with four respondents operating their businesses with no help, twenty-nine with between two to five employees, and twelve with between six to fifteen employees. Only four of the entrepreneurs declared having more than thirty employees, and these were all in manufacturing or construction. In these businesses, over two-thirds of Portuguese entrepreneurs employ family members and seven-eighths employ Portuguese workers. It appears that a regional orientation is also at work in the hiring process, with the region of origin in Portugal (from the mainland or the islands of Azores and Madeira) of the entrepreneur influencing his determination of who to hire. Moreover, for some types of Portuguese businesses (e.g., real estate agencies, travel agencies, or grocery stores which specialize in regional products such as sausages, cheeses, etc.), the regional orientation of employees mirrors the region of origin of the business's clients. In a highly concentrated and intimate community such as Toronto's Little Portugal, Portuguese clients are not only looking for specific ethnic products but also a highly personalized type of service where trust and good reputation in the community are important considerations (see Teixeira 1998).

When asked how Portuguese entrepreneurs recruited their employees, 84 percent cited their reliance on informal channels such as Portuguese friends and relatives. This heavy reliance may partly explain the tendency of the Portuguese to hire employees from the same region and/or island of Portugal. Moreover, many Portuguese entrepreneurs advertise their businesses through ethnic sources of information, particularly Portuguese telephone directories and "ethnic" media. In general, it appears that for this group of Portuguese entrepreneurs, few have sought advice outside their group regarding the operation and advertising of their businesses.

We also asked respondents how important the hiring of co-ethnic employees was to the success of their businesses. Not surprisingly, two-thirds of respondents cited it as very important and, when asked for specifics, overwhelmingly cited knowledge of the Portuguese language followed by knowledge of the client base. In this regard, it is clear that Portuguese entrepreneurs regard insider knowledge of the group's language and cultural preferences to be important. As one respondent observed: "My business is ninety percent in the Portuguese community. Having Portuguese people as employees makes our clients very comfortable and happy."

Although Toronto's Portuguese community has migrated over the last three decades along the immigrant corridor from the downtown core to the suburbs (e.g., Mississauga, Brampton, Oakville), the majority of Portuguese businesses still continue to operate within Little Portugal. In many respects, this concentration of Portuguese businesses represents an ethnic economy that exists to serve a Portuguese clientele. The responses of entrepreneurs reflected this ethnic orientation. As one entrepreneur put it, "We can live an entire life here speaking and living only in Portuguese." This view reflects the general location pattern of ethnic enclave businesses, which are usually conspicuous by their proximity to their community. As figure 4.2 suggests, approximately half of the Portuguese businesses cited in the survey are located in Little Portugal, with a few located along the immigrant corridor or in Mississauga. The types of business owned by Portuguese are characteristic of ethnic enclave economies where the majority of business owners, employees, and clients are of the same group/ethnicity—retail business (39 percent); followed by finance, insurance, and real estate (22 percent); and medical, legal, and other services (15 percent). In this context, we asked respondents why they located their businesses where they did. In reply, about half indicated that proximity to the Portuguese community was the most important reason for selecting their present business location (table 4.1). These entrepreneurs seemed to agree that their proximity to the Portuguese community was an important factor in their business success.

As one respondent noted: "I always lived in the neighborhood. I knew a lot of people there. I felt I had a better chance of success in this neighborhood than in a neighborhood that I didn't know nobody."

Clearly, Portuguese entrepreneurs consider the residential patterns of the Portuguese community, their primary clientele, in their choice of business locations. In recent years some Portuguese entrepreneurs have ventured to locate their businesses outside the core of the Portuguese community. These businesses—grocery stores, restaurants, and real estate agencies—have followed the Portuguese community in its migration along Toronto's northwest-oriented immigrant corridor along the path previously followed by the Italian group. Indeed, the response of one entrepreneur—a real estate agent—suggests that Portuguese businesses have considered the residential settlement

**Table 4.1. Reasons for Present Business Locations of
Portuguese Ethnics**

	N	%
Proximity to Ethnic Community	29	53.7
Central Location		
Public Transportation/Parking	12	22.2
Ethnic/Community Oriented Business	12	22.2
Occupancy Costs—Buy/Rent	5	9.3
Location of Suppliers	2	3.7
Proximity to Residence	1	1.9
Ethnic/Racial Composition of Area		
Potential for Expansion		
Other	7	13.0
Total	**54**	

Source: Questionnaire Survey.

patterns of both Italian and Portuguese groups in the location of their businesses: "Obviously my main market was the Portuguese and Italian communities. The Portuguese clientele has a preference for buying houses previously owned by Italians. Since my main customers [buyers] were Portuguese, my preoccupation was to place my centre of activity accessible to both communities."

This orientation of Portuguese entrepreneurs toward a geographically segregated co-ethnic market is likely to continue for years to come. However, the question as to whether or not Portuguese entrepreneurs will survive outside of the geographical boundaries of Little Portugal—a choice between the enclave and the mainstream—remains unanswered.

ENTREPRENEUR BUSINESSES
AND COMMUNITY RESOURCES

The nature of the Portuguese migration to Canada—being primarily through sponsorship and chain migration—contributed to the formation of a relatively homogeneous group. Portuguese immigrants relied extensively on networks of friendship and kinship ties both to find jobs and in the selection of the neighborhood of settlement upon arrival in Canada (Anderson 1974). In the case of Toronto, these complex ethnic networks of contacts helped build a highly visible Little Portugal in the core of the city (Anderson 1974; Teixeira 2000). Given that an important characteristic of the Portuguese immigration

to Toronto has been their tendency to form highly visible, institutionally complete neighborhoods and economies, we asked respondents about the importance of ethnic networks of information to the establishment and operation of
their businesses.

Table 4.2 reveals that Portuguese entrepreneurs used a wide variety of sources
to obtain information and/or advice about starting and operating their businesses.
The main source of business information and advice for the Portuguese entrepreneurs was ethnic friends and relatives. Overall, results indicate that Portuguese entrepreneurs rely extensively on their own community (ethnic) resources. Respondents also cited community resources as being particularly
important in providing information about clients/potential customers and about
the business climate (table 4.3). These findings lend support to the main thesis
that Portuguese entrepreneurs' involvement in the network of kinship/friendship
and community ties is integral to their business success.

Entrepreneurs' participation in community organizations is a key indicator of
their degree of community involvement. Not surprisingly, approximately 85
percent of Portuguese entrepreneurs declared being somewhat or highly involved in the social-cultural life of the Portuguese community. Also, approximately half of the Portuguese entrepreneurs indicated being a member and/or
participating actively in the life of their community's business-professional organizations and sociocultural associations. Most Portuguese entrepreneurs em-

**Table 4.2.   Most Important Information Source Used to
Start/Operate Current Business**

	Portuguese N=54	
	N	%
Ethnic Sources		
Ethnic Friends/Relations	23	42.6
Ethnic Media	4	7.4
Ethnic Organizations/Institutions	2	3.7
Sources Used:	29	63.0
Non-Ethnic Sources		
Non-Ethnic Friends	7	13.0
Non-Ethnic Organizations/Institutions	4	7.4
Non-Ethnic Media	1	1.9
Other	5	9.3
Sources Used:	17	37.0
Not Used Source	5	9.3

Source: Questionnaire Survey.

**Table 4.3.   Degree of Importance of "Ethnic Sources" in the
Following Aspects Related to the Establishment/Operation of
Current Business**

	Portuguese N=46	
	N	%[1]
Recommending Clients	26	56.5
Providing Information about Market / Climate for Business	22	47.8
Providing Information About Business Site	15	32.6
Recommending Employees	14	30.4
Providing Information About Government Assistance, Legal Matters	11	23.9
Providing Mutual Aid and Assistance in Acquiring Training in Business	11	23.9
Providing Capital to Establish and/or Expand Current Business	11	23.9
Other	2	4.3

Source: Questionnaire survey.
[1]Percentage of entrepreneurs who indicate ethnic sources being "very important" or "important" in the establishment/operation of current business.

phasized the importance of their participation in the life of community organizations. As one entrepreneur observed: "[Portuguese organizations] are a network of vital information and contacts with different people, in different types of businesses, and regional cultures [islands and the mainland Portugal]."

The Portuguese community continues to show a high degree of group cohesiveness and institutional completeness as well as of culture identification, language retention, and residential segregation (Murdie and Teixeira 2003). Portuguese entrepreneurs also depend heavily on clients from the same ethnic background for their market. More than two-thirds of the entrepreneurs indicated that over half of their clients are Portuguese, and explain this by citing the "community oriented" nature of their business. As one entrepreneur observed: "We cater to the language, culture and other aspects of the [Portuguese] clients." Thus, we can conclude that Portuguese entrepreneurs are still heavily dependent upon an ethnic (Portuguese) clientele for their markets and have yet to make major advances into mainstream markets.

Portuguese entrepreneurs expressed mixed attitudes regarding the evaluation of success and the future. Four out of five Portuguese entrepreneurs described themselves as very or moderately successful. They identified the most important contributors to this success as being a good reputation in the community, reliance on Portuguese market, and the location of the business in and around the Portuguese community. Regarding Portuguese entrepreneurship in general, 45 percent said it was going to be stable with the rest divided between those who thought it would grow or decline. Contributing to the pessimistic outlook are the decrease in Portuguese immigration to Canada, the competitiveness of the ethnic market, and the lack of new generations of Portuguese entrepreneurs entering ethnic business. Generational change in the Portuguese community was also cited as a reason for this pessimism. As one respondent noted, "Our customers' children are all growing and most of them don't want/like traditional European styles and quality in children's clothes." Another said, "Decrease in immigration, ageing population and integration . . . new generation is not 'Portuguese' but 'Canadian.' They want American brands."

Given these responses, it is surprising to note that an overwhelming 84 percent of Portuguese entrepreneurs interviewed would encourage other Portuguese to go into business. Although Portuguese entrepreneurs appear aware of their dependency on the co-ethnic market and the implications of declining Portuguese immigration to Canada, they remain nonetheless highly positive regarding the importance of their entrepreneurship. For Portuguese entrepreneurs, their ethnic business symbolizes not only economic success but also visibility and influence in both the Portuguese community and mainstream Canadian society.

CONCLUSION

In the context of economic globalization, Canada's increasingly multicultural population represents a significant national economic asset in terms of both the domestic economy and Canada's ability to access international markets. The Portuguese have been a highly visible part of Canada's rich and complex cultural mosaic, and their impact is evident in the physical landscape of Toronto's Little Portugal. Portuguese homeowners, organizations, and businesses have all contributed to transforming the cultural, social, and economic geography of Toronto.

The factors responsible for the formation of Little Portugal—an institutionally complete community and self-sufficient ethnic economy—in Toronto are varied. These include factors internal to the Portuguese group, such as the retention of cultural traditions and the need to live close to friends and relatives from the same ethnic background. From this perspective, the Portuguese ethnic enclave is in large part an expression of cultural preferences. The shared religious, social, and economic needs of this enclave's residents and community leaders have served as the basis for their integration into Canadian society as a whole. This cultural preference to live and work close to other members of the Portuguese group has played an integral role in the formation of a strong and visible ethnic economy.

Portuguese entrepreneurs have followed a community-oriented strategy in their business practices. Portuguese immigrants and entrepreneurs remain one of the most concentrated groups in Toronto (Qadeer 2003; Teixeira and Murdie 1997). Not surprisingly, Portuguese entrepreneurs were highly involved in co-ethnic networks of kinship, friendship, and community ties. These allowed them to build, in a relatively short period of time, an ethnic economy in Little Portugal in the core of Toronto. Portuguese entrepreneurs also display a high degree of social embeddedness, being both highly concentrated and largely dependent on their own ethnic economy for their business success.

In this context, we can see not only how an institutionally complete community has been important to the economic success of Portuguese immigrant businesses but also how immigrant community networks and cultural values have shaped the physical, social, and economic landscapes of one of Canada's major metropolises. In this way, the visible presence of a dynamic and prosperous Portuguese community has contributed to the reputation Toronto enjoys today as a multicultural "city of homelands" and bears witness to the power of immigration as an engine of economic growth and social transformation.

NOTE

1. The main source data for this study was a questionnaire survey administered to a sample of self-employed Portuguese entrepreneurs in the Toronto CMA. Nine out of ten of the Portuguese entrepreneurs interviewed were born in Portugal. This group of respondents are culturally homogeneous and are typical of a relatively recent immigrant group. All respondents were of the same ethnic background (Portuguese) and declared Portuguese as their "mother tongue." Half of the Portuguese entrepreneurs arrived in Canada during the period 1954–1969, and 86 percent emigrated for economic reasons and/or came to join the family. Not surprisingly, sponsorship and family reunification characterizes the immigration process of these respondents. In regard to education, 28 percent of Portuguese entrepreneurs did not attend school in Canada, in part because of age (more than 18 years of age) upon arrival in Canada, while 30 percent completed high school or university.

REFERENCES

Anderson, G. M. 1974. *Networks of contact: The Portuguese and Toronto*. Waterloo, Ontario: Wilfrid Laurier University Publications.

Anderson, G. M., and D. Higgs. 1976. *A future to inherit: The Portuguese communities of Canada*. Toronto: McClelland and Stewart.

Anisef, P., and M. Lanphier. 2003. Introduction: Immigration and accommodation of diversity. In *The world in a city*, ed. P. Anisef and M. Lanphier, 3–18. Toronto: University of Toronto Press.

Breton, R. 1964. Institutional completeness of ethnic communities and the personal relations of immigrants. *American Journal of Sociology* 70:193–205.

Dakan, W. 1998. Ethnic segregation and concentration in Canadian cities. Paper presented at the Association of American Geographers, Boston.

Hiebert, D. 1994. Focus: Immigration to Canada. *The Canadian Geographer* 38:254–58.

Jansen, C., and L. Lam. 2003. Immigrants in the greater Toronto area: A sociodemographic overview. In *The world in a city*, ed. P. Anisef and M. Lanphier, 63–131. Toronto: University of Toronto Press.

Ley, D. 2003. Seeking *homo economicus*: The Canadian state and the strange story of the business immigration program. *Annals of the Association of American Geographers* 93:426–41.

Lo, L., C. Teixeira, and M. Truelove. 2002. Cultural resources, ethnic strategies, and immigrant entrepreneurship: A comparative study of five immigrant groups in the Toronto CMA. CERIS Working Paper Series, no. 21, Joint Centre of Excellence for Research on Immigration and Settlement, Toronto.

Murdie, R. A. 1996. Economic restructuring and social polarization in Toronto. In *Social polarization in post-industrial metropolises*, ed. J. O'Loughlin and J. Friedrichs, 207–58. New York: Walter de Gruyter.

Murdie, R. A., and C. Teixeira. 2003. Towards a comfortable neighborhood and appropriate housing: Immigrant experiences in Toronto. In *The world in a city*, ed. P. Anisef and M. Lanphier, 132–91. Toronto: University of Toronto Press.

Preston, V., and L. Lo. 2000. "Asian theme" malls in suburban Toronto: Land use conflicts in Richmond Hill. *The Canadian Geographer* 44:182–90.

Qadeer, M. 2003. Ethnic segregation in a multicultural city: The case of Toronto, Canada. CERIS Working Paper Series, no. 28, Joint Centre of Excellence for Research on Immigration and Settlement, Toronto.

Rath, J., and R. Kloosterman. 2000. Outsiders' business: A critical review of research on immigrant entrepreneurship. *International Migration Review* 34:657–81.

Razin, E., and A. Langlois. 1996. Metropolitan characteristics and entrepreneurship among immigrants and ethnic groups in Canada. *International Migration Review* 30:703–27.

Ribeiro, M. A. 1970. Jose Freitas inaugurou os novos escritorios de real estate. *Correio Portugues*, 15 February: 11.

———. 1990. *O Canada e a presenca Portuguesa*. Toronto: Correio Portugues.

Teixeira, C. 1998. Cultural resources and ethnic entrepreneurship: A case study of the Portuguese real estate industry in Toronto. *The Canadian Geographer* 42:267–81.

———. 2000. On the move: Portuguese in Toronto. In *The Portuguese in Canada: From the sea to the city*, ed. C. Teixeira and V. Da Rosa, 207–20. Toronto: University of Toronto Press.

———. 2001. Community resources and opportunities in ethnic economies: A case study of Portuguese and Black entrepreneurs in Toronto. *Urban Studies* 38:2055–78.

———. 2002. A village of dream homes: The Portuguese in Mississauga. In *Mississauga: The first 10,000 years*, ed. F. Dieterman, 244–63. Mississauga, ON: Mississauga Heritage Foundation.

Teixeira, C., and R. A. Murdie. 1997. The role of ethnic real estate agents in the residential relocation process: A case study of Portuguese homebuyers in suburban Toronto. *Urban Geography* 18:497–520.

Troper, H. 2003. Becoming an immigrant city: A history of immigration into Toronto since the Second World War. In *The world in a city*, ed. P. Anisef and M. Lanphier, 19–62. Toronto: University of Toronto Press.

Tuck, S. 2003. Ottawa eases up on immigration guidelines. *Globe and Mail*, 19 September.

Turner, D. 1973. The Portuguese find "making it" has a new twist. *Toronto Star*, 8 December.

Waldinger, R., H. Aldrich, and R. Ward. 1990. Opportunities, group characteristics, and strategies. In *Ethnic entrepreneurs*, ed. R. Waldinger, H. Aldrich, and R. Ward, 13–48. Newbury Park, CA: Sage Publications.

Chapter Five

Race, Space, Crime, and the African American Entrepreneur: Business Owner Attitudes, Business Success, and the Neighborhood Context

David H. Kaplan and Bessie House-Soremekun

Compared to several other populations, African Americans have lower rates of business ownership (Boyd 1990; Light and Gold 2000). This gap has been attributed to many factors, such as financial capital, education and training, and social capital (Light 1972; Fratoe 1998; Butler 1991; Bates 1997; House-Soremekun 2002b, 2002c). While all of these factors play a significant role, scholars have tended to neglect the immediate neighborhood environment in which Black businesses operate and how this may help or hinder their overall business success.

Of interest to this chapter is the issue of crime—both in regard to the reality and the perception of crime. Crime can affect businesses in several ways. First, it can result in damage or property loss to the business itself. Second, it can require increased overhead through expensive security measures and higher insurance rates. Third, it can deter people from shopping in an establishment. These factors and others can make the operation of a business in a high-crime neighborhood problematic (House-Soremekun 2002a). Therefore, geographic location, and the crime-related aspects attributed to particular locations, plays a substantive role in shaping the experiences of African American entrepreneurs.

This chapter explores the linkage between Black business success, crime rates, and perceptions of crime at the neighborhood level. We argue that business success must be understood contextually in relationship to the attributes of the neighborhoods within which they operate. Most Black businesses exist within a context of spatial segregation, and many operate within communities that are economically and socially challenged. We address the issue of how the neighborhood context, particularly in relation to crime, influences business success.

RACE, GEOGRAPHIC SPACE, AND CRIME

A number of scholars have examined how racial dynamics influence the development of African American businesses in the United States across time and space (Walker 1998; Butler 1991; Feagin and Sikes 1994; House-Soremekun 2002b, 2002c; Bates 1993, 1997). These studies emphasize the salience of racial discrimination in prohibiting the growth and maturation of the Black-owned business sector in the United States. Walker (1998) demonstrates that the establishment of a business ethos amongst African Americans was of longstanding duration. According to Walker (1998, xiv):

> Africans in America, slave and free, seized every opportunity to develop enterprises and participate as businesspeople in the commercial life of a developing new nation. While they established a tradition of Black business participation in colonial America, slavery and racism defeated attempts by Blacks to develop enterprises competitive with those established by whites.

Many of the difficulties experienced by Black entrepreneurs generally are seen within particular sectors of the economy. Feagin and Sikes (1994) argue that racial discrimination has diminished the numbers of African American entrepreneurs owning businesses in the construction industry. An "old boys network" continues to inhibit the formation of new alliances between Black entrepreneurs and white contractors. Blacks often have trouble getting construction bids and are excluded from receiving critical information about bidding and contracting processes. There continue to be ongoing problems in acquiring bonding, which is important in receiving construction contracts. Feagin and Sikes (1994, 581) attribute this to "institutional racism," which includes arrangements of "dominant white businesses with a history of mutually supporting, racially exclusive or restrictive networks."

Several scholars have also examined the effects of geography and spatial factors on minority business development. Waldinger, McEvoy, and Aldrich (1990) emphasize that spatial factors can have a very important impact on the development of ethnic entrepreneurial communities. They argue that historically, immigrant and newly emerging groups tended to locate themselves in particular geographical areas of the community, isolating themselves from members of the dominant community. Community residents needed certain types of products and services and often depended on their own ethnic entrepreneurial community members to satisfy their cultural preferences. Geographical space can be considered to be a resource that under certain conditions can actually bring positive benefits to ethnic entrepreneurs (Kaplan 1998).

While spatial concentration has benefited many ethnic groups in the United States, it has not necessarily enhanced the economic condition of African American entrepreneurs. The role of the neighborhood context has significant impacts on Black business development. African American businesses are often located in communities where the majority of residents are Black. These communities often have higher rates of joblessness, lower per capita incomes, and increasing levels of criminal activity (House-Soremekun 2002a). They are also more likely to be areas where fewer employment opportunities exist (Kaplan 1999). According to Coulton and Chow (1995, 202), "modern urban poverty is embedded in a set of mutually reinforcing economic and social forces at the regional, neighborhood and individual level."

The neighborhood effect would pertain to Black entrepreneurial success as well, one of the most critical elements of a dynamic neighborhood. Research indicates that African American entrepreneurs tend to be located in neighborhoods that are demographically, economically, and socially different from those inhabited by white entrepreneurs. Within these neighborhoods, there are often limited sources of capital available to Black entrepreneurs (Bates 1997). Businesses located within the segregated community often rely on customers inside the neighborhood (Texeira 2001), but the existing customer pool may be fairly poor (Cummings 1999).

Prior studies have shown that crime is an unwelcome interloper in economically disadvantaged neighborhoods (Krivo and Peterson 1996), precisely those neighborhoods where many Black businesses are established. Linkages between race, poverty, segregation, and crime have already been established in the literature. For example, Massey (1990, 329) finds that racial segregation was a critical variable that led to the development of an urban underclass during the the 1970s in the United States; he states that "increases in poverty concentration are, in turn, associated with other changes in the socioeconomic character of neighborhoods, transforming them into physically deteriorated areas of high crime, poor schools, and excessive mortality where welfare dependent, female-headed families are the norm." It follows, therefore, that there is a relationship between living in very disadvantaged neighborhoods and high incidences of criminal activity (Krivo and Peterson 1996). Thus, crime is one of the key neighborhood characteristics that may make it more difficult for Black entrepreneurs to maintain their businesses.

Hakim and Schachmurove (1996) focus attention on several suburban areas of Philadelphia in order to determine which variables can be used to predict when burglaries are likely to occur. They find that businesses were less likely to experience a burglary if they were found within a three block area of heavy traffic and that business owners who had been in operation for less than a year were more likely to have been burglarized than those who had been in operation for longer periods of time. Kuratko et al. (2000) also examine the impact of crime on small businesses. They focus on a number of key areas that include the types of criminal activities that business owners experience, the amount that each of these crimes costs, preventive measures being taken by the entrepreneurs, whether the entrepreneurs are investing in a significant way in crime preventive security systems, and whether firms subsumed under different business sectors of the economy experience crime in different ways. The results of the study indicate that the most common and costly crimes experienced by the business owners were shoplifting of merchandise/money and employee theft. Although the participants in the study by Kuratko and colleagues were not seriously concerned with criminal activity in regard to their business enterprises, they were actively engaged in using preventive measures to reduce the possibility of criminal activity in the future. Last, entrepreneurs that owned businesses in the service and retail sectors of the economy believed that it was important to take measures against crime more than did entrepreneurs who owned manufacturing companies.

BLACK BUSINESS ACTIVITY IN THE CLEVELAND CONTEXT

To begin the discussion of how Black-owned businesses operate within Cleveland, it helps to consider the larger scale portrait of Black-owned businesses in the United States and in Ohio. Compared with businesses overall, Black businesses generally 1) are less likely to have employees, 2) have on average fewer employees even among those firms with employees, 3) are far smaller when measured in terms of their sales volume, 4) pay slightly less per employee, and 5) constitute a smaller share per 1,000 population. Black business development lags behind the population as a whole. Part of this has to do with lower rates of capital formation, but Black business owners are also often concentrated in less lucrative businesses. As a whole, Black-owned firms concentrate on construction, retail, and consumer services. Even among these industry groups, however, Black-owned businesses receive much lower average receipts (U.S. Bureau of the Census 2001). For example, the average yearly receipts for a construction firm is $405,000, whereas it is only $136,000 for a Black-owned construction company.

As for the Black business share of the overall economy, Black-owned firms constitute about four percent of the total for all firms, but less than two percent for those firms with employees (a much more exclusive pool). In regard to sales, payroll, and employees, the contribution is well under one percent. This compares to a population proportion of just over 12 percent (11.5 percent in Ohio).

Cleveland and Cuyahoga County (where Cleveland is located) are the largest centers for Black business activity within Ohio. At the same time, a very small proportion of the African American population owns a business in these localities. Cleveland is still one of the most residentially segregated cities in the United States, and poverty levels increased in Cleveland after 1970. One of the major factors that contributed to the increase in poverty from 1970–1980 was the population loss that the city experienced as more people moved from the city to the suburbs and to other states. Although the population of Cleveland continued to decrease after 1980, the number of poor people increased and about 30 percent of the residents of the city of Cleveland were living below the poverty line (Colton and Chow 1995). Poverty levels were, however, more pronounced for non-white residents than for white residents.

The persistent and geographically concentrated poverty in Cleveland was affected by several factors that are demographic, economic, regional, and local. During the decade of the 1980s, Cleveland experienced a loss in the number of jobs in the manufacturing sector as many manufacturing companies moved to other areas in search of greater levels of profit. This geographic change accompanied population losses to the city because employed individuals also moved their residences from the central city areas (Colton and Chow 1995).

BUSINESS DATA IN NEIGHBORHOOD CONTEXT

Data on individual business establishments were collected from February 1998–Spring 2000.[1] There is no existing list of all African American entrepreneurs that are located in Cleveland. However, data from a sample of sixty businesses was collected. Each of these business establishments was geocoded and compared with data from the 1990 U.S. Census and crime statistics for the years 1990–1997. This allowed for the comparison of business characteristics and contextual variables. Because our sample respondents reported on previous experiences with crime and other business activities, we felt that the use of data from 1990, as opposed to 2000, was more relevant.

Many of the businesses surveyed were located in areas where there was a great deal of crime, but several businesses were found in relatively low crime areas. The approximate median for the city of Cleveland as a whole was 1,000 property crimes per census tract for the eight years studied and about 500 violent crimes. Property crimes include arson, auto theft, burglary, and larceny. Violent crimes include assault, homicide, rape, and robbery.

Figures 5.1 and 5.2 place the surveyed businesses within the context of Cleveland's crime landscape. As background to the study, it is interesting to

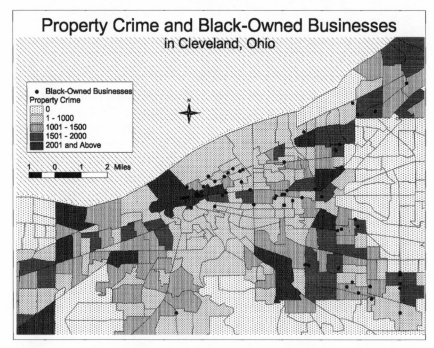

Figure 5.1.   Surveyed Businesses on Map of Property Crimes

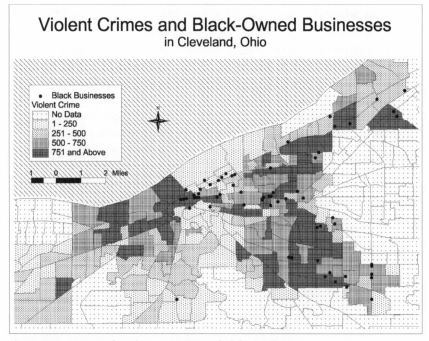

Figure 5.2.   Surveyed Businesses on Map of Violent Crimes

Table 5.1.   Number of Tracts in Each Category

Crime Levels	Property	Violent
Up to Median	27	24
1 to 1½ Median	18	25
1½ to 2X Median	19	11
More than 2X Median	16	20
Total	80	80

note most businesses are located within primarily African American neighborhoods but within all sorts of crime contexts. Figure 5.1 places the surveyed Black-owned businesses on a map that shows levels of property crimes. Figure 5.2 superimposes these same businesses on the incidence of violent crime. There is a wider and higher range of violent crime within segregated Black neighborhoods. Businesses fall into several categories here as well.

In response to our initial questions, we decided that it was appropriate to divide the neighborhoods into various crime categories: up to the median level, one to one and a half times the median, one and a half to twice the median, and more than twice the median. The breakdown of tracts, shown in table 5.1, indicates that the businesses were located in a range of crime contexts. These figures help to demonstrate that, although this is a mid-level sample of sixty Black-owned businesses, these businesses are located within neighborhoods that represent a range of Cleveland's racial and criminal environments.

NEIGHBORHOOD CONTEXT AND BUSINESS SUCCESS

The analysis yields several findings regarding how crime rates affect the experience and perception of crime and how these rates affect business success among African American entrepreneurs.

Experience and Perception of Crime

Of the several questions asked in the survey, the most relevant ones that dealt with business owners' experience and perceptions of crime were whether the business owners had personally experienced criminal activity (in this case burglary), whether they had taken security measures, and whether they felt that crime and drug-related violence had a negative impact on the community and the business environment. Table 5.2 demonstrates how the answers to these questions varied by the extent of property and violent crime in the neighborhood.

Table 5.2.   Crime Experience and Perception, Black Business Owners

Business Burglarized?

	Property Crime (%)		Violent Crime (%)	
	No	Yes	No	Yes
Up to median	37	63	57	43
1 to 1½ median	43	57	32	68
1½ to 2× median	47	53	60	40
More than 2 median	60	40	43	57
Over median	49	51	41	59
Total	**45**	**55**	**45**	**55**

Security Measures

	Property Crime (%)			Violent Crime (%)		
	None	One	Two+	None	One	Two+
Up to median	21	37	42	29	29	43
1 to 1½ median	14	50	36	23	55	23
1½ to 2× median	41	29	29	10	50	40
More than 2× median	30	50	20	43	21	36
Total	**27**	**40**	**33**	**27**	**40**	**33**

Crime Violence Impacts Community

	Property Crime (%)			Violent Crime (%)		
	Disagree	Agree	Strongly Agree	Disagree	Agree	Strongly Agree
Up to median	11	68	21	36	57	7
1 to 1½ median	29	7	64	9	50	41
1½ to 2× median	12	41	47	10	10	80
More than 2× median	30	20	50	21	21	57
Total	**18**	**38**	**43**	**18**	**38**	**43**

Burglaries were common among the sampled businesses and were experienced by more than half. However, the level of property crime in the census tract had absolutely no effect. Violent crime, on the other hand, did have an effect. Those businesses located in tracts with violent crime rates lower than Cleveland's median experienced far fewer burglaries than those in tracts above the median. Overall, only about two out of five businesses in the lowest violent crime areas experienced burglary, compared to three out of five in the higher violent crime zones.

The data demonstrate that there are substantial economic, physical, and psychological costs to doing business in minority communities. Entrepreneurs reported that various items had been stolen from their facilities, including money from their cash registers, safes, typewriters, adding machines, computers, and other items. One entrepreneur linked the existence of criminal activity against business owners to the bigger issue of chronic unemployment, poverty, and malaise that is endemic to many minority communities. As one African American entrepreneur clearly articulated,

> Crime is personally related to unemployment. The statistics people are getting do not include minorities. . . . My business is in a high unemployment neighborhood. People who have too much time on their hands—whether black or white—will steal. It's all connected. Some business owners can only afford to be in the lowest-income areas. . . . I cannot go out and hire the very best people. My cash flow affects the kind of employees I hire in my businesses. I usually hire someone from my neighborhood. (Participant in study 1999)

Interestingly, the use of security measures did not increase as crime levels increased. These measures included locking doors, hiring guards, reducing store hours, carrying a gun, installing a security system, increasing security overall, developing safety rules, putting up fences, hiring neighorhood children to keep a lookout, changing locks on their doors, and putting more lights on the exterior areas of the businesses. Businesses in areas with less violent and property crime were more likely to utilize these measures. Paradoxically, businesses located in high property crime zones were far less likely to use any security measures. Among businesses that had been burglarized, there was a slight increase in the propensity to introduce more security measures. However, there was no relationship among those businesses with a strong perception of crime.

The strongest relationship was found in regard to how the actual crime rate affects the perception of crime. Crime perceptions are often strangely at odds with reality. Today, many people feel that crime is worse when most objective evidence indicates that crime rates have dropped. Small business owners have more reason to fear a rise in crime, since they are often on the front lines. In this sample, the levels of property crime had less bearing on perceptions, but there was some. Overall, about one-fifth of sampled business owners in lower property crime areas strongly agreed that crime violence was a major problem, compared to majorities of sampled owners whose businesses were located in tracts where property crime was greater than Cleveland's median. The levels of violent crime had an even more powerful effect. In neighborhoods where crime rates were at least fifty percent above the median, over two-thirds of respondents strongly felt that criminal violence was a serious threat. This relationship was significant—overall, the actual levels of violent crime accounted for thirty-nine percent of the perception of crime.

Crime and Business Success

So how much does crime affect business success? The cost of doing business in minority communities can be prohibitive, especially in terms of being able to pay expensive premiums on insurance policies for the business. Previous studies have discussed the continual persistence of the policy of "redlining," where the costs of capital and insurance premiums are much more expensive in poor minority communities than in predominantly white communities (Squires 2003). The higher economic costs borne by minority entrepreneurs are significant, as are the physical costs they incur as they move from one neighborhood to another in search of safe and secure locations for themselves, their employees, and their clients. One African American entrepreneur described his situation in the following way:

> Insurance premiums declined as you moved out into a safer neighborhood. I had an earlier location on Kinsman Road in Cleveland six years ago. There was a higher crime rate [there]. They used alarms and gates on the windows. . . . Clients were afraid to come into the neighborhood. The perception was that it was really dangerous. It was important to move before something happened. We were losing customers. (Participant in study 2000)

Responses varied from the participants in terms of whether they felt that they had access to police protection and the extent to which police patrolled their neighborhoods. Police presence can be considered an important indicator of the extent to which citizens feel some degree of safety and security within the neighborhood context. One African American entrepreneur stated, "It's safer in Beachwood [one of the affluent suburbs of Cleveland]. I left the city of Cleveland because of lack of police protection. Two-thirds of the police were not doing their basic patrol" (Participant in study 1999).

Other entrepreneurs in the study voiced similar concerns. One entrepreneur stated that "the relationship between the police officers and white owners in their neighborhood was good, while the relationship between police officers and black owners was poor." In his words, "Police don't look upon you as a business owner but [as] a black man and suspicion [is] dependent upon race" (Participant in study 1999). Another respondent stated, "Police hardly come by. They come only when you call that there is a problem" (Participant in study 1999). One of the entrepreneurs, whose business was located in one of the inner city communities of Cleveland, related one of his own experiences with crime. He spoke of an occasion when one of his customers parked a truck outside of the front of his business and came in to patronize his facility. While the customer was inside, someone stole his truck and rode off with it. When the customer left the store, he found that his truck had been stolen, and he and the business owner quickly phoned the police department. It took the police officers several hours to respond to their call. Later on, the truck was finally found but only because it had been wrecked and left in an abandoned area. According to the business owner, the slow response of the police to residents of the inner city communities is fairly common (Participant in study 1999).

With regard to whether the extent of crime has a direct impact on the success of the entrepreneurs, the relationships are not as clear as might be expected (see table 5.3). In regard to the number of years the business has been in operation (one of our measures of business success), no clear relationship exists. There are a few more long-term businesses (eleven or more years) in areas with lower levels of property and violent crime, but the association needs further study. In some respects, high crime rates could increase the proportion of long-term businesses by deterring new business start-ups. On the other hand, it could cause more businesses to succumb to the higher overhead costs and difficulties in attracting new customers. The muddled character of this relationship is reflected in the data.

There is a significant relationship between violent crime and the number of employees in the businesses. In general, it appears that bigger businesses—as measured by the number of workers employed—operate in neighborhoods where violent crime is below or just above the median. Fewer such businesses exist in high crime zones. Profit levels do not seem to be affected at all by violent or property crime rates. If anything, businesses in the highest crime areas earn the largest profits, although that relationship is not statistically significant. When we asked the entrepreneurs whether their profits had increased in the last five-year period, most business owners responded positively. Ironically, businesses in the highest crime zones were most likely to experience a boost.

A question might be raised as to whether there were any other primary effects or any important interaction effects that may alter the results presented here. There are a few, but these need to be studied further, preferably with a larger sample size. We know from the literature and the Economic Census that Black businesses are smaller, less capitalized, and experience greater obstacles than white-owned businesses. This would probably cause some variations in the way they function. However, there are only a few clear variations on the findings presented here. One variation results from business longevity. Black businesses in lower violent crime neighborhoods are more likely to have remained over ten and some over twenty years than those Black businesses in higher violent crime neighborhoods. Respondents sometimes mentioned their desire to move to a safer area; this may be borne out by the data.

We also wonder whether the perception of crime, as opposed to the reality of crime, is a factor in business success. In this case, we did see a strong relationship with profits but in a complicated way. Respondents who strongly felt that crime was a serious problem were more likely to report

Table 5.3. Impacts of Crime on Business Success, Black Business Owners

Years in Operation

	Property Crime (%)				Violent Crime (%)			
	<5	6–10	11–20	21+	<5	6–10	11–20	21+
Up to median	32	21	21	26	29	29	43	0
1 to 1½ median	21	21	29	29	27	23	0	50
1½ to 2× median	41	24	6	29	50	10	20	20
More than 2× median	22	56	0	22	23	46	8	23
Total	**31**	**27**	**15**	**27**	**31**	**27**	**15**	**27**

Number of Employees

	Property Crime (%)			Violent Crime (%)		
	<5	6–10	11+	<5	6–10	11+
Up to median	58	5	37	64	14	21
1 to 1½ median	79	7	14	32	27	41
1½ to 2× median	47	29	24	100	0	0
More than 2× median	22	56	22	46	31	23
Total	**54**	**20**	**25**	**54**	**20**	**25**

Total Profits per Year

	Property Crime (%)			Violent Crime (%)		
	<$40K	$40–100K	$100K+	<$40K	$40–100K	$100K+
Up to median	37	32	32	36	43	21
1 to 1½ median	31	31	38	55	18	27
1½ to 2× median	63	19	19	40	30	30
More than 2× median	30	40	30	25	33	42
Total	**41**	**29**	**29**	**41**	**29**	**29**

Profit Increased during Past Five Years

	Property Crime (%)		Violent Crime (%)	
	No	Yes	No	Yes
Up to median	27	73	18	82
1 to 1½ median	42	58	50	50
1½ to 2× median	40	60	33	67
More than 2× median	0	100	18	82
Total	**32**	**68**	**32**	**68**

higher profits but were less likely to say that their profits had increased in the last five years. It could be that business owners were partially blaming their context for their troubles.

CONCLUSION

We know from the data that the numbers of Black-owned businesses, while increasing, still lags behind white-owned businesses. Previous studies have explained this disparity in terms of African Americans' lower levels of financial capital, human capital, economic culture, and racial discrimination. We argue that the neighborhood context also exerts a significant impact on the success and survival of any business. That being said, the levels and perception of crime should be considered issues that are especially germane to Black-owned businesses. First, Black businesses tend to be located in Black neighborhoods, which tend to experience higher levels of violent crime. Second, the effect on owner experience and perception is clear: businesses that are located in high violent crime areas are more likely to experience burglary and their owners have a stronger perception of crime. The effect on business success is less clear, however. The number of years that the business has been in operation may be affected, as may the number of employees. But the relationships are not particularly strong or significant. Further research—which would involve the construction of a larger survey sample that allows for the development of cross tabulations by business type—may help us in the future to more clearly examine the influence of the neighborhood crime context.

Especially noteworthy is that, of the two crime measures, violent crime clearly casts the greater shadow over business experience, perception, and success. While property crime annoys, violent crime terrifies. High levels of violent crime create a landscape of fear and thus make it more difficult for business owners to attract customers and employees and to foster business relationships. Sadly, it is precisely in these high crime neighborhoods, where desperation runs rampant and stabilizing institutions are scarce, that Black-owned businesses are needed the most.

NOTE

1. Special thanks goes to the Ohio Board of Regents for providing economic support to collect the original data on African American entrepreneurs and crime, upon which this chapter is based. The authors would also like to thank the Ohio Urban University Program for research funds to perform the analysis on the original data set.

REFERENCES

Bates, T. 1993. *Banking on Black enterprise: The potential of emerging firms for revitalizing urban economies.* Washington, DC: Joint Center for Political and Economic Studies.

——. 1997. *Race, self-employment and upward mobility: An illusive American dream.* Washington, DC: Woodrow Wilson Center Press.

Boyd, R. 1990. Black and Asian self-employment in large metropolitan areas: A comparative analysis. *Social Problems* 37:258–74.

Butler, J. S. 1991. *Entrepreneurship and self-help among Black Americans: A reconsideration of race and economics.* Albany: State University of New York Press.

Coulton, C., and J. Chow. 1995. The impact of poverty on Cleveland neighborhoods. In *Cleveland: A metropolitan reader*, ed. W. D. Keating, N. Krumholz, and D. Perry, 202–27. Kent, OH: Kent State University Press.

Cummings, S. 1999. African American entrepreneurship in the suburbs: Protected markets and enclave business development. *Journal of the American Planning Association* 65 (1): 50–61.

Feagin, J. R., and M. Sikes. 1994. *Living with racism: The Black middle-class experience.* Boston: Beacon Press.

Fratoe, F. 1998. Social capital of Black business owners. *The Review of Black Political Economy* 16:33–50.

Hakim, S., and Y. Schachmurove. 1996. Spatial and temporal patterns of commercial burglaries: The evidence examined. *The American Journal of Economics and Sociology* 55 (4): 444–55.

House-Soremekun, B. 2002a. *Confronting the odds: African American entrepreneurship in Cleveland, Ohio.* Kent, OH: Kent State University Press.

——. 2002b. The impact of criminal activity on Black business success: Implications for public policy. In *Black business and economic power*, ed. A. Jalloh and T. Falola, 444–69. Rochester, NY: University of Rochester Press.

——. 2002c. The impact of economic culture on the business success of African American entrepreneurs. In *Black business and economic power*, ed. A. Jalloh and T. Falola, 424–43. Rochester, NY: University of Rochester Press.

Kaplan, D. H. 1998. The spatial structure of urban ethnic economies. *Urban Geography* 19:489–501.

——. 1999. The uneven distribution of employment opportunities: Neighborhood and race in Cleveland. *Journal of Urban Affairs* 21:189–212.

Krivo, L., and Peterson, D. 1996. Extremely disadvantaged neighborhoods and urban crime. *Social Forces* 75:619–50.

Kuratko, D., J. Hornsby, D. Naffziger, and R. Hodgetts. 2000. Crime and small business: An exploratory study of cost and prevention issues in U.S. firms. *Journal of Small Business Management* 38:1–13.

Light, I. 1972. *Ethnic enterprise in America: Business and welfare among Chinese, Japanese, and Blacks.* Berkeley: The University of California Press.

Light, I., and S. Gold. 2000. *Ethnic economies.* San Diego: Academic Press.

Massey, D. 1990. American apartheid: Segregation and the making of the underclass. *American Journal of Sociology* 96:329–57.

Squires, G. 2003. Racial profiling, insurance style: Insurance redlining and the uneven development of metropolitan areas. *Journal of Urban Affairs* 25 (4): 391–410.

Texeira, C. 2001. Community resources and opportunities in ethnic economies: A case study of Portuguese and Black entrepreneurs in Toronto. *Urban Studies* 38 (11): 2055–78.

U.S. Bureau of the Census. 2001. *1997 economic census, survey of minority owned business enterprises: Black*. Washington, DC: U.S. Department of Commerce.

Waldinger, R., D. McEvoy, and H. Aldrich. 1990. Spatial dimensions of opportunity structures. In *Ethnic entrepreneurs: Immigrant business in industrial societies*, ed. R. Waldinger, H. Aldrich, and R. Ward, 106–30. Newbury Park, CA: Sage Publications.

Walker, J. 1998. The history of Black business in America: Capitalism, race, entrepreneurship. New York: Macmillan.

Chapter Six

Changing Geography of Toronto's Chinese Ethnic Economy

Lucia Lo

With forty-four percent of its population born outside Canada and over one hundred languages spoken in those homes, the Toronto Census Metropolitan Area is arguably the most ethnically diverse region in the world. It houses a large number of ethnic economies, ranging from those owning a few restaurants and grocery stores serving a specific ethnic group to those with a full range of economic activities serving a mixed clientele (Lo et al. 2000). Some, like the Greektown, are visible in a single concentration. Others, such as the Indian and Korean ethnic economies, are found in several locations or are dispersed throughout the metropolitan area. These variations reflect the dynamic nature of both the ethnic populations and the businesses they create.

Recently, there has been a revived interest in ethnic economies as a contested urban phenomenon. Most studies, however, focus on the economic incorporation of the ethnic entrepreneurs and the social barriers they face (see Lo, Teixeira, and Truelove 2002). There are few studies on the determinants of entrepreneurialism and the shifting nature of ethnic economies in both geographical and non-geographical terms. The role of space and place is particularly neglected, although some studies have shown that ethnic businesses can act as important agents of urban renewal and that ethnic economies may have territorial impacts such as helping a neighborhood to develop a place identity or reviving a local economy (Teixeira 1998; Buzzelli 2000).

Generally speaking, the kind of economy (enclave, non-enclave, or mixed) associated with an ethnic group at any point in time and in any location reflects the group's degree of integration into the larger economy (Nee, Sanders, and Sernau 1994). While this may be true, it does not acknowledge the contextual and structural factors under which ethnic groups and their businesses arrive, survive, and propagate. Ethnic business development relates not only to the size and composition of the group, but also to the conditions under which subsequent flows are added to the stock. Similar to other forms of immigrant economic incorporation, ethnic business development in any country is embedded within global economic-political structures and national policy domains (Piore 1979; Portes and Böröcz 1989; Lo and Wang 2004). To this end, this chapter examines the spatial dynamics of the Chinese ethnic economy in Toronto, with a focus on if and how ethnic residential concentration may aid ethnic business development.

FROM CHINATOWN TO ETHNOBURBS: THE SETTLEMENT PATHS

Chinese migration to Canada has a long and varied history. Over the last century, the political and economic changes in Greater China (China, Hong Kong, and Taiwan) and the policy changes in Canada determined for different time periods who the migrants were, where they originated, what resources they brought to Canada, and where they settled in Toronto (Lo and Wang 1997). The first Chinese in Toronto, mostly originating from rural China, faced residential, educational, and occupational segregation. They settled in an inner city enclave: Chinatown. Through upward mobility, some subsequently moved to the suburbs. Recent Chinese migrants, depending on their social positions, either followed the pathway of their predecessors or went straight to the suburbs. Movement to the suburbs began in earnest in the 1970s, with two distinctive waves. The first wave, to the inner suburban ring (i.e., North York and Scarborough) in the 1970s and the early 1980s, was characteristic of upward mobility and spatial assimilation. The second wave, which saw drastic growth in the outer suburbs (Richmond Hill, Markham, and Mississauga) throughout the 1990s, was due largely to the political uncertainty in Hong Kong. The agreement reached by China and Britain in 1984 on the future of Hong Kong pressed a panic button and caused many to leave for Toronto. The generally affluent newcomers preferred to settle into the modern homes with generous living and green spaces in the outer suburbs of Toronto.

Amidst the suburbanization trends, the Chinese enclaves in the city core, however, have continued to flourish. Those leaving the enclave were replaced in the late 1970s and early 1980s by "boat people" from Vietnam and Cambodia, in the 1980s by family-class immigrants (family members sponsored by those already in Toronto) from mainland China, and in the early 1990s by the well-educated but financially unresourceful mainland Chinese professionals and scholars who chose to stay in Canada after the Tiananmen Incident of 1989. As a result of these concurrent settlement trends, a multinucleated Chinese landscape, with distinct pockets inhabited by those from Hong Kong, Taiwan, China, and Vietnam (Lo and Wang 1997), emerged in Canada's largest city.

FROM MIDDLEMEN TO CORPORATIONS:
THE STRUCTURAL SHIFT

In a similar vein, the business development path taken by the Chinese migrants in Toronto is intricately related to their history of immigration to Canada (see table 6.1). At the beginning, institutional discrimination not only produced Chinatown, but also prompted early Chinese involvement in laundry and restaurant businesses (Anderson 1991). In 1923, the discriminatory Chinese Exclusion Act blocked the entry of Chinese into Canada. The 2,500 Chinese at that time operated 203 restaurants, 47 laundries, and nine grocery stores (Thompson 1979 cited in Rhyne 1982, 31). These relatively large proportions of restaurants and laundries indicate a somewhat broader-than-enclave economy among the early generation of Chinese migrants.

When the Exclusion Act was repealed in 1947, it opened the door for family-class immigrants. The Chinese ethnic economy grew to 448 firms in 1966. The enclave portion expanded substantially to include import and export firms; gift shops; real estate, insurance, and travel agents; and professionals. The 1967 Immigration Act, which allowed immigrants of any race to enter Canada, began a new chapter. Chinese businesses diversified and a true enclave economy emerged. In fact, of the 187 firms surveyed by Chan

Table 6.1.   Distribution of Chinese Businesses in the Toronto CMA, 1923–1994

Percent Type	1923	1966	1980	1994
N	(203)	(448)	(1333)	(3698)
Laundries and cleaners	18.0	32.6		
Food and grocers	3.0	18.1	18.2	9.3
Restaurants	78.0	38.8	28.0	13.8
General merchandise and other retailing		2.2	30.4	19.2
Financial, real estate, and other business services		1.3	4.8	16.2
Medical and other professional services		3.5	2.8	11.5
Personal and recreational services		0.7	3.6	10.9
Household furniture and services			7.3	11.7
Automotive				4.7
Miscellaneous		2.7	4.4	2.5
	100.0	100.0	100.0	100.0

Source: Rhyne (1982), Thompson (1989), and Wang (1996).

and Cheung (1985), consumer services (i.e., restaurants, dry cleaners, and herbal stores), commercial outlets (i.e., grocery stores, photo shops, and newspapers), and professional services (i.e., physicians, accountants, and interior decorators) predominated. Interestingly, half of these firms were located outside Toronto's two Chinatowns. As the Chinese population suburbanized, an enclave economy fueled by demand took a firm hold in multiple locations across Toronto.

The Chinese ethnic economy was further transformed by the influx of immigrants from Hong Kong since 1984 and the much-promoted Canadian business immigrant program. Marger and Hoffman (1992), using evaluation reports on immigrant entrepreneurs entering Ontario in 1986 and 1987, found that Chinese businesses established by business migrants from Hong Kong and mainland China comprised three-fifths retail/wholesale trades and services and about one-third small manufacturing.[1] Geographically, only one-tenth of the firms were located outside the Toronto CMA. Within the Toronto CMA, half of the firms were in the inner city core, one-third in the inner suburbs, and one-sixth in the outer suburbs. This distribution shows that the Chinese ethnic economy in the mid-1980s shifted not only spatially, but also changed in structural and functional terms.

Many Chinese immigrants today come with human and financial capital, management experience, business acumen, and transnational connections (Li 1992; Tseng 1994). Their businesses are not necessarily consumer-oriented, and they do not need to stay in or around Chinese residential enclaves (Olds 1996; Saxenian 1999; Zhou 1998). The modern Chinese business sector has taken a new form, consisting of an enclave component and an integrated component.

The Enclave Component

Unlike traditional enclaves with street-front stores on restricted retail strips, contemporary Chinese enclaves in Toronto are found in multiple locations with many indoor malls. Since the first Chinese shopping mall was introduced in Scarborough in the early 1980s, a flurry of "Chinese malling" activities has taken place. There are now over 65 Chinese malls in Toronto and a few more are under construction. Many of them would not be here if not for the huge exodus from Hong Kong. Seeing many Chinese arriving as entrepreneurs, investors, and wealthy retirees, local Chinese developers began converting existing plazas in Scarborough into Chinese retail spaces and building enclosed shopping or retail/commercial structures. These plazas and malls were generally small, but they filled up quickly.

Seeing mall development as a lucrative business, non-Chinese developers joined the bandwagon at the onset of the 1990 recession. Advised by Chinese real estate agents and supported by the Richmond Hill City Council, the Iranian-owned Times Development Inc. converted two planned retail commercial buildings along the main thoroughfare in Richmond Hill into a retail condominium targeting exclusively migrants and investors from Hong Kong. Others soon followed. The municipal governments of Scarborough, Markham, and Mississauga, in their effort to fight off the worst recession since the Oil Crisis of the early 1970s, accommodated the change by quickly passing bylaws that allowed the sale of commercial units within their jurisdiction. Some Chinese migrants took this as a means to fulfill their immigration requirements. Others hoped that the postwar "miracle" in Hong Kong that had profited them could repeat in Toronto.

Whatever the motive, the outcome is a proliferation of Chinese shopping malls in Scarborough, Markham, Richmond Hill, and Mississauga where Chinese residential concentrations are found (see figure 6.1). These malls, as well as the traditional Chinatowns in the inner city, highlight a thriving enclave ethnic economy defined by the increase in Chinese residential concentrations.

Chinatown Central

Relocated to its present site at the crossroads of Spadina Avenue and Dundas Street to make way for the construction of the "new" Toronto City Hall at its former location on Dundas and Elizabeth Streets in the early 1960s, Chinatown Central is still bustling with activity. The grocery stores extend their retail space onto the sidewalk with makeshift stands displaying fruits and vegetables. On the floor near the entrance, a small Buddhist shrine is often installed to protect the store against evil spirits, and tiny golden cups of tea and pieces of apples and oranges are placed as offerings. Traditional Chinese herbal stores flash in neon red the message "Herbalist and Acupuncturist on Duty." In their storefronts are barrels mounded with different varieties of ginseng and dried mushrooms. In both Chinese and English, an occasional board sign promotes the service of an astrologer or geomancer. There is no difficulty in finding a place to eat in this neighborhood; restaurants abound, offering Vietnamese and northern Chinese tastes, evidence of the continuing transformation of Chinatown when the younger generations growing up there chose to move to the suburbs and were replaced by immigrants from Vietnam and China.

Although the majority of enterprises in the area are located in traditional shop-houses, there are two mall developments, more similar to the suburban

88   *Lucia Lo*

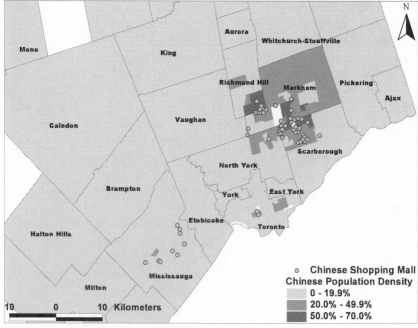

Figure 6.1.   Distribution of Chinese Shopping Malls in Toronto CMA

enclaves than to the rest of Chinatown. The two-story Chinatown Centre, on
the southern edge of Chinatown Central, has glassed-in stores built around an
open middle, selling such diverse items as shoes, electronics, Asian CDs, and
popular tourist chinoiserie such as silk slippers. In the basement level is a
food court with outlets prominently displaying a green "Pass" certificate is-
sued by the Toronto Health Department. Dragon City, in the center of Chinatown, is smaller, with a food court in the basement, retail stores on the ground
floor, and professional offices on the third floor. The top story once hosted the
Mandarin Club, a membership club exclusive to the Chinese elites and professionals of Toronto in the 1980s.

   Chinatown Central, like its sisters elsewhere in the Western world, serves
two groups of clients. The majority are the newer arrivals from China and
Vietnam who cannot afford the suburbs and the older Chinese migrants of an
era or two ago who still feel attached to the area. To some of them, life in Chinatown is an everyday struggle, toiling at the back of the restaurants and grocery stores. Then there are the occasional local non-Chinese population and
tourists to the city who visit for lunch and Chinese products. To the non-reg-
ulars, the visit is sometimes considered an exotic experience.

The Suburban Malls

The Chinese malls in suburban Toronto are the outcomes of planned and joint responses from both the public and the private sectors to affluent immigrants arriving in droves during an economically hard time. These malls assume names like Times Square and Pacific Mall after the popular shopping centers in Hong Kong. The individual retail units within them are generally small except for the anchoring restaurants, supermarkets, and banks (Qadeer 1998; Wang 1999). They house a wide array of consumer goods and services, from low-priced food outlets to high-end jewelry stores, from video-rentals to professional services. Two are particularly popular: the Pacific Mall/Market Village complex bordering Markham and Scarborough and First Markham Place, which is located next to a complex of big box stores in Markham.

Pacific Mall, built in the late 1990s, is the largest Chinese mall in North America. The adjacent Market Village was transformed into a Chinese mall in the early 1990s. Its outside looks like a block of old-fashioned row houses, but the inside layout is similar to a typical unified Western mall. Together they make up the largest indoor Chinese shopping complex in North America, with over 350 stores. These malls, occupying the site of the former Weal and Cullen Country Barn, share the same parking lot. The first floor of the Pacific Mall is anchored by the Bank of East Asia and is arranged in a uniform grid of glass cubicles. The aisles are named after the popular streets in Hong Kong. The stores are numbered, but numbers 4, 14, and 24 are conspicuously left out because *four* sounds like *death* in Cantonese. The second floor has a large restaurant, a food court, a Japanese-run table-art store, and a section called "Pacific Heritage Town," with traditional Chinese decor. Pacific Heritage Town is a mall within a mall and has its own stores and a food court offering a variety of food and non-food items from East and Southeast Asia. One can easily spend an entire day shopping in these two malls, going through cellular phone and accessories stores, CD/DVD stores selling Chinese titles, Hong Kong–style jewelry stores, and Japanese fashion trend boutiques. These malls attract shoppers from all over and even beyond the Greater Toronto Region. They differ from traditional ethnic enclaves in both design and intent. Just like most suburban malls, they are meant to keep customers indoors for a long stay, away from the harsh winter winds and the sweltering summer heat.

In these malls, Cantonese is the main tongue, and most of the items are marked in Chinese text. They offer the Chinese immigrant population opportunities to shop in familial, albeit transplanted, environments with the convenience of one-stop shopping. The larger malls are also sites of recreational and cultural activities. They have a center stage with special events scheduled throughout the year, including such things as Tai Chi and line dancing classes in the morning, and calligraphy, singing, and debating competitions on the weekend. Many retirees and the non-working population visit these malls every day to get fresh groceries, socialize, or spend their leisure time. On weekends, Chinese teenagers (sometimes with their non-Chinese friends) descend into the most popular Chinese malls, enjoying a glass of bubble tea or browsing through the many boutiques and video game arcades. As Lilian Lau, 17, says, "Chinese malls provide the identity that many Canadian Chinese want." She avoids stores like Gap and Stitches, which are nowhere to be seen in Pacific Mall. "I don't want to look like everyone else. Chinese designers have different ideas" (Doctorow 2002).

It is common to find in each mall several stores offering the same goods or services. It is also common to see the same store appearing in different malls. Unlike enclave businesses of an earlier era, contemporary Chinese enclave businesses have expanded to include multiple outlets and even warehouses. The supermarket chain Big Land Farm, the Chinese herbal giant Uncle Bill, the Hong Kong–based jeweler Luk Fook, and the popular Mr. Wong's Congee are just some examples. They are cloaked in modern management and actively engaged in ethnic marketing. Many of these businesses have to compete fiercely not only against mainstream stores but also co-ethnic vendors.

The Integrated Component

Stores and firms in the Chinese enclaves are visible representations of the Chinese business sector, yet they do not tell the full story about contemporary Chinese business development in Toronto. To understand the nature, structure, and geography of an expanded Chinese ethnic economy, Lo and Wang (2000) sampled 634 medium and large Chinese-owned businesses from the 1997 Dun & Bradstreet Business Directory.

First, the study finds, Chinese-owned businesses are diversifying and the Chinese ethnic economy has moved away from its traditional focus on consumer goods and services to one that covers nearly the whole array of industrial activities. Evidence shows that Chinese businesses are represented in 78 percent of all industrial sectors except mining and public administration (the latter is largely government-run). Moreover, those industrial concentrations that do exist are not in the traditional ethnic niches.

Second, Chinese-owned firms are expanding. Although the majority of them are as small as most other businesses in the general economy, one out of fifty Chinese firms hire more than two hundred workers and one-tenth have annual sales of over US$10 million. More significantly, while Chinese firms account for only one-thousandth of Toronto businesses, they account for one percent of the largest one thousand Toronto firms. In addition, twelve percent of the sample are headquartered firms. The large firms are all incorporated and cover wholesale, retail, manufacturing, realty, hotel accommodation, business, and transport services.

Third, the locations of Chinese businesses are not tied to their residential locations; they are everywhere. The concentration indices (also known as location quotients) in table 6.2 highlight a mismatch between the share of Chinese businesses and Chinese population in most of the municipalities making up the Toronto CMA. For example, in North York, Richmond Hill, and Scarborough where there is a large Chinese population in concentrated neighborhoods, Chinese businesses are relatively few. But in Etobicoke, Vaughan, Aurora, and Caledon where there are fewer and more dispersed Chinese residences, the share of Chinese businesses is relatively higher. This phenomenon can be explained first by the fact that close to half of the firms in the sample are producer firms which have different site and location requirements from those offering consumer goods and services. Producer firms are often restricted to areas designated for industrial use. In Markham,

Table 6.2. Municipal Share of Chinese Population and Chinese Businesses in the Toronto CMA

Municipality	Relative Share of Chinese Business (A)	Relative Share of business Employment (B)	Relative Share of Chinese Population(C)	Concentration Index Business (A/C)	Concentration Index Employment (B/C)
Aurora	0.32	0.17	0.13	2.34	1.25
Brampton	1.58	1.27	1.45	1.09	0.88
Caledon	0.16	0.05	0.03	6.21	2.01
East York	0.16	0.51	2.03	0.08	0.25
Etobicoke	5.52	7.41	1.85	2.99	4.02
Markham	14.83	20.09	13.28	1.12	1.51
Mississauga	13.41	12.68	8.99	1.49	1.41
Newmarket	0.32	0.25	0.40	0.79	0.63
North York	7.57	6.88	15.25	0.50	0.45
Oakville	0.95	0.57	0.81	1.17	0.71
Pickering	0.79	0.55	0.48	1.65	1.16
Richmond Hill	4.42	2.33	6.24	0.71	0.37
Scarborough	19.72	19.83	28.03	0.70	0.71
Toronto	26.97	24.18	17.98	1.59	1.35
Vaughan	2.84	2.98	1.83	1.55	1.63
York	0.47	0.24	1.24	0.38	0.19

Note: A concentration index of 1 means a municipality's share of Chinese businesses is proportional to its share of Chinese population. An index greater than 1 means its share of businesses is greater than its share of population.
Source: Lo and Wang (2000).

Mississauga, Etobicoke, Vaughan, and Scarborough, Chinese business clusters are found in industrial and business parks, not near Chinese residential neighborhoods (compare figures 6.1 and 6.2). Secondly, many Chinese retail operators locate outside the Chinese enclaves. They are dispersed all over urban Toronto. For example, when the city core and Etobicoke respectively hold eighteen percent and two percent of the CMA's total Chinese population, they house instead thirty-four percent and six percent of the Chinese retail establishments, proportions much higher than what the local Chinese population needs.

The current Chinese business sector has diversified in scale, space, and structure. These businesses are well integrated into the general economy. They are results of Canada's immigration policy changes in the last three decades; the capital, talents, and business experience brought along by the Chinese immigrants have accelerated the process of business integration.

The integration has followed different paths. We can begin with ATI, the world's largest supplier of 3D graphics and multimedia technologies, which is located in the heart of Toronto's high-tech zone in Markham. Its success illustrates the vision and the leadership of Kwok-Yuan Ho, a business immi-

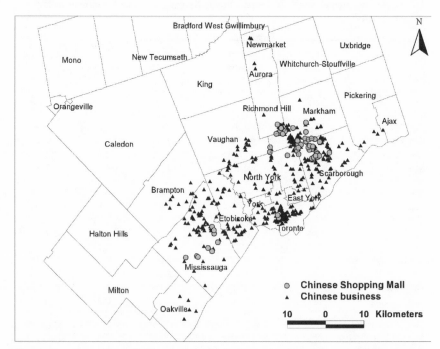

Figure 6.2.   Locations of Chinese Enclaves and Integrated Business Establishments

grant from Hong Kong who started in 1985 by producing graphic chips in the basement of his home (Acharya 1998). On the other hand, Shui Pong Developments Ltd. delineates a business development path commonly undertaken by migrants. Starting by building retail and residential complexes aimed at the Chinese community, it went on to develop Canada's first themed high-tech development complex in Richmond Hill and bring the concept of the wide loft to Toronto's residential development (Wong 1999a, 1999b). Alternatively, the presence of Viva Magnetics—a Hong Kong–based private company and one of the world's largest optical disc and packaging manufacturers—in Toronto is due to Toronto's trade missions to Hong Kong. According to the *Ontario Economic Development Network Newsletter* (1999), its two plants in Scarborough, totaling 633,000 square feet, are key to the continued development of Toronto's growing music industry network.

CONCLUSION

The Chinese have been the fastest growing immigrant group in Canada since the revamping of the Canadian Immigration Act in the mid-1960s. They have drastically transformed the social, cultural, and economic landscapes of Toronto. The population suburbanizes, and their businesses proliferate as a result of the mass entry of a skilled and affluent class. In particular, the middle-class migrants have the capital and know-how to develop and sustain different types of businesses, giving rise to a mature ethnic economy with large and small firms locating all over the metropolitan area and serving both Chinese and non-Chinese clients.

In the Chinese ethnic economy, an enclave component visibly displayed by numerous Chinese shopping malls runs side-by-side with a functionally and structurally integrated component that shows no visible Chinese traits. The overall spatial distribution is "concentrations within dispersion." While some concentrations are justified by proximity to a co-ethnic pool of clients and labor, others are outcomes of industrial linkages and agglomeration economies, a kind of economies of scale due to the clustering of many similar and/or related businesses.

The parallel growth of an enclave and an integrated component confirms that geography is a complex commodity. Space alone, as that represented by residential concentrations, can define where ethnic businesses go. Space can also interplay with other factors, such as the nature of a business or the composition and maturity of an ethnic economy, in a location choice process. Essentially, we can argue that depending on the type of group resources utilized, the type of businesses established, and the stage of business development, space can be used differently to affect the concentration or dispersion of ethnic firms (Kaplan 1998). This Toronto example illustrates that geography has played both a defined and an added role in the development of Chinese businesses. It also shows that the growth of enclave and integrated businesses can take place at the same time and within the same ethnic economy.

NOTE

1. These figures were adapted from table 2 in Marger and Hoffman (1992) and adjusted according to the standard industrial classification scheme. The manufacturing figure includes food processing, and import/export is grouped with wholesale/supply.

REFERENCES

Acharya, M. 1998. Turning a vision into a reputation: ATI chief built high-tech dream in tough niche. *Toronto Star*, 9 October.

Anderson, K. J. 1991. *Vancouver's Chinatown: Racial discourse in Canada, 1875–1980*. Montreal: McGill Queen's University Press.

Buzzelli, M. 2000. Toronto's postwar Little Italy: Landscape change and ethnic relations. *The Canadian Geographer* 44:298–305.

Chan, J. B. L., and Y-W Cheung. 1985. Ethnic resources and business enterprise: A study of Chinese businesses in Toronto. *Human Organization* 4:142–54.

Doctorow, C. 2002. Boing Boing: Hong Kong comes to Toronto. March 21. boingboing.net/2002/03/21/hong_kong_comes_to_t.html (accessed 6 April 2004).

Kaplan, D. 1998. The spatial structure of urban ethnic economies. *Urban Geography* 19:489–501.

Li, P. 1992. Ethnic enterprise in transition: Chinese business in Richmond, B.C. 1980–1990. *Canadian Ethnic Studies* 24:120–38.

Lo, L., V. Preston, S. Wang, K. Reil, H. Harvey, and B. Siu. 2000. *Immigrants' economic status in Toronto: Rethinking settlement and integration strategies*. CERIS Working Paper, no. 15, Joint Centre of Excellence for Research on Immigration and Settlement, Toronto.

Lo, L., C. Teixeira, and M. Truelove. 2002. *Cultural resources, ethnic strategies, and immigrant entrepreneurship: A comparative study of five immigrant groups in the Toronto CMA*. CERIS Working Paper, no. 21, Joint Centre for Research on Immigration and Settlement, Toronto.

Lo, L., and L. Wang. 2004. A political economy approach to understanding the economic incorporation of Chinese sub-ethnic groups. *Journal of International Migration and Integration* 5:107–40.

Lo, L., and S. Wang. 1997. Settlement patterns of Toronto's Chinese immigrants: Convergence or divergence? *Canadian Journal of Regional Science* 20:49–72.

——. 2000. Chinese businesses in Toronto: A spatial and structural anatomy. Paper presented at the Conference on Comparative Perspectives on Chinese Ethnic Economies, Toronto, September.

——. Forthcoming. The new Chinese business sector in Toronto: A spatial and structural anatomy of medium- and large-sized firms. In *Chinese ethnic economy: Global and local perspectives*, ed. E. Fong and C. Luk. Philadelphia: Temple University Press.

Marger, M. N., and C. A. Hoffman. 1992. Ethnic enterprise in Ontario: Immigrant participation in the small business sector. *International Migration Review* 26:968–81.

Nee, V., J. M. Sanders, and S. Sernau. 1994. Job transitions in an immigrant metropolis: Ethnic boundaries and the mixed economy. *American Sociological Review* 59:849–72.

Olds, K. 1996. Developing the trans-Pacific property market: Tales from Vancouver via Hong Kong. Working Paper 96-02, Research on Immigration and Integration in the Metropolis, Vancouver.

Ontario Economic Development Network Newsletter. 1999. Viva Magnetics builds jewel box plant. 20 January. www.edco.on.ca/news/news990120.htm

Piore, M. 1979. *Birds of passage: Migrant labor and the industrial society*. Cambridge: Cambridge University Press.

Portes, A., and J. Böröcz. 1989. Contemporary immigration: Theoretical perspectives on its determinants and modes of incorporation. *International Migration Review* 23:606–30.

Qadeer, M. 1998. Ethnic malls and plazas: Chinese commercial developments in Scarborough, Ontario. CERIS Working Paper, No. 3, Joint Centre for Research on Immigration and Settlement, Toronto.

Rhyne, D. 1982. Visible minority business in metropolitan Toronto: An exploratory analysis. Toronto: Race Relations Division, Ontario Human Rights Commission.

Saxenian, A. 1999. *Silicon Valley's new immigrant entrepreneurs*. San Francisco: Public Policy Institute of California.

Teixeira, C. 1998. Cultural resources and ethnic entrepreneurship: A case study of the Portuguese in real estate industries in Toronto. *The Canadian Geographer* 42:267–81.

Thompson, R. H. 1979. The state and the ethnic community: The changing social organization of Toronto's Chinatown. PhD diss., University of Michigan.

——. 1989. *Toronto's Chinatown: The changing social organization of an ethnic community*. New York: AMS Press.

Tseng, Y-F. 1994. Chinese ethnic economy: San Gabriel Valley, Los Angeles County. *Journal of Urban Affairs* 16:169–89.

Wang, S. 1996. *New development patterns of Chinese commercial activity in the Toronto CMA*. Toronto: Centre for the Study of Commercial Activity, Ryerson Polytechnic University.

——. 1999. Chinese commercial activity in the Toronto CMA: New development patterns and impacts. *The Canadian Geographer* 43:19–35.

Wong, T. 1999a. High-tech office complex to rise in Richmond Hill. *Toronto Star*, 13 May.

———. 1999b. New Canadians with global connections: What is the legacy of immigration programs that drew many enterprising Chinese to Canada? Major Canadian businesses with links around the world. *Toronto Star*, 10 May.

Zhou, Y. 1998. Beyond ethnic enclaves: Location strategies of Chinese producer service firms in Los Angeles. *Economic Geography* 74:228–51.

Chapter Seven

Gendered Landscapes of Ethnic Economies: Turkish Entrepreneurs in Berlin

Felicitas Hillmann

In the last few years, the striking concept of ethnic economies has caught the interest of town planners and local politicians in various European countries. In some German towns, especially Berlin, there is a widespread hope that flourishing ethnic entrepreneurship will revive the urban labor markets that suffer from de-industrialization and high unemployment. From this perspective, self-employment is seen as an opportunity for the immigrants themselves—a chance for success in the precarious employment market after the economic restructuring processes of recent years. As I shall argue here, the proliferation of ethnic economies is only *one* variant of internationalization processes, ethnicization, and informalization of urban labor markets.

This chapter concentrates on the fluid but vague concept of ethnic economies in theoretical and empirical terms. The case study presented is Berlin. Particular attention is paid to a gender-differentiated view, since closer empirical study shows the gender-structuring effect of migration on the labor market. The migration process opens up different possibilities depending on the gender of the immigrants. These processes are not supposed to be gender-neutral, so they exhibit clear differences for men and women (Phizacklea 2003; Erel, Shinozaki, and Lenz 2003). First, this chapter considers the connection between the migration system and the development of urban labor markets and outlines the basic concept and theories relating to ethnic economies in international urban research relevant to the presented case. The second section of the chapter consists of a critical empirical consideration of the positioning of the Turkish ethnic economy in the Berlin labor market and highlights the scope of the ethnic economy. The third section concentrates on the gendered nature of the Turkish ethnic economy in Berlin.

URBAN LABOR MARKETS AND THE MIGRATION
SYSTEM IN EUROPE AND IN GERMANY

The process of globalization changed existing local labor markets in the European Union. Forms of ethnic structure of the labor market and of ethnic economies have developed in almost all Western industrialized countries. Depending on the prevalent immigration policy and the structuring of the labor market (by age, gender, or qualifications), various groups of immigrants have established themselves in the urban labor markets. In countries that tend to welcome immigration and implement a market-oriented *laissez-faire* policy, strong ethnic economies emerge and minorities assume mediating functions. In countries with no explicit tradition of immigration and where migration is closely linked to a rotation system, ethnic economies develop differently: often despite the absence of political regulation rather than because of it (Fassmann 1997). Empirical studies on the gender differences in the setting of ethnic entrepreneurship are still rare. Apitzsch and Kontos (2003, 169) argue that "women still need to be more generally recognized as agents, that is, as active protagonists in the complex dynamics between (ethnic) communities, (ethnic) networks, and labor market conditions."

There have been three general trends since the 1990s. First, the presence of illegal immigrants (including those who overstay their visas and persons without legal status of any sort) and their employment in informal work arrangements became more common during the 1990s. The European Council estimates that up to one million people were without valid residence status in Germany; the number in Berlin is estimated at between 100,000 and 500,000 (Lederer 1999; Erzbischöfliches Ordinariat 2000; Rath 1999). Second, globalization and metropolitan internationalization spurred a Europe-wide increase in the mobility of highly qualified workers and fostering "brain circulation" (Stalker 2000; OECD 1998; Sassen 1991, 2000; Rudolph and Hillmann 1998). Berlin's city administration now regards the recruitment of highly qualified employees and international businessmen as an essential factor in enhancing Berlin's attraction as a business location. Third, foreign workers are more concentrated in the so-called 3D jobs (dirty, dangerous, dreadful), a trend which continues partly with the next generation (Faist, Hillman, and Zühlke-Robinet 1996). In light of the fact that unemployment in the foreign population is about double that of the German nationals raises concerns of whether a new underclass is being created (Bremer and Gestring 1997; Freudenberg 2000; Häußermann 1998).

During the 1990s, exclusion of foreign labor became part of Germany's urban development. Previously, postwar cities functioned as "integration machines" for foreigners, but in the 1990s they seem to have entered a crisis (Heitmeyer, Dollase, and Backes 1998). Their integration potential dwindled, and in many German towns sociospatial developments led to polarization and, increasingly, fragmentation. In the cities, planning for immigration became divided as plans to recruit top-level employees coexisted with agendas for coping with victims of poverty and political persecution (Schmals 2000). In the midst of these changes during the 1990s, an intermediate position between internationalization and ethnicization emerged during the 1990s: the ethnic economies. Many parties, especially employers' associations, now credit the Turkish ethnic economy as a considerable potential for growth. Berlin's politicians have recently shown a growing interest in incorporating ethnic business into the economy. In the context of the URBAN program on urban development and in other EU networks, male and female immigrant entrepreneurs were identified as an important resource on the urban labor markets.

Theoretical literature on ethnic economies suggests a substantial difference in the perception and regulation of ethnic economies between the United States and Europe. In contrast to Anglo-Saxon countries, where the myth of the self-made man has positive social connotations and the increase in "ethnic niches" was interpreted as a rational response to limited access to the labor market (Waldinger 1996), the self-employment of immigrants in European countries is regarded as more of a solution to an inaccessible labor market than a confident decision to enter a specific form of employment. Immigrants and minorities in most European countries function within relatively heavily regulated labor markets, mainly in its least attractive segments and on the margins of the formal sector. This means that immigrants are more exposed to fluctuations and changes in the labor market connecting them to the informal sector. The simultaneous growth of informal economies (Mingione 1999) and the (re)burgeoning of sweatshops in labor-intensive industries indicate a changing trend in labor organization and a regionalization of production that particularly affects immigrants (Anderson 1999; Raes 2000).

The marginalization and exclusion of migrants from the formal labor market lead to a revival of those (usually informal) labor market segments that require minimal start-up money, are labor-intensive, and face keen price competition (Wilpert 1998; Reyneri 1998). The ethnic occupation of such sublabor markets is interpreted as a stratification phenomenon rather than a culture-related relationship between certain ethnic groups and labor preferences (Häußermann and Oswald 1997). Analysis of ethnic entrepreneurship in European countries analyzes it as closely connected to processes of social exclusion (Samers 1998) or, more recently, focuses on immigrant regimes by putting the focus on the socioeconomic affiliation of the ethnic entrepreneurs rather than on individual enterprises (Kloosterman 2000).

In Germany, *ethnic economies* are generally defined as "all forms of self-employment by foreigners." The word *foreigner* has different meanings here. For the authorities it is an established statistical term that refers solely to the nationality and the attribute "non-German," whereas the general public and the lobbyists of the ethnic economies count all self-employed persons who have immigrated into Germany as part of ethnic business. This ambivalence—in both the legal interpretation of the term *foreigner* and in the definition of an immigrant as a "minority" owing to his or her cultural affiliation—is also reflected in this chapter. Details about the ethnic structure of the labor market here relate to the legal definition of *foreigner*, while the remarks on ethnic economies refer to ethnic minorities living in Germany or specifically in Berlin.

BERLIN'S LABOR MARKET AND ITS TURKISH ETHNIC ECONOMY

In August 2003, 304,500 people were unemployed in the Berlin region; of these more nearly 51,000 were foreigners. Among the foreign unemployed, just under forty-five percent are Turkish, three percent are Italians, ten percent come from former Yugoslavia, three percent are Greek, and less than one percent each were Spanish or Portuguese. In absolute figures, the number of unemployed foreigners (including all those not holding German citizenship) in Berlin doubled in the decade after the collapse of East Germany. Since the end of the 1990s, more than a third of all foreigners in Berlin and in the surrounding Brandenburg state were unemployed.

Comparison of structural data on unemployment makes it clear that the formal qualifications of the foreign population are lower than average and unemployment affects the younger generation. Three-quarters of the unemployed foreigners have no vocational training (as opposed to a third of all unemployed), fifteen percent have had company training (in comparison to over half of all unemployed), and one-tenth attended a technical school, college, or university (compared to one-eighth of all unemployed). Unemployed foreigners are also a bit younger than the general population of unemployed and tend to focus in construction, cleaning, and food sectors. On the other hand, the proportion of foreigners among the social insurance contributors in Berlin dropped continuously between 1990 and 2003, indicating an increasingly difficult insertion of migrants in the formal parts of the labor market.

At the same time, the number of self-employed rose during the 1990s in both the German and non-German populations. The number of self-employed

Germans rose from 122,000 in 1991 to 158,000 in 1996 while the number of self-employed foreigners rose from 9,500 to 21,800 during the same period. In 1996, the proportion of self-employed foreigners stood at twelve percent, four percentage points above the German average. In 1997 about 440,000 people of foreign nationality were registered as (primarily) resident in Berlin. About a third of them (some 150,000 people) have Turkish passports. The number of Turkish-stemming people is much higher since many have naturalized in the past years or grew up as children of Turkish descent born and raised in town. This creates a solid background for the evolution of an ethnic economy among that immigrant group.

The general public perceives this increasing Turkish self-employment either as an indicator of the worsening chances of Turks on the Berlin labor market or as a sign of growing integration. Newly unemployed foreigners relying on self-employment as a last economic survival strategy signals exclusion from the German economy, while foreigners seizing the opportunities offered by an ethnic economy signals their integration into the economy. In fact, ethnic economies are active in both directions. Positioned at the margins of the formal and informal economies, they function as revolving doors by allowing certain social groups to move between the formal and informal labor markets.

Scope of the Turkish Ethnic Economy

At the local level, ethnic economy is now an established fact (Goldberg and Sen 1997; Zentrum für Turkeistudien 1999). Several official programs have been launched to create training places in enterprises run by foreigners, hopefully stimulating Berlin's labor market. In accordance with Berlin's plans to sharpen its profile as a European business location, start-ups and business activity by foreigners are seen as a significant factor of local economic life. Since unification, ethnic business has been steadily integrated into Berlin's economy. In the mid-1990s, the Turkish-German Employers' Association of Berlin-Brandenburg estimated that there were about 5,000 enterprises (with some 20,000 employees) run by Turkish individuals. At the end of the 1990s, the association was already speaking of "more than 6,000 companies of entrepreneurs and tradespeople of Turkish descent. Their number is growing by about 200 to 400 units per year. These enterprises employ some 20,000 workers. Their annual turnover reaches thousands of millions DM" (Turkish-German Employers' Association of Berlin-Brandenburg). In supraregional terms, too, self-employment by immigrants of Turkish origin is credited with the enormous potential to provide as many as 500,000 jobs in the near future (Arslan 2000).

The Zentrum für Turkeistudien (1999) assumes 51,000 Turkish self-employed with 265,000 employees and an annual turnover of about 46 billion DM (equivalent to 23 billion Euro) in the Federal Republic. In Berlin the Turkish-based ethnic economic community is so well established that the Turkish-German Employers' Association of Berlin-Brandenburg sporadically publishes a journal for the Turkish economy (*Türk Ekonomi Dergisi*). However, precise data relating to self-employed entrepreneurs in Berlin are only available at a rudimentary level.[1]

The Turkish yellow pages *Is Rehberi*, published annually since 1996, listed just under 3,596 enterprises in 1998, up from 2,467 in 1996. The entries for 1999, however, show a substantial drop of nearly 700 entries. This confirms an impression gained through survey research that ethnic economies are affected by heavy pressure from competitors, price trends, and falling purchasing power in the districts where ethnic enterprises are primarily located—Kreuzberg, Tiergarten, Wedding, Neukölln (see figure 7.1). In such neighborhoods the de-industralization processes of the 1990s disproportionately affected highly concentrated Turkish immigrants working in the industrial sector, leading to high unemployment. This negative trend is also confirmed by the editors of *Is Rehberi*, whose enquiries into the whereabouts of the many missing enterprises came up with the same answer again and again: "misinvestment," which means business failure

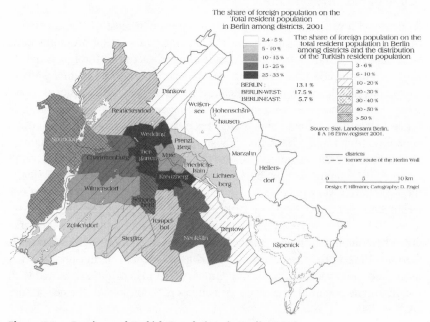

Figure 7.1.   Foreign and Turkish Populations in Berlin, 2001

due to bad or mistaken investments and wrong assumptions on the potential market.

There are clear variations in the fortunes of different ethnic business sectors. In 1999 it was the marginal areas of self-employment—such as the small kiosks—that continued to expand, whereas many other trades and services stalled and sometimes declined. This may be connected to the rapidly increasing competition from newspaper peddlers: the number of Germans running kiosks has decreased in the past years. It is just as plausible to assume that the increase in Turkish butchers' shops is linked to the fact that the German population has lost interest in this trade. In the food sector, the number of entries fell rapidly and is now below the 1996 level. Wholesale businesses have also expanded, whereas the retail trade is clearly losing ground. There are fewer Turkish restaurants, bakers, and especially typical Turkish cafés. Recent studies on the turnover of Turkish-stemming entrepreneurs confirm the trend of lower returns and point to the often problematic economic dimension of the Turkish ethnic entrepreneurship (see also Pütz 2003).

In our previous study of Turkish ethnic businesses in the food sector, we found that most Turkish enterprises were concentrated in those districts with a high percentage of residents of Turkish origin (Kreuzberg, Wedding, Tiergarten) (see figure 7.1). Most self-employed businesspeople reported that they had deliberately chosen this spatial strategy to be near family and friends. In addition, most businesses were very small, with only a few employees who were all of Turkish origin. Four-fifths of the employees were family members. Only one-tenth of the businesses surveyed said that they could survive without family help. Conversely, this means that the help of family members was essential to the function of these small businesses (Rudolph and Hillmann 1997).

Gendered Turkish Ethnic Economy in Berlin

In our previous study, all of the respondents were male although we did not explicitly focus on gender differences. We decided to conduct a second study on the Turkish ethnic economy in Berlin that specifically dealt with the labor market situation of Turkish businesswomen and female employees in ethnic businesses. Case studies on the form and scope of ethnic economies in Germany do exist, especially for the Turkish-stemming immigrants, but gender-sensitive studies are still missing (see Haberfellner 2000). Our interviews included women of Turkish origin in various sectors (Hillmann 1998).[2] Among the female entrepreneurs, results suggested strong similarities with their male counterparts. Most businesswomen had started up businesses after unification, mainly between 1994 and 1996. Their motives were often entrepreneurial; only one-fifth of the interviewees gave unemployment as the deciding factor. Similarly, the female Turkish respondents worked in small to very small businesses in terms of investment volume, spatial size, and number of employees. Like the men, none of the women owned their own business property.

However, the research results indicate that there are considerable differences with regard to embeddedness of the women within the ethnic community concerning the spatial allocation, the recruitment of labor, and the identification with the Turkish community.

In considering spatial allocation, most of our respondents lived in districts in western Berlin that have a high concentration of foreign residents: Neukölln and Kreuzberg. Few women lived in the former eastern districts of the city. Comparing the place of residence with the place of work, women who worked as dependent employees in the Turkish ethnic economy were more likely to work in their own neighborhood than the female (Turkish) entrepreneurs. While the entrepreneurs chose to live in those districts (because they were familiar with them), the employed women said that they "happened to find work there." Only one female entrepreneur said that proximity to the Turkish ethnic community was of some relevance in deciding the location of her business. Many preferred opening up their business in German districts, figuring that Germans would have more money to spend than their Turkish neighbors.

The recruitment of labor also becomes important. Whereas Turkish businessmen preferred to employ Turkish people and have relatives working for them, saying that the businesses could not survive without their help, Turkish businesswomen apparently would rather turn away from the ethnic community in order to keep their businesses going. The personnel structure of their enterprises did not suggest reliance on primarily Turkish staff; family members were employed as the exception rather than the rule. In the view of the female entrepreneurs, the greatest advantage of hiring family members was the high degree of trust they could place in their family.

However, in the interviews, the businesswomen emphasized the difficulties of employing family members. They said that family members "had their own work too," and initial attempts to involve them were soon abandoned. The entrepreneurs further underlined that they accepted this decision of relatives not to be involved in their business. Reasons varied by sector. For instance, some businesswomen like beauticians were in need of qualified, trained labor. In other cases, the explanation pointed more to hierarchical problems that they would face if they employed male family members. The outcome of the survey indicates that the Turkish women were not able or willing to use the "resource (informal) family help" to the same extent as their male counterparts. In fact, most interviews stressed the problematic aspect of employing family members. A recent study on Turkish female entrepreneurs in Hanover reaffirms this argument (Alberts 2003).

The clientele of most of the businesses mainly consisted of German clients. Six enterprises reported that they had no Turkish clients at all, and only one enterprise had exclusively Turkish clients. Also, businesswomen were oriented toward recruiting German clientele. Only three women planned to place advertisements in the Turkish media, while nine women planned to do so in German newspapers and media. Our study also showed that beauticians and hairdressers had no Turkish suppliers at all, and in other sectors there were at least as many German as Turkish suppliers.

Few businesswomen felt that they belonged to the Turkish ethnic economy. They did not generally define themselves as an "ethnic business," whereas the male interviewees specifically emphasized their Turkish origin (often also mentioning the "Turkish entrepreneurial spirit"). A typical comment among female entrepreneurs was "I don't want to be typically Turkish, because I offer something special and good quality" (Beautician, 30 years old). Two-thirds of the women interviewed did not consider their business to be ethnic; one-third, overwhelmingly active in the food sector, said that they offered Turkish specialities and thus belonged to the ethnic community. Most women answered that quality was more important than ethnic background—and that they preferred not to be judged by nationality, especially when they grew up in Germany and passed the national German schooling system. The most frequent explanation was that they were not offering a common service or product, such as the ubiquitous *Döner Kebab*, but a more sophisticated assortment. Some had explicitly moved away from the Turkish community and located their business in an area mainly frequented by German customers. Three-quarters of the women entrepreneurs did not consider their own professional biography to be typical.

By contrast, Turkish women wage-earners rated a "Turkish" environment much higher than the businesswomen. Some women responded that "this is typical for Turkish immigrant women. You came as a guest worker and then in the case of unemployment you had to look for alternatives—as self-employment or work in the business of a co-ethnic is" (Dependent worker in a Turkish food sector enterprise, 44 years old). This break in the biography became more prominent among the women that were older than forty and that had experienced another type of formal employment before.

Young Turkish women, our study suggests, have more consciously chosen to turn away from their own ethnic community than men and actively pursue a strategy of ethnic diversification. Seventy-two percent of the women were in steady contact with other entrepreneurs, while the rest said that they had no contacts with other entrepreneurs at all. Colleagues or family were the next best source for advice when problems arose. Only three women were members of the chamber of commerce or an association. The female entrepreneurs co-operated mostly with German enterprises (twenty-four interviewees) and less with Turkish enterprises (sixteen interviewees), which indicates that they still hold a certain bond with their ethnic and cultural background, even if the main focus of their cooperation was with the overall local setting.

CONCLUSION

Today the emergence of an active ethnic economy is no longer a marginal phenomenon in the urban economy. But ethnic economies are located within a field of tension. They are positioned between the formal and informal labor market segments and concentrate in particular sectors. They relate to processes of marginalization and informalization in the overall labor market and constitute a new form of labor market integration.

Our research findings suggest that there are clear gender differences in the Turkish ethnic economy. These are reflected in the statements and the actions of the women—sometimes not in a conspicuous way. This gender-specific view of Turkish ethnic enterprise is one step toward more differentiated analysis on the local scale. Our research results suggest that the usual definition of *ethnic business* refers implicitly only to the group of male entrepreneurs belonging to a certain generation of immigrants. For them, the frequently emphasized interaction with the informal labor market and the possibility of using family members for help are positive effects. For these businessmen, the ethnic economies act as revolving doors between the formal and informal segments of the labor market. By successfully combining these two resources, they are able to safeguard their intermediary position.

Things are different for Turkish businesswomen. First, their own self-perception distances them from the ethnic economy; second, they cannot reckon with (generally cheap) family capacities to the same extent; and third, they often have to deliberately distance themselves from their own ethnic community in order to achieve business success. For them, the ethnic economy represents a revolving door away from the informal and toward the formal segment of the labor market. What can generally be interpreted as a business asset for the male entrepreneur—namely easier access to reliable family help—does not apply to their female counterparts.

NOTES

1. Conclusions about the structure of the foreign self-employed segment can also be drawn from the number of applications for adjustment of residence status in order

to set up a business that were submitted to Berlin's Senate Department of Economics and Technology. The number of applicants does not give direct information about the real level of self-employment, since it is not known how many applications are actually implemented, but it gives a good idea of the business structure of foreign tradespeople. There is a clear trend toward service industries. On average, 127 people of Turkish nationality made an application in 1994–1999 per year. This corresponds to 8.5 percent of all applicants. During this period, on average one-fifth of the Turkish applications related to restaurants, etc., and only three percent to professional occupations. Seventeen percent were active in services, thirteen percent in retail, about ten percent in the travel business, and about twenty percent in skilled trades.

2. In this study a total of fifty women were interviewed, two-thirds of whom were businesswomen and one-third of whom were employees. The women worked in the following branches: food and restaurants, textiles and clothing, cosmetic services (hairdressers, beauticians), travel agencies, cleaning, and kiosks.

REFERENCES

Alberts, H. 2003. Researching self-employed immigrant women in Hanover, Germany. In *Crossing borders and shifting boundaries*, ed. U. Erel, K. Shinozaki, and I. Lenz, 285–97. Opladen: Leske and Budrich.

Anderson, P. 1999. From the wailing wall to the "dignified juggler": Making a living as an undocumented migrant in the United Kingdom. In *Migration und Illegalität*, ed. E. Eichenhofer, 195–212. Osnabrück: IMIS-Schriften.

Apitzsch, U., and M. Kontos. 2003. Self-employment, gender and migration. *International Review of Sociology* 13 (1): 67–76.

Arslan, B. 2000. Integration als Zukunftsaufgabe. *Das Parlament* 17 (3).

Bremer, P., and N. Gestring. 1997. Urban underclass: Neue Formen der Ausgrenzung auch in deutschen Städten? *Prokla: Zeitschrift für kritische Sozialwissenschaft Heft* 106 (27.1): 55–76.

Erel, U., K. Shinozaki, and I. Lenz, eds. 2003. *Crossing borders and shifting boundaries*. Opladen: Leske and Budrich.

Erzbischöfliches Ordinariat. 2000. *Illegal in Berlin*. Berlin: Erzbischöfliches Ordinariat.

Faist, T., F. Hillmann, and K. Zühlke-Robinet. 1996. Neue Migrationsprozesse: Politisch-institutionelle Regulierung und Wechselbeziehung zum Arbeitsmarkt. Working Paper of the Zentrum für Sozialpolitik Bremen, no. 6.

Fassmann, H. 1997. Die ethnische Segmentierung des Wiener Arbeitsmarktes. In *Leviathan*, ed. H. Häußermann and I. Oswald, 157–69. Sonderheft 17, Zuwanderung und Stadtentwicklung: Darmstadt.

Freudenberg Stiftung. 2000. *Towards emerging ethnic classes in Europe?* Weinheim: Author.

Goldberg, A., and F. Sen. 1997. Türkische Unternehmer in Deutschland: Wirtschaftliche Aktivitäten einer Einwanderungsgesellschaft in einem komplexen Wirtschaftssystem. In *Leviathan,* ed. H. Häußermann and I. Oswald, 63–84. Sonderheft 17, Zuwanderung und Stadtentwicklung: Darmstadt.

Haberfellner, R. 2000. Ethnische Ökonomien als Forschungsgegenstand der Sozialwissenschaften. *SWS-Rundschau* 40 (1): 43–61.

Häußermann, H. 1998. Zuwanderung und die Zukunft der Stadt: Neue ethnisch-kulturelle Konflikte durch die Entstehung einer neuen sozialen Unterklasse? In *Die Krise der Städte*, ed. W. Heitmeyer, R. Dollase, and O. Backes, 145–75. Frankfurt am Main: Suhrkamp.

Häußermann, H., and I. Oswald. 1997. Zuwanderung und Stadtentwicklung. In *Leviathan*, ed. H. Häußermann and I. Oswald, 9–29. Sonderheft 17, Zuwanderung und Stadtentwicklung: Darmstadt.

Heitmeyer, W., R. Dollase, and O. Backes, eds. 1998. *Die Krise der Städte*. Frankfurt am Main: Suhrkamp.

Hillmann, F. 1998. Türkische Unternehmerinnen und Beschäftigte im Berliner ethnischen Gewerbe. Discussion Paper FS I–107, Wissenschaftszentrum, Berlin.

Kloosterman, R. 2000. Immigrant entrepreneurship and the institutional context: A theoretical exploration. In *Immigrant businesses*, ed. J. Rath, 90–106. Houndmills, UK: Macmillan Press.

Landesarbeitsamt Berlin-Brandenburg. 1999. *Statistics on the employment among nationality*. Berlin: Landesarbeitsamt Berlin-Brandenburg.

———. 2002. *Statistics on the employment among nationality*. Berlin: Landesarbeitsamt Berlin-Brandenburg.

———. 2003. *Statistics on the employment among nationality*. Berlin: Landesarbeitsamt Berlin-Brandenburg.

Lederer, H. W. 1999. Typologie und Statistik illegaler Zuwanderung nach Deutschland. In *Migration und Illegalität*, ed. E. Eichenhofer, 53–72. Osnabrück: IMIS-Schriften 7.

Mingione, E. 1999. Introduction: Immigrants and the informal economy in European cities. *International Journal of Urban and Regional Research* 23 (2): 209–11.

Organisation for Economic Co-operation and Development. 1998. *SOPEMI: Trends in international migration: 1998 edition*. Paris: OECD.

Phizacklea, A. 2003. Transnationalism, gender and global workers. In *Crossing borders and shifting boundaries*, ed. U. Erel, K. Shinozaki, and I. Lenz, 79–100. Opladen: Leske and Budrich.

Pütz, R. 2003. Unternehmer türkischer Herkunft in Deutschland. *Geographische Rundschau* 55 (4): 26–31.

Raes, S. 2000. Regionalization in a globalising world: The emergence of clothing sweatshops in the European Union. In *Immigrant businesses*, ed. J. Rath, 20–36. Houndmills, UK: Macmillan Press.

Rath, J. 1999. The informal economy as bastard sphere of social integration. In *Migration und Illegalität*, ed. E. Eichenhofer, 117–36. Osnabrück: IMIS-Schriften 7.

Razin, E. 2002. The economic context, embeddedness and immigrant entrepreneurs. *The International Journal of Entrepreneurial Behaviour and Research* 8:3–4.

Reyneri, E. 1998. The role of the underground economy in irregular migration to Italy: Cause or effect? *Journal of Ethnic and Migration Studies* 24 (2): 313–31.

Rudolph, H., and F. Hillmann. 1997. Döner contra Bulette—Döner und Bulette: Berliner türkischer Herkunft als Arbeitskräfte und Unternehmer im Nahrungsgütersektor. In *Leviathan,* ed. H. Häußermann and I. Oswald, 106–20. Sonderheft 17, Zuwanderung und Stadtentwicklung: Darmstadt.

———. 1998. The invisible hand needs visible heads: Managers, experts and professionals from western countries in Poland. In *The new migration in Europe*, ed. K. Koser and H. Lutz, 60–84. Basingstoke, UK: Macmillan Press.

Samers, M. 1998. Immigration, "ethnic minorities," and "social exclusion" in the European Union: A critical perspective. *Geoforum* 29 (2): 123–44.

Sassen, S. 1991. *The global city: New York, London, Tokyo*. Princeton, NJ: Princeton University Press.

———. 2000. Dienstleistungsökonomien und die Beschäftigung von Migrantinnen in Städten. In *Migration und Stadt*, ed. K. Schmals, 87–114. Opladen: Entwicklugen.

Schmals, K., ed. 2000. *Migration und Stadt*. Opladen: Entwicklugen.

Stalker, P. 2000. *Workers without frontiers*. Boulder, CO: Lynne Rienner Publishers.

Waldinger, R. 1996. *Still the promised city?* Cambridge, MA: Harvard University Press.

Wilpert, C. 1998. Migration and informal work in the new Berlin: New forms of work or new sources of labour? *Journal of Ethnic and Migration Studies* 24 (2): 269–94.

Zentrum für Türkeistudien. 1999. Die ökonomische Dimension der türkischen Selbständigen in Deutschland: Neueste Untersuchungsergebnisse des Zentrums für Türkeistudien. Mimeo from Zentrum für Türkeistudien, Essen.

Part Two

HOW THE ETHNIC ECONOMY
SHAPES THE URBAN LANDSCAPE

Chapter Eight

How Ethnic Banks Matter: Banking and Community/Economic Development in Los Angeles[1]

Wei Li, Gary Dymski, Maria W. L. Chee,
Hyeon-Hyo Ahn, Carolyn Aldana, and Yu Zhou

Paralleling a trend of increasing Asian immigration, the number of businesses owned by Asian Americans[2] in the United States has grown markedly in recent decades. As of 1997, businesses owned by Asian and Pacific Islanders (API) numbered 913,000 nationwide (4.4 percent of all businesses in the country). The total for API-owned businesses lags behind that of Hispanic businesses but is larger than that for African American and Native American businesses. Moreover, there are 105.6 Asian-owned companies for every 1,000 Asian adults, nearly twice the rate for Hispanics and more than three times the rate for African Americans.[3] Further, API-owned businesses have higher average revenues ($336,000) than other minority-owned businesses.

The mainstream media, the general public, and many scholars have attributed Asians' high rates of business ownership and success to cultural attributes, to their disproportionate use of government loans, and/or to the extensive use of informal lending circles within Asian American communities (Brandon 1999; Geertz 1956; Hopkins 2002; LeDuff 2002; Light 1972; Light and Bonacich 1988). However, these factors do not fully account for the reality of Asian American businesses today. Increasingly, Asian American businesses rely on formal financial institutions for starting up and operating their businesses. The growing population of Asian American–owned banks has also expanded API businesses' access to capital; by exploiting their familiarity with the language and business practices of their Asian American customers (Lee 1999), these banks have both offered alternatives to and competed with mainstream banks. As of 31 March 2002, for instance, 35 of the 102 minority-owned banks registered with the Federal Reserve were owned by Asian Americans, exceeding the totals for African Americans (30), Hispanics (17), and Native Americans (14).[4] Many of the government loans that flow to API businesses are made by these Asian American-owned banks (Kesmodel 2000).

Ethnic minority–owned banks have become an increasingly important component of minority community development. The shifting nature of ethnic banks over time tracks the intertwined trajectories of financial exclusion and immigration in the United States. This chapter draws on our accumulated research on this topic to describe the origins, evolution, and impact of ethnic banking in Los Angeles County. Our focus is primarily on the historical case of Japanese American banks and the contemporary cases of Chinese American and Korean American banks.[5]

Ethnic banks are defined here as U.S. chartered commercial banks and savings and loans that are owned, controlled, and/or managed by members of U.S. ethnic minority groups and that focus on meeting the specific needs of minority businesses and residents (Li et al. 2001). The term *ethnic bank* is reserved for banks as defined in the economics literature—that is, financial firms that make loans and supply insured deposits. Just as Li's (1998a) ethnoburb concept represents a new phenomenon not encompassed in earlier notions of ethnic enclave, the notion of an ethnic bank represents a phenomenon not previously encompassed in earlier analyses of financial activities in minority communities. The process of defining the population of ethnic banks necessarily involves making some decisions about classification. In our definition, the population of ethnic banks incorporates both banks created by members of ethnic minorities and U.S. subsidiaries of foreign banks domiciled in countries of origin for those classified as ethnic minorities in the United States.[6] Our list is based not just on federal government information but also on published and unpublished research; articles in English, Chinese, and Korean newspapers; and Chinese and Korean Yellow Pages.

The first ethnic bank in Los Angeles was created by Japanese Americans at the turn of the twentieth century. At the current time, most ethnic banks in Los Angeles are Asian American–owned, and most of these are Chinese and Korean. As of 31 October 2002, Los Angeles contained seven Korean American and 27 Chinese American banks. These banks had a total of 187 branches (table 8.1).

This phenomenon deserves urban theorists' and policymakers' attention for two principal reasons. First, this institutional innovation can be traced to several ongoing trends in large urban centers: cross-border inflows of population and capital, shifting strategies and roles of non-ethnic banks, emergence of minority-population majorities in urban areas, and a shift from government-directed to market-based urban community development. Second, the structural comparison of ethnic banks' role in urban economic development gives some insights into the potential of community development financial institutions as mechanisms for urban revitalization, especially in lower income areas.

Table 8.1. Chinese and Korean American Banks Operating in Los Angeles County

	Headquarter City	No. of Offices		Total Assets ($ mil.)		Date Opened
		6/30/99	10/31/02	6/30/99	10/31/02	
Korean American Banks						
Hanmi Bank	Los Angeles	10	11	739.7	1292.4	Dec-82
California Korea Bank	Los Angeles	10	10	593.8	830.6	Sep-74
Nara Bank	Los Angeles	6	8	358.9	793.7	Jun-89
California Center Bank	Los Angeles	4	8	351.7	655.7	Mar-86
Wilshire State Bank	Los Angeles	5	8	300.5	577.3	Dec.-80
Saehan Bank	Los Angeles	2	6	121.5	250.9	Jun-91
California Cho Hung Bank	Los Angeles	1	1	89.3	157.1	Oct-88
Subtotal		38	52	2555.4	4,557.7	
Chinese American Banks						
United Commercial Bank	San Francisco	6	6	2282.8	3192.1	Mar-86
East West Bank	Los Angeles	20	25	2150.3	3030.5	Jun-72
Cathay Bank	Los Angeles	10	10	1995.5	2547.5	Apr-62
General Bank	Los Angeles	9	10	1738.5	2528.7	Mar-80
Chinatrust Bank (USA)	Torrance	7	7	1305.9	1766.6	Apr-65
Bank of Canton of California	San Francisco	2	4	910.4	1448.8	May-37
Far East National Bank	Los Angeles	7	7	856.4	1297.9	Dec-74
Standard Savings Bank	Monterey Park	6	5	701.1	853.6	Jun-85
United National Bank	San Marino	6	7	486.0	654.9	Jun-83
Preferred Bank	Los Angeles	6	6	496.6	652.3	Dec-91
Universal Bank	West Covina	7	6	359.5	358.6	Nov-54
First Continental Bank	Rosemead	3	3	270.6	310.6	Mar-91
First Commercial Bank (USA)	Alhambra	2	2	129.3	221.3	May-97
Trust Bank FSB	Monterey Park	3	3	185.6	217.0	Jan-77
						(continued)

Table 8.1. (continued)

	Headquarter City	No. of Offices 6/30/99	No. of Offices 10/31/02	Total Assets ($ mil.) 6/30/99	Total Assets ($ mil.) 10/31/02	Date Opened
Evertrust Bank	City of Industry	2	2	114.3	201.2	May-95
International Bank of California	Los Angeles	6	6	131.2	184.0	Apr-73
Omni Bank	Alhambra	4	4	189.7	181.9	Feb-80
Los Angeles National Bank	Buena Park	2	2	142.3	176.5	Dec-82
Grand National Bank	Alhambra	2	2	142.5	166.5	Feb-83
Pacific Business Bank	Santa Fe Springs	7	4	176.9	153.6	Apr-84
United Pacific Bank	City of Industry	2	2	151.9	135.3	May-82
Guaranty Bank of California	Los Angeles	3	3	106.6	134.2	Nov-76
First United Bank	San Diego	1	1	75.1	133.5	May-91
InterBusiness Bank	Los Angeles	n.a.	3	n.a.	113.0	Sep-00
Golden Security Bank	Alhambra	1	1	90.3	103.9	Dec-82
Eastern International Bank	Los Angeles	2	2	73.5	84.3	Feb-85
Asian Pacific National Bank	San Gabriel	2	2	39.7	49.1	Jul-90
Lippo Bank	San Francisco	1	n.a.	21.1		Nov-89
Subtotal		134	135	15323.6	20897.4	

Note: Ranked by total assets as of 6/30/02; Chinese American bank data is updated from Li et al. (2001, table 1); 1999 figure for "number of offices" includes those of American International Bank.

Note: California Korea Bank is now known as Pacific Union Bank.

The following Chinese American banks were acquired by other banks and no longer exist:

American Int'l Bank	Los Angeles	Bought out by East West Bank, 1/15/2000
First Central Bank	Cerritos	Bought by East West Bank, 5/29/1999
First Global Bank	Los Angeles	Bought by Hanmi Bank, 10/1/1998

Lippo Bank ceased to exist as of 5/31/2000.
Pacific Business and Universal became Chinese American banks in 1994 and 1980 respectively.

The asset totals here represent the holdings of the entire commercial bank, not the bank's assets in LA. All figures are based on FDIC reports. The "date opened" reported here may not accurately depict when an institution became an ethnic bank. Only institutions that have FDIC-reported branches are reported here.

Total assets for inactive institutions were taken from the last reported Call Report or Thrift Financial Report.

Source: FDIC 2004.

Households and businesses in Los Angeles's urban landscapes, as in previous generations, require financial institutions that can channel their savings into community-building investment. The inadequate response of mainstream banks to the county's new populations has opened the way for ethnic banks to play this role. The study of ethnic banks will shed light on an underlying meta-question: how does ethnic banking matter as a socioeconomic phenomenon? What roles do ethnic banks play in contemporary immigrant and/or minority community building and in the transformation of local economic landscapes?

The discussion below shows that ethnic banks may represent important, independent determinants of ethnic communities' growth and prosperity or of these communities' failure to grow and prosper. Given their unique origins, ethnic banks diverge from many banking industry trends. For example, they largely maintain relationship banking at a time when many financial institutions have turned to "by-the-numbers" banking; they use traditional branches to deliver most services, whereas many mainstream banks have attempted to redefine the role of branches; and they encourage culturally specific growth rather than "plain vanilla" growth. Ethnic banks also differ considerably in their focus: some target customers of a single ethnicity, while others target customers of multiple ethnic-minority backgrounds. Their market areas include not just the inner city but Los Angeles's growing ethnoburbs.

ASIAN IMMIGRATION AND ETHNIC BANKS

Asian immigrants have the tradition of creating their own informal savings pools; however, these arrangements involved tiny levels of finance, too small to change communal outcomes (examples are the Chinese *Hui* and Korean *Kye*; see Geertz 1956; Light 1972; Light and Bonacich 1988). However, "new migrations" from Mexico, Central and Latin America, and Asia[7] (Portes and Rumbaut 1996) have now altered the conjuncture of race and financial structure. One element of difference is the simultaneous arrival of economically heterogeneous groups of immigrants from many countries. These immigrants have created urban niches that are spatially substantial and structurally dense. While many cities have had Chinatowns for decades, the scale and rapid growth of these new communities have created a new phase in multiethnic settlement (Fong 1994; Horton 1995; Li 1998a; Lin 1998; Saito 1998; M. Zhou 1992; Y. Zhou 1998). The concentrated economic and residential spaces initially occupied by migrants from Korea, Haiti, and elsewhere have been termed *ethnic enclaves*. Social scientific discourses about ethnic urban communities shifted in response to this transition: the internal-colony/ethnic-succession duality of the 1970s gave way to the ethnic-enclave/ethnic-economy model of the 1990s.

The presence or absence of community-building capacity matters due to the economic heterogeneity of the new immigrants. Even among immigrants from the same country, a wide range of skill, education, and wealth levels exists. Those with high skill levels, professional credentials, and good English-speaking ability are positioned to succeed with little help from ethnic/immigrant networks (even with financial wealth that is initially modest). Only a small proportion of new entrants, however, can qualify for this position. More commonly, an immigrant with professional skills may lack U.S. credentials and English-speaking ability. An immigrant who possesses substantial financial wealth—due to inheritance or home-country enterprise—may lack professional credentials, language skills, and any credit history in destination countries. Many immigrants, especially women, are disadvantaged in terms of formal education, language skills, or wealth.[8] A bank offers the means to acquire fair arms-length savings and credit when informal methods are not viable. It can provide a mechanism for continual relationships at terms that permit widespread wealth building for both savers and borrowers. Most ethnic banks originate to fill these banking gaps—the double needs for job generation and financial services. How and when ethnic banks are created depends on the relationship between inflows of ethnic residents and businesses and inflows of these units' financial wealth. Banks can rise quickly when those in the first wave of ethnic entry have sizable resources; otherwise, they become feasible only after a gradual build-up of financial wealth through sweat equity and saving.

Ethnic Banking as Ethnic Economy

Ethnic banks started as the result of mainstream banks' negligence of and discrimination against minority and immigrant neighborhoods. In 1899, immigrants founded the first ethnic-financial firm in California, Nichibei Kinyusha (the Japanese American Financial Company).[9] In 1903, this company was chartered as a California state bank, the Nichibei Ginko (Japanese American Bank), and a Los Angeles branch was established. The Kinmon Ginko followed in 1905. Both banks were centered in the downtown portion of a Japanese community that totaled 1,200 in Los Angeles County in 1900 (Fogelson 1993).

The creation of two ethnic banks testified to this community's financial exclusion, stemming from the deep-seated segregation and discrimination of those years. These institutions' founding was linked to the opening of some Japanese small businesses. A financial panic in 1907 and a subsequent severe recession led to these banks' failure by 1909. Bank examiners cited mismanagement and embezzlement at these institutions. The Gentlemen's Agreement of 1907 then severely limited further migration of Japanese labor to the U.S. mainland. Though the Japanese population of Los Angeles grew steadily— due to migration within the United States and natural growth—prohibitions against Japanese landownership came about with the 1913 and 1920 California Alien Land Laws, which inhibited the sort of asset accumulation that banks might nurture. As of 1913, an overseas branch of the Japan-based Yokohama Specie Bank handled remittances to Japan from Japanese workers based in the United States. Rotating-credit associations (lending circles) were widely used to support small businesses and family expenses, and savings associations linked to prefectural residence in Japan flourished. Mutual-aid and group-lending institutions organized on the basis of geographic origin also proliferated among white immigrants to California (Dymski and Veitch 1996). When practiced by Asian immigrants, it was not only linked to ethnic exclusion but to preexisting cultural traits.

During these years, legal assaults on Japanese ownership rights reduced community wealth, culminating in the expropriation of Japanese American property during the World War II internments. After the war, the Japanese American community created several credit unions to pool their financial resources. In 1962, Merit Savings Bank was established under Japanese American ownership and a commercial bank, Marina del Rey National Bank, soon followed. Coupled with the lack of Japanese immigration inflow and continuous assimilation of later-generation Japanese Americans, these Japanese American banks withered over the years. After a downturn in the residential real estate market in 1988, other thrifts absorbed these Japanese American thrifts. Japanese Americans' experience with ethnic banks demonstrated their fragility. Making loans on a character basis may be valid, especially when it penetrates the veil of prejudice, but when made on a small scale for undercapitalized businesses in communities with low-wealth levels, there is a thin margin for error. Any external downturn can plunge lenders and community alike into crisis: banks are only large enough to affect individual economic units, not the community as a whole.

While the Japanese American migration of the early twentieth century was known for its drama and controversy, it was only one of numerous significant Asia-based migrations to Los Angeles. Chinese and Filipino immigrants in particular have as long and complex a history in Los Angeles. Koreans too have been present in Southern California in smaller numbers, since the late nineteenth century. None of these other Asian immigrant populations created formal banks, however, until well into the second half of the twentieth century.

The economic and banking opportunities for Asian Americans in Southern California were gradually transformed from the mid-1960s onward, due to the conjuncture of several factors—enhanced opportunities for international migration, financial globalization, and changes in U.S. domestic and geopolitical policies. The key event was the 1965 Immigration Act, which facilitated new large-scale Asian immigrations, with Los Angeles as a prime destination. This act, combined with subsequent geopolitical developments, led to a large influx of immigrants from Korea, Vietnam, and other Southeast Asian countries and to a significant inflow of Chinese.

This chapter focuses on the Chinese and Korean cases because these two groups have created the largest number of ethnic banks in Southern California. Further, these two groups' transnational ties permit us to identify some of the drastic differences between these new groups' ethnic banks and the ethnic banks created by Japanese Americans, not to mention those created in the African American and Latino communities (Dymski et al. 2000).

As major beneficiaries of the 1965 Immigration Act, the pace of community and economic development within the Chinese and Korean American communities became notably quicker after the mid-1960s. The Chinese and Korean migratory streams differ in a variety of ways, which are reflected in the banking institutions these communities' members have created. The Korean migration largely involves the movement of individuals and families between South Korea and the United States. The Chinese migration is more diasporic and multicentered—Chinese individuals and families moving between various origin and destination countries. Ethnic Chinese immigrants come to Southern California from a wide range of Asian countries: Taiwan, Hong Kong, mainland China, Indonesia, Vietnam, other Southeast Asian countries, and other parts of the world. Therefore, studying the similarities and differences of these two ethnic banking sectors and their relationships to their respective communities and Southern California at large will shed light on how Asian ethnic banking, as a new ethnic economy sector, has made its mark in transforming existing ethnic communities and in creating new economic possibilities in the contemporary era.

Chinese American Banks

The small Los Angeles Chinese American community of the early 1950s (about 10,000 according to the 1950 U.S. Census) began exploring creating their own formal financial institutions. Regardless of their financial and educational backgrounds, local Chinese Americans at the time were unable to secure loans from mainstream banks for their business activities and home financing. In April 1962, after repeated defeats and setbacks during a ten-year period of enduring efforts to establish their own formal financial institutions to battle discrimination, the first Chinese American commercial bank in Los

Angeles, Cathay Bank, opened its doors in the heart of Chinatown. It took another ten years (1972), for the second Chinese American bank, East-West Federal Savings, to receive its charter. The creation of East-West was partially due both to a new federal government minority banking program and to personal connections between a key official of this program and local Chinese American bankers. The origins of the first wave of Chinese American banks thus had some similarities to earlier efforts to create banks serving the Japanese American community (Li et al. 2000; Wang 1998).

The pace of Chinese American banking activity—and its success in community building—has picked up since the 1970s. Several Chinese banks were founded then, but the 1980s saw their number in Los Angeles County double (from six to twelve). Between 1980 and 2000, the number of Chinese in Los Angeles County increased almost eightfold—from 41,000 to more than 329,000 (table 8.1) due largely to immigration. These immigrants found themselves in a robust economy fueled by defense-related spending and a real estate boom. At the same time, the center of Los Angeles's Chinese community experienced a geographic shift from Chinatown to the western suburban San Gabriel Valley (SGV), which also involved a shift in the Chinese American banks' primary clientele from "old-timer" Chinatown generation to "newcomer" immigrants who bypassed Chinatown and moved directly to SGV (Fong 1994; Horton 1995; Li 1998a, 1998b, 1999; Li et al. 2002; Saito 1998).

Earlier generations of Chinese immigrants consisted largely of laborers (before World War II) and of students (who were primarily from Taiwan in the 1970s and later prospered). Many of the new immigrants came from wealthy families or were owners of established-overseas businesses. Their immigration to the United States often was motivated not by economic or social advancement but by their desire for a financial and political "safe haven" from the geopolitical changes affecting members of the Chinese Diaspora in the international arena (Li 1998a; Y. Zhou 1998). These wealthy Chinese immigrants were sophisticated financially and possessed the means to form banks and to fuel rapid growth in existing banks' assets. In effect, these new Chinese immigrants brought the financial capital, the human capital, the social capital, and the customer bases required to start successful banks.

Accompanying the transformation of this Chinese American residential population was the ensuing change of Chinese banks' ownership in Los Angeles from old-timer Chinatown Chinese to newcomer Chinese transnational immigrants and overseas ethnic Chinese and their enterprises. In seeking the initial capital required for the creation of the third Chinese American bank in Los Angeles, for instance, the founder of the Far East National Bank went to Taiwan in the early 1970s (Bank interview 1999).

Beginning in the 1980s, overseas Chinese financial groups and individuals based in Taiwan, Indonesia, and the Philippines began to purchase Chinese American banks in California and to increase their capital base (Flanigan 1998; Li et al. 2000; Wang 1998). Five new banks were founded in the early 1990s and another in 2000.

As of 31 October 2002, Los Angeles had a total of 27 Chinese American banks (10 of them partially foreign–owned) with 135 branches. These banks, equipped with strong capitalization at both their local bases and their Asian home countries—along with the twenty ethnic Chinese foreign bank branches in Los Angeles—have formed extensive networks for financing local Chinese American communities. As figure 8.1 demonstrates, many of their bank offices are highly associated with the geographic distribution of Chinese Americans.

At the same time, these banks have branched out to other areas. These latter branching activities are also reflected in the spatial distribution of their commercial loan activities. Instead of financing only in those areas that have a high concentration of Chinese Americans' commercial activities, Chinese American banks also provide construction loans to projects outside the core Chinese American communities in Los Angeles County. For instance, an extension of "University Village" outside University of California Riverside was financed by Far East National Bank, a Chinese American bank headquartered in Los Angeles's financial district. Therefore, contemporary Chinese American banks have been moving beyond the traditional boundaries of

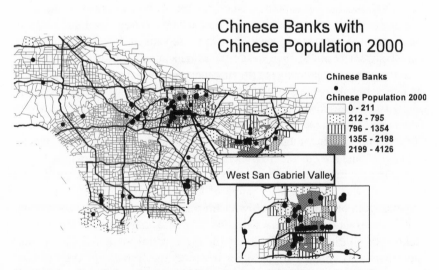

Figure 8.1.   Correlations between Chinese Banks and the Chinese Population

the ethnic economy and instead are increasingly functioning as an integral component of Los Angeles's core investment processes.

Korean American Banks

The Korean immigration to the United States did not begin in significant numbers until the 1970s and has grown rapidly since. In Los Angeles County, the number of Koreans has risen from 8,900 to 186,350 in Los Angeles County between 1970 and 2000 (table 8.1). The Korean entrepreneurship rate is among the highest in the nation (Yoon 1996). The first Korean bank, California Korea Bank, was established in 1974. For almost a decade, it remained the county's only Korean American bank. As in the case of the Chinese American banks, most Korean American banks were established during the 1980s. For example, a Korean immigrant bought Wilshire State Bank from its former African American owners and turned it into a Korean American bank in 1980. Several other Korean banks were started later in the 1980s: Hanmi Bank (1982); California Center Bank (1986); Seoul Bank of California, later California Cho Hung Bank (1988); and United Citizens National Bank, later Nara Bank (1989). Saehan Bank was established in 1991. Among these institutions, banks headquartered in South Korea control California Korea Bank and California Cho Hung Bank (Ahn and Hong 1999; Pak and Huh 1995). With some exceptions, these Korean American banks locate their branches in areas where Asian Americans are concentrated. They are especially clustered in Koreatown. Figure 8.2 illustrates the presence of Korean American banks in the Koreatown community in the western part of central Los Angeles, an area whose residents consist primarily of Latinos and Koreans.

Korean American banks are smaller than Chinese ethnic banks. As of 30 June 2002, the former have average assets of $651 million versus $774 million for Chinese ethnic banks; average deposits for Korean American banks are $567 million versus $647 million for Chinese banks. While smaller, Korean American banks have been growing much more quickly than even the surging Chinese American banking sector—their total assets increased 78 percent between 1999 and 2002, compared with 36 percent for Chinese American banks. The assets of the largest Korean American bank (Hanmi Bank) are equivalent to those of the seventh largest Chinese American bank. While total numbers of offices of all the other three ethnic bank subsectors stabilized in the same three-year period, the number of Korean American banks increased from 38 to 52 (FDIC 2002).

In addition to facilitating individual entrepreneurs' success (a role played by African American banks on a limited scale), Korean banks have played a significant role in the commercial resurgence of Koreatown within Los

Korean Banks with
Korean Population 2000

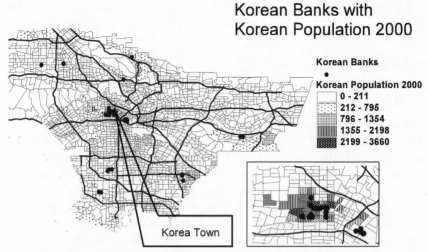

Korean Banks
●
Korean Population 2000
☐ 0 - 211
▦ 212 - 795
▨ 796 - 1354
▩ 1355 - 2198
■ 2199 - 3660

Korea Town

Figure 8.2.   Correlation between Korean Banks and the Korean Population

Angeles (a role played by Chinese American banks in supporting both business operations and commercial development in selected portions of the San Gabriel Valley).

But in contrast to Chinese American banks, whose financing of residential loans has helped to build up the residential clustering of Asian American populations in the San Gabriel Valley, Korean American banks make limited numbers of residential real estate loans (figure 8.3). Korean American banks

Loans 1998 - 2000 and
Asian Household Change 1990 - 2000

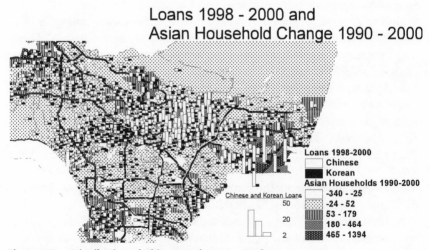

Loans 1998-2000
☐ Chinese
■ Korean
Asian Households 1990-2000
☐ -340 - -25
▦ -24 - 52
▥ 53 - 179
▩ 180 - 464
■ 465 - 1394

Chinese and Korean Loans
50
20
2

Figure 8.3.   Distribution of Chinese and Korean Bank Loans

have largely bypassed the residential loan market, focusing instead primarily on small business financing for Korean American businesses (see Ahn and Hong 1999; Li et al. 2002). While the Korean population has prospered and moved out to dispersed suburban communities in the San Gabriel Valley and the San Fernando Valley (figure 8.2; Allen and Turner 2002), Korean American banks have not financed many of these residential loans nor have they followed the community into these suburban areas as steadfastly as have Chinese American banks. As the result, the majority of Korean American bank offices have continuously concentrated in Koreatown area (figures 8.2 and 8.3).

In sum, Korean American banks engage in community building, but in a limited way, especially compared to the Chinese American banking sector. It remains to be seen whether the rapidly growing financial capacity of this ethnic banking sector will lead to an expanded role in community building in future years.

ETHNIC BANKING AND ETHNIC ECONOMY

The key economic role of ethnic banks within the ethnic economy is to finance other ethnic economic activities. As such, these banks can be an important life support for other ethnic economic sectors, providing the financing that permits them to make vital backward and forward linkages.

The primary mission of Korean American banks has been nurturing and serving Korean small businesses. For instance, after the 1992 riots in Los Angeles, one Korean American bank offered all its existing customers loans of up to $100,000 without collateral in order to revitalize hard-hit Korean American businesses. Nationwide, more than half of Korean businesses have accounts at Korean American banks (Palmeri 2003). Almost all Korean American banks concentrate on making business loans. The portion of business loans in the overall loan portfolio averages 86 percent at Korean American banks, with consumer loans and mortgage loans accounting respectively for only 6.6 percent and 7.3 percent of loan portfolios. Korean banks depend on small business both in their loan and deposit markets and are very active in community-based banking activities. Korean American banks provided for trade and financial flows, including remittances, between the United States and Korea (Ahn and Hong 1999).

By focusing so exclusively on Korean businesses and trading companies, these banks have been instrumental to Korean Americans' ethnic business development. However, these banks' small size limited the scope of their operations; they sometimes could not provide the loan volumes their customers required due to their limited capital base. Consequently, some of the larger Korean loan customers have been forced to seek credit from Chinese American or mainstream banks. Korean American banks may, after nurturing Korean small businesses in their initial growth periods, have systematically lost their more successful loan customers due to their small scale of operation.

By contrast, Chinese American banks have played important roles in transforming the traditional downtown Chinatown and in facilitating the creation of the San Gabriel Valley multiracial and multicultural ethnoburbs. Their role is entrepreneurial in precisely the manner described by Schumpeter in his classic work on the role of banking in economic development—meaning they are active players who have built the market and not simply followed the lead of the market. In the earlier days of Chinese American banking, bankers in this sector actively financed land and housing purchases and also the construction of residential real estate, thus permitting the rapid growth of Chinatown's population and the emergence of its robust consumer base. They tutored local Chinese business owners on how to utilize bank services to maximize their business profits and were instrumental in transforming Chinatown's cash economy to one that utilizes institutionalized financial services (Li et al. 2002).

Reflecting their customers' multinational character, Chinese American banks have developed considerable expertise in international banking practices, notably trade financing; many of their customers have import/export business ventures involving other Pacific Rim countries. Further, many of the new immigrants required frequent international monetary transactions, including remittances and foreign exchange. Even compared with mainstream banks, Chinese American bankers feel they have certain advantages in international banking because of the seasoning of their staff in this area.

Both Chinese and Korean American banks heavily rely on their co-ethnic depositors, which make up to 70 percent of their deposit bases. As for loan borrowers and portfolios, Chinese American banks are more diverse than Korean American banks; the latter make some 70 percent of their loans to co-ethnic borrowers, notably businesses (Ahn and Hong 1999; Li et al. 2001).

Because of stiff competition from non-ethnic banks and the need to broaden their customer bases, Chinese and Korean American banks in Los Angeles County have made conscious efforts to reach beyond their co-ethnic customers and areas. Most Chinese American banks have tried several methods of developing business with other ethnic groups. Most Korean American banks have also diversified their market focus by trying to expand their markets; in particular, they are targeting Hispanic customers as a means of expanding their loan and savings volumes.

Chinese American bank loans are balanced between commercial and residential loans. Some 58 percent of Chinese banks' loan portfolios consists of commercial and industrial loans, another 41 percent are residential real estate–based loans, and less than one percent are allocated to loans to individuals. However, due to their large numbers and substantial total assets, Chinese American banks underwrite many commercial projects and provide start-up and working capital to their co-ethnic businesses (Ahn and Hong 1999; Li et al. 2001; Li et al. 2002; Li and Dymski forthcoming).

As two ethnic banking sectors primarily serving their co-ethnic clients, Chinese and Korean American banks share many similarities, despite their differences. As with other community banks, both Chinese and Korean American banks in Los Angeles County have close ties with the local communities they are serving. As ethnic banks, they also fit the definition of a niche bank, which prospers by developing its own area of expertise and becoming more efficient and better informed about its specialty area than are non-specialist banks. As both community banks and niche banks, two characteristics differentiate the Chinese and Korean American banks from mainstream banks: their mission of serving the ethnic community by nurturing community and economic development and their focus on relationship banking.

First and foremost, Chinese and Korean American banks have clear missions of serving Asian American communities, especially these communities' business ventures. Chinese and Korean American bankers acknowledge the importance of the relationship between banks and community development and think their banks play vital roles in the local community's economic growth and social well-being. Some banks state in so many words (in interviews) that serving the Chinese and/or Korean American community is among their primary missions.

A second point of difference for these banks is Chinese and Korean American banks' emphasis on relationship banking—that is, on business practices that depend on sustained links and information exchanges between bankers and their customers. The majority of our interviewees stressed the importance of relationship banking in developing and implementing their strategies. Chinese and Korean American bankers consider this to be a key difference from the practices of large mainstream banks. They build the rapport to maintain trust relationships with their customers through regular face-to-face meetings and continuous close contacts.

Table 8.2 provides figures on bank branch density for the period 1970 to 2000 and summarizes their relationship with Chinese and Korean American populations and businesses as compared to Los Angeles County as a whole. It demonstrates rapid growth in the number of Chinese American banks and

Table 8.2. Chinese and Korean American Population, Business and Banking (1970-2000)

Year (Year of E-census)	Chinese Population	Chinese Business	Chinese Branch	Chinese Population/ Branch	Chinese Business/ Branch	Overall Population/ LA County	Overall Business/ Bank Branch
1970 (1972)	40,978	1,378	1	40,978	1,378	8,037	n/a
1980 (1982)	93,747	7,611	9	10,416	846	n/a	n/a
1990 (1987)	248,033	16,049	70	3,543	229	7,045	n/a
1994 (1992)	248,033	n/a	105	2,362	n/a	5,144	387
2000 (1997)	329,352	40,352	128	2,573	315	6,313	516

Year (Year of E-census)	Korean Population	Korean Business	Korean Branch	Korean Population/ Branch	Korean Business/ Branch
1970 (1972)	n/a	398	0	n/a	n/a
1980 (1982)	60,618	7,906	2	30,309	3,953
1990 (1987)	145,431	17,165	19	7,654	903
1994 (1992)	145,431	n/a	26	5,594	n/a
2000 (1997)	186,350	21,777	38	4,904	573

Sources: Pollard 1996; Li et al. 2002; U.S. Bureau of the Census 1997, n.d.; 1990, 2000 Census.

Note: 1994 ratios based on 1990 population data. Population: 1990, 2000 Census.

2000 — http://factfinder.census.gov/servlet/DTTable?_bm=y&-context=dt&-reg=DEC_2000_SF2_U_PCT001:001|016|023&-ds_name=DEC_2000_SF2_U&-CONTEXT=dt&-mt_name=DEC_2000_SF2_U_PCT001&-tree_id=402&-all_geo_types=N&-geo_id=05000US06037&-format=&-_lang=en

1990 — http://factfinder.census.gov/servlet/DTTable?_bm=y&-context=dt&-reg=DEC_2000_SF2_U_PCT001:001|016|023;&-ds_name=DEC_1990_STF1_&-mt_name=DEC_1990_STF1_P001&-CONTEXT=dt&-tree_id=100&-redoLog=true&-all_geo_types=N&-geo_id=05000US06037&-format=&-_lang=en

Business1997 — http://www.census.gov/epcd/mwb97/metro/p4480.html

1992 — county total only: http://www.census.gov/epcd/www/92profiles/county/06037.TXT

1988 — county pop total: http://www.census.gov/population/cencounts/ca190090.txt

in their branch density, compared to Korean American banking sector. While the numbers of banks and branch totals for the Korean American banking sector have grown during the same time period, the ratios of ethnic population and ethnic business to ethnic bank branches for this sector are still higher than for Chinese American banks.

For the most part, Chinese and Korean residential and business populations overall enjoy a higher level of access to banking services than other populations in Los Angeles County in recent decades—a testimony to ethnic banks' role in ethnic community and economic development.[10] East-West Bank, a Chinese American bank, follows in the footsteps of mainstream banks by establishing branches inside 99 Ranch Market, the largest Chinese supermarket chain in the country.

CONCLUSION

In this chapter, we have compared and contrasted the differential trajectories of Asian ethnic banking development in Los Angeles. We have found that each ethnic banking sector is unique; their trajectories are history bound, time dependent, and path specific. No common evolutionary trajectory emerges. Hence, there is no blueprint for success in community economic development which all minority and immigrant financial institutions and communities can follow.

Our work does reveal that ethnic banks have been created, both in the historical and contemporary periods, to serve their respective minority population and businesses. Thus, their activities have some commonalities. Nonetheless, their roles in community building vary significantly due to differences in their capital sources, in the scale and number of ethnic banks in a given community, in community members' wealth assets, and in the degree and character of economic connections, especially transnational connections.

In the Chinese American community, ethnic banks are primary conduits for savings and credit flows; these banks' substantial scale has provided them the opportunity to play the entrepreneurial role. More than any other ethnic banking subsectors, the Chinese American banks have tapped into transnational financial resources and become part of the financial web across the Pacific Ocean. In the Korean community, the banks have supported business start-ups and community commercial flows.

In sum, the Chinese and Korean American banks in Los Angeles County resulted from the new migration that occurred after changes in immigration law in 1965 and in the wake of shifting geopolitical dynamics and global economic structures. Both these ethnic bank subsectors heavily rely on capital sources and customer markets brought by newer immigrants with transnational ties. This path to autonomous community development through creating a capable ethnic-banking sector would be difficult to replicate for other minorities that lack access to such diverse immigrant inflows.

NOTES

1. This project has been partially funded by a National Science Foundation grant (SES-00747754/SES-0296136) and faculty research grants from the College of Public Programs and Office of the Vice Provost for Research and Economic Affairs, Arizona State University, the University of California, and California State University. An earlier version of this paper was presented at the 2000 meeting of the Urban Affairs Association in Los Angeles and the 2000 International Geographic Congress in Seoul, Korea. The authors thank session participants for helpful discussion, while remaining responsible for errors. We are also grateful to Mary Fran Draisker, Jianfeng Zhang, and Yun Zhou at Arizona State University, Marian Fu at the University of California Riverside, and Rob Garcia at California State University, San Bernardino, for research and editorial assistance. Mailed correspondence regarding this chapter should be directed to Wei Li or Gary Dymski; individual coauthors may also be contacted at their e-mail addresses.

2. The term *Asian American* is used here at its broadest meaning, including both Asian immigrants and native-born Americans of Asian descent.

3. The U.S. 2000 Census reveals there are 35,238,481 Hispanic/Latinos, 33,707,230 African Americans, and 10,067,813 Asians in the nation; see U.S. Bureau of the Census American FactFinder. Business data is from the U.S. 1997 Economic Census (U.S. Bureau of the Census 2001) and Hopkins (2002).

4. Calculation based on data from Federal Reserve (2001).

5. The authors' research has involved developing an extensive database and conducting over fifty detailed, multilingual interviews (conducted since summer 1999) with ethnic bank officers and managers. In this paper, the terms *ethnic banks* and ethnobanks are used interchangeably.

6. Note that foreign banks' U.S. offices are excluded, as these offices cannot operate as banks in U.S. markets. Clearly, U.S. subsidiaries of foreign-owned multinational banks are very different from community-based banks founded by domestic minority residents. Note that the population of ethnic banks included in our research is larger than the list of ethnic banks maintained by the Federal Reserve.

7. For example, Japanese Americans have been present in Los Angeles for over a century, and Little Tokyo was a long-established feature of that city's downtown. The number of Japanese Americans, however, has remained under a million nationally during this entire period. By contrast, the Korean population in Los Angeles has grown explosively since the 1970s. Consequently, Los Angeles' Koreatown is Portes and Rumbaut's (1996) leading example of the impact of the "new migration."

8. Table 11 of Portes and Rumbaut (1996, 59) shows that even when immigrants have high average wealth and education levels, a large proportion of them lack secondary education.

9. The discussion on Japanese American banks is based primarily on Chee (2000).

10. Table 8.2 presents a hypothetical scenario when minorities only utilize their co-ethnic banks. In reality, mainstream banks have actively courted Chinese and Korean customers in recent decades, which makes their banking accessibility even higher than table 8.2 portrays.

REFERENCES

Ahn, H., and J. Hong. 1999. The evolution of Korean ethnic banks in California. *Journal of Regional Studies* (Korea) 7 (2): 97–120.

Allen, J. P., and E. J. Turner. 2002. *Changing faces, changing places: Mapping Southern Californians*. Northridge: California State University.

Brandon, K. 1999. Catalyst for change—and dollars. *Chicago Tribune*, November 2.

Chee, M. 2000. The political economy of ethnic banking: The presence and absence of the Japanese American banking sector in Los Angeles. Mimeo from Department of Anthropology, University of California, Riverside.

Dymski, G., W. Li, C. Rodriguez, M. Chee, H. H. Ahn, J.-P. Hong, and Y. Zhou. 2000. The development of ethnic banking in Southern California. Mimeo from Department of Economics, University of California, Riverside.

Dymski, G., and J. Veitch. 1996. Financial transformation and the metropolis: Booms, busts, and banking in Los Angeles. *Environment and Planning A* 28 (7): 1233–60.

Federal Deposit Insurance Corporation (FDIC). 2002. FDIC A to Z. www.fdic.gov (accessed 4 November 2002).

Federal Reserve. 2001. *Minority owned banks as of June 30, 2003*. www.federalreserve.gov/releases/mob/min_bnk_lst.pdf (accessed 16 February 2006).

Flanigan, J. 1998. Immigrant banks: A model for Asia, a boon to U.S. *LA Times*, 14 January.

Fogelson, R. 1993. *The fragmented metropolis: Los Angeles, 1850–1930*. Berkeley: University of California Press.

Fong, T. 1994. *The first suburban Chinatown: The remaking of Monterey Park, California*. Philadelphia: Temple University Press.

Geertz, C. 1956. *The Rotating Credit Association: An instrument for development*. Cambridge: Massachusetts Institute of Technology, Center for International Studies.

Hopkins, J. 2002. Shift in power creates tension in minorities. *USA Today*, 4 March.

Horton, J. 1995. *The politics of diversity immigration, resistance, and change in Monterey Park, California*. Philadelphia: Temple University Press.

Kesmodel, D. 2000. Korean American banks in top ranks of SBA lending. *Los Angeles Times*, 13 September.

LeDuff, C. 2002. When origin becomes a competitive issue. *New York Times*, 11 May. www.nytimes.com/2002/05/11/national/11MOTE.html (accessed 11 May 2002).

Lee, D. 1999. Divergent trends for entrepreneurs. *Los Angeles Times*, 17 September.

Li, W. 1998a. Anatomy of a new ethnic settlement: The Chinese *ethnoburb* in Los Angeles. *Urban Studies* 35 (3): 479–501.

———. 1998b. Los Angeles' Chinese *ethnoburb*: From ethnic service center to global economy outpost. *Urban Geography* 19 (6): 502–17.

———. 1999. Building ethnoburbia: The emergence and manifestation of the Chinese *ethnoburb* in Los Angeles' San Gabriel Valley. *Journal of Asian American Studies* 2 (1): 1–28.

Li, W., M. Chee, Y. Zhou, and G. Dymski. 2000. *Development trajectory of Chinese American banking sector in Los Angeles*. Mimeo from Asian American Studies Institute, University of Connecticut.

Li, W., and G. Dymski. Forthcoming. Globally connected and locally embedded financial institutions: Analyzing the ethnic Chinese banking sector. In *Chinese ethnic economy: Global and local perspectives*, ed. E. Fong. Philadelphia: Temple University Press.

Li, W., G. Dymski, Y. Zhou, M. Chee, and C. Aldana. 2002. Chinese American banking and community development in Los Angeles County. *Annals of Association of American Geographers* 92 (4): 777–96.

Li, W., Y. Zhou, G. Dymski, and M. Chee. 2001. Banking on social capital in the era of globalization: Chinese ethnic banks in Los Angeles. *Environment and Planning A* 33 (4): 1923–48.

Light, I. 1972. *Ethnic enterprise in America: Business and welfare among Chinese, Japanese, and Blacks*. Berkeley: University of California Press.

Light, I., and E. Bonacich. 1988. *Immigrant entrepreneurs: Koreans in Los Angeles, 1965–1982*. Berkeley: University of California Press.

Lin, J. 1998. *Reconstructing Chinatown: Ethnic enclave, global change*. Minneapolis: University of Minnesota Press.

Mach, W. 1998. Break out: An evolution or a revolution? Mimeo from the Pacific Coast Banking School, Seattle.

Pak, H. S., and S.-K. Huh. 1995. Comparative analysis of Korean banks' performance. *Journal of Interdisciplinary Studies* 8: 143–50. http://www.csupomona.edu/~jis/1995/pak.pdf (accessed 16 February 2006).

Palmeri, C. 2003. For Korean banks, truly a golden state: They thrive serving loan-hungry small business in California. *Business Week*, 17 February.

Pollard, J. 1996. Banking at the margins: A geography of financial exclusion in Los Angeles. *Environmental and Planning A* 28 (7): 1209–32.

Portes, A., and R. Rumbaut. 1996. *Immigrant America: A portrait*, 2nd ed. Berkeley: University of California Press.

Saito, L. 1998. *Race and politics: Asian Americans, Latinos, and Whites in a Los Angeles suburb*. Chicago: University of Illinois Press.

U.S. Bureau of the Census. 2001. 1997 economic census minority- and women-owned business United States. www.census.gov/epcd/mwb97/us/us.html (accessed 24 February 2006).

——. n.d. American factfinder. factfinder.census.gov (accessed 1 June 2005).

Wang, E. 1998. Retrospectives of Chinese American banks. *Chinese International Daily*, Section C, 28 April–3 May.

Yoon, I. 1996. *On my own: Korean businesses and race relations in America.* Chicago: University of Chicago Press.

Zhou, M. 1992. *Chinatown: The socioeconomic potential of an urban enclave.* Philadelphia: Temple University Press.

Zhou, Y. 1998. How do places matter? A comparative study of Chinese ethnic economies in Los Angeles and New York City. *Urban Geography* 19 (6): 531–53.

Chapter Nine

Ethnic Diversity and the Ethnic Economy in Cosmopolitan Sydney

Jock Collins

Sydney is Australia's largest city with a population of just under four million, one-fifth of the nation's total population. It is also Australia's largest immigrant city, generally receiving over 40 percent of Australia's annual immigrant intake. Today Sydney accommodates people from over 180 nations, with 58 percent of the population in 2001 first- or second-generation immigrants. Sydney is unmistakably a cosmopolitan city, with the smell, taste, feel and look of its contemporary downtown and suburban areas reflecting its two centuries of immigration (Collins and Castillo 1998). Much of the cosmopolitan character of Sydney stems from its ethnic economy (Light and Gold 2000, 4) and from Sydney's immigrant entrepreneurs who have shaped the economic, social, and cultural landscape of the city.

This chapter explores Sydney's ethnic economy through the lens of immigrant entrepreneurship (Kloosterman and Rath 2003; Collins et al. 1995; Collins 2003), including the role of clusters of immigrant entrepreneurs, particularly those in the restaurant and food business, in shaping the contemporary cosmopolitan feel of Chinatown, Little Italy, and Cabramatta neighborhoods.

ETHNIC ENTREPRENEURS IN COSMOPOLITAN SYDNEY

According to the 2001 National Census, Sydney includes nearly 2.5 million people born in Australia and over 180,000 born in the UK. The other immigrant groups exceeding populations of 20,000 are from China, New Zealand, Vietnam, Italy, Lebanon, Hong Kong, India, Greece, Korea, Fiji, and South Africa. In addition, Sydney has another thirteen immigrant groups with a population between 10,000 and 20,000 and over one hundred immigrant groups

135

with a population of less than 10,000. The 2001 Census also revealed other dimensions of cosmopolitan Sydney. Sydney's population born in Southeast Asia comprises six percent of the total population and sixteen percent of those born overseas. Over 180,000 Sydney-siders speak a Chinese language at home and 130,287 people speak Arabic at home (Australian Bureau of Statistics 2002).

Immigrant entrepreneurs are the backbone of Sydney's ethnic economy. While this is the case for ethnic economies everywhere, Sydney's ethnic economy is, in relative terms, one of the largest. First-generation immigrants comprise a quarter of all self-employed and employers in Australia, a rate of immigrant entrepreneurship higher than in any other major country belonging to the Organisation for Economic Co-operation and Development (OECD) (OECD 1998, 36). The ethnic diversity of Australian society is reflected in Australian entrepreneurship, though the relationship between birthplace and rate of entrepreneurship varies considerably.

Census data shows that some immigrant groups—such as the Koreans, Taiwanese, Greeks, Italians, Dutch, and Germans—are fifty percent more likely to be entrepreneurs than those born in Australia. First-generation Korean immigrants have the highest rate of entrepreneurship, nearly double the rate of people born in Australia (Collins 2003). But other groups of immigrants—those born in China, Singapore, Malaysia, Egypt, Lebanon, Poland, Ukraine, and Yugoslavia—have similar rates of entrepreneurship to the Australian average. Moreover, immigrants from Japan, India, Sri Lanka, Vietnam, Indonesia, and Turkey have lower rates of entrepreneurship than average. Immigrants born in the United Kingdom, New Zealand, Canada, and the United States also have rates of entrepreneurship very similar to people born in Australia.

Immigrant entrepreneurs in Australia are conspicuous in the retail sector of the economy in much the same way as they are in Britain, Europe, and the United States (Waldinger, Aldrich, and Ward 1990). Census data for Sydney, as shown in table 9.1, reveals that a number of ethnic niches exist in the city's retailing industry. Entrepreneurship related to food is a core part of the ethnic economy in Sydney, as it is in other cities around the world (Warde 1997; Warde and Martens 2000). First-generation immigrants comprise about half of entrepreneurs who own fish shops, takeout food shops, grocers, and fruit and vegetable stores. Italians are the most prominent immigrant group in fruit and vegetable stores, where they comprise twenty-two percent of the total employers—and eighteen percent of the self-employed[1]—despite being less than two percent of the total population. Similarly Greeks, with a smaller population, alone account for eighteen percent of employers and twenty-one percent of the self-employed in the fish shops, take-out food, and milk bars

Table 9.1. First-Generation Immigrants as a Proportion of All Entrepreneurs in Sydney's Retail Sector, 1991 Census

Retail Industry Sector	% Born Overseas
General stores	17.8
Clothing stores	34.2
Footwear, shoe repair	30.5
Fabrics, textiles	21.1
Floor coverings, furniture	24.4
Hardware stores	33.1
Watchmakers, jewelers	39.7
Music stores	24.4
Household appliance stores	26.3
Motor vehicles, petrol	21.6
Service stations	33.3
Smash repairs	26.1
Boats, caravans	22.7
Tires, batteries	12.3
Milk bars	14.3
Food stores, grocers	41.9
Butchers	22.2
Fruit, vegetable	48.2
Liquor stores	21.6
Bread, cake stores	37.3
Fish shop, take away food	57.3
Pharmacies	17.9
Photography, sport, toys	33.7

segment of the retail industry. Other parts of the Australian retail industry with a relatively high immigrant presence are clothing and footwear shops, service stations, watchmakers and jewellers, and bread and cake shops. They are least represented in general stores, tire and battery stores, milk and bread vendors, newsagents and booksellers, and pharmacies.

ETHNIC PRECINCTS IN SYDNEY

Ethnic precincts visually reflect the ethnic economy and ethnic diversity of Sydney's landscape. Like so many Western cities (Zhou 1992; Lin 1998; Fong 2000; Anderson 1991), Sydney has a prominent and long-established China-town in the downtown area. Sydney's other ethnic precincts are located in the suburbs of southwestern Sydney (Collins and Poynting 2000) and include Leichhardt (Little Italy), Campsie (Little Korea), Petersham (Portuguese), and

Marrickville (once Greek, now Vietnamese) in Sydney's inner ring. In the middle-ring suburbs, ethnic precincts include Auburn (Arabic), Lakemba and Punchbowl (Middle Eastern), and Bankstown (Asian and Middle Eastern). Cabramatta, further west, has become an Asiatown (Collins and Castillo 1998). One exception to the southwestern location of Sydney's ethnic precincts is the north-shore Chinese precinct of Chatswood, the center of professional and well-educated middle-class Chinese immigrants. In addition, the Bondi Beach area in the eastern suburbs has a prominent Jewish history and presence.

Chinatown

The history of Chinese settlement in Sydney dates back over 150 years. Responding to community prejudice and drawing on the attraction of co-ethnic provision of goods, services, language, and company, the concentrated settlement patterns of Chinese immigrants and entrepreneurs reflected the residential and labor discrimination the Chinese faced. Sydney's early Chinese settlement was in the 1860s around George Street, close to the wharves, and by the 1890s Sydney's Chinatown moved to the Gipps Ward, west of the central business district (Anderson 1990). By 1901 there were 799 Chinese shopkeepers and grocers in New South Wales (NSW), and half of these were in the Sydney area. Many became greengrocers, fruit and vegetable distributors, cafe owners or general dealers, hawkers, and importers (Choi 1975, 33), while others moved into the laundry business or opened small furniture shops (Yuan 1988, 305). In the 1940s Chinatown moved to its current location on Campbell Street and Dixon Street (Collins and Castillo 1998, 278–89; Fitzgerald 1997). In the post-1945 decades, Chinese immigrant–run cafes and restaurants sprang up all over the metropolitan and rural areas across the nation. By the mid-1980s, Chinese cafes or restaurants were a feature of Australian suburban and small town landscapes. According to Chin (1988), there were 700 cafes operated by Chinese in NSW, with 300 in Sydney at that time, most of them employing Chinese labor. Today Chinatown is a very vibrant and lively precinct (see figure 9.1).

Local government authorities shaped Sydney's Chinatown, demonstrating how regimes of regulation influence ethnic entrepreneurial outcomes in different countries in different ways (Kloosterman and Rath 2001). The redevelopment of Dixon Street began in 1972 by introducing porticos, lanterns, and trash bins with "traditional" Chinese symbols in order to make the area more Chinese. According to Anderson (1990, 150), this redevelopment was driven by the fact that Sydney planners were envious of San Francisco developments and thought their Chinatown shabby by comparison. In the 1980s, Dixon Street became a pedestrian thoroughfare with Chinese dragons at the Paddy's Market end and Chinese trees along the streetscape. It was linked to the new

SYDNEY'S CHINATOWN

1 Emperor's Garden Barbecue and Noodles
2 Burlington Centre.
3 Wong's Barbecue.
4 DNA Meat Market.
5 Central Fish Market.
6 Emperor's Garden Butcher.
7 Dong Nam A Grocery.
8 Chinese Ginseng & Herb Co.
9 Fuji-san
10 Marigold
11 Silver Spring
12 Wing Hing.
13 Wai Wong Barbecue & Butcher.
14 David Duong Top Quality Butchery.
15 China Town Fish Market.
16 BBQ King.
17 Thai Kee Supermarket.
18 Marigold.
19 The Regal.
20 Golden Century
21 Sussex Food Centre.
22 Everspring Supermarket.
23 Dixon House.
24 Chinatown Food Centre.
25 Golden Harbour
26 Superbowl Chinese Restaurant.
27 Kam Fook

Figure 9.1.   Map of Chinatown

Darling Harbour development via the Chinese Gardens (Fitzgerald 1997). Hong Kong Chinese capital financed much of this development.

However, according to Anderson (1990, 150), Sydney's Chinatown has been revitalized in ways that reflect white Australia's image of *Chinese-ness*: "Making the area more 'Chinese' seemed to make the area appear more consistent with the architectural motifs and symbols of ancient China." A related point is the way in which, during this process of "developing" Chinatown, the Chinese were seen as a homogenous Other rather than a community divided along regional, class, and commercial lines. There are more than one hundred ethnic Chinese community organizations in Sydney, refuting the notion of a homogenous Chinese ethnicity or community. The planning process to redevelop Sydney's Chinatown has always involved representatives of Sydney's Chinese community and, in turn, led to internal struggles among members of Sydney's Chinese community over the right to gain representation and influence over the development of Sydney's Chinatown (Anderson 1990).

Nevertheless, Sydney's Chinatown is a vibrant component of Sydney's ethnic economy and a landmark to Sydney's immigrant history. Walk through the dragons and along the pedestrian mall in Dixon Street or along adjoining streets any lunchtime, and Chinatown is awash with people. Many of the Asian faces are Sydney residents, permanent immigrants, some who live nearby in the new downtown apartments built before and since the Sydney 2000 Olympic Games. The others live in Sydney's suburbs and come down to Chinatown to have *yum cha* with friends or family, to do business, to see a doctor or dentist, and to shop.

Equally large numbers of Asians are temporary immigrants who call Sydney home for the three years or so it takes them to finish their education in Sydney's universities, colleges, and schools. Other Asians are tourists, part of the more than four million international tourists who visit Sydney every year. Sydney's Chinatown thus smells, tastes, and looks Asian and is an enduring and dynamic part of the landscape of Sydney's ethnic economy. Like other ethnic precincts, Chinatown is also the main site of Chinese ethnic festivals throughout the Chinese calendar, and the nearby Darling Harbour is used for the annual Dragon Boat Festival and races.

Little Italy

Italian immigration history in Sydney has been strongly linked to entrepreneurship and to the inner-western suburb of Leichhardt, Sydney's Little Italy (Pascoe 1988; Collins 1992). Leichhardt has been the original home of Sydney's Italian immigrant community since 1885 when the fishmonger Angelo Pomabello and the Bongiorno Brothers were among the first Italians to settle in Leichhardt and open shops on Parramatta Road. But it was not until after the 1920s that the growth of Leichhardt's Italian community began to expand dramatically, particularly in the late 1950s and early 1960s. For the postwar Italian immigrants, Leichhardt offered cheap housing, proximity to employers of unskilled labor, Italian shops, and other businesses. Religion and commerce were at the center of this flourishing community. The Saint Fiacre church and parish, still run by the Italian-speaking Capuchin fathers, became the hub of Italian life in the area.

This residential concentration began to be reflected in the business composition of the area. By 1958 Italian entrepreneurs established a range of businesses including "travel agencies, imported wine shops, women's fashion shops, radio stores, and a second phase of comparison goods stores following earlier more basic convenience stores—delicatessens, fruit sellers, pastry shops, and seafood stores" (Burnley 2001, 161). In the early 1960s, half of the members of the Leichhardt Chamber of Commerce were Italian (Burnley 2001). By 1976, there were 175 Italian businesses in Leichhardt—fruit sellers, greengrocers, cafes, restaurants, pastry shops, furniture shops, real estate agents, and mixed businesses—which served Italians and other local customers (Burnley 1988).

In recent decades, Leichhardt has undergone significant changes. The Leichhardt municipality was home to 6,000 Italians in 1961, but by 1981 it had only 1,000 Italians (Burnley 1988, 627). Many Italian families have moved to other middle-ring suburbs such as Drummoyne, Ashfield, Haberfield, Concord, and Burwood or to outer-ring suburbs in the Fairfield area. Today there are more British- and New Zealand–born immigrants living in the Leichhardt municipality than Italian-born immigrants.

It is not the population of Leichhardt that confers on it the status of an ethnic precinct but rather the first- and second-generation Italian immigrant entrepreneurs who dominate the retail shopping and restaurant businesses in the area. Burnley (2001, 171) lists 325 Italian-owned businesses in Leichhardt and neighboring Five Dock. In all, 190 were involved in general retail (including 33 restaurants, 18 cafes, 13 butchers, and 11 pasticceria), 58 were light industrials (including terrazzo tiles and pasta food manufacture), and 72 were professionals (doctors, accountants, dentists, optometrists, solicitors, and paramedics). It is those ethnic entrepreneurs in the professional and service areas that attract Italians to Leichhardt, while for non-Italians the food, coffee, and ambiance of Little Italy are most critical.

The Leichhardt Municipal Council has supported the development of Little Italy along Norton Street via street beautification programs and as a sponsor of the annual Norton Street Festival (Collins and Castillo 1998, 169). During the festival, held in March or April each year, Norton Street (see figure 9.2) is closed and lavishly decorated in the Italian colors of green, red, and white. Food, market stalls, art exhibitions, and other entertainments take place, attracting over 100,000 people each year, highlighting the popularity of this event. A recent development, the Italian Forum near the Parramatta Road end of Norton Street, financed by Italian immigrant millionaire Franco Belgiorno-Nettis, reproduces an Italian village piazza atmosphere in five-story apartment

Figure 9.2.   Map of Leichhardt

blocks with juliet balconies overlooking an internal square around a clock tower that is ringed by two levels of restaurants. Whether the Italian Forum represents a Disneyfication of Italian urban life or an authentic representation is a matter of debate, though the strong representation of first- and second-generation Italians as owners, workers, customers, and members of the "passing parade" adds to the authenticity of Leichhardt's Italian feel.

Asiatown

While Chinatown is in Sydney's CBD and Little Italy close to it, Cabramatta is forty kilometers west of the city. Cabramatta is a suburban Asiatown, or an *ethnoburb*, to use the term coined by Li (1998) to describe suburbs of multi-ethnic immigrant settlement in the United States. In the 1980s, migrant camps in the Cabramatta area received a large number of Indo-Chinese refugees — mainly Vietnamese who fled following the collapse of Saigon in 1975 (Viviani 1984). They were Sydney's first large intake of Asian immigrants since the White Australia policy was adopted at Federation in 1901. When they moved out of the camps, they settled in the local area, which had low rents because it was largely comprised of a traditional white or European immigrant working class living in fibro houses and was thus affordable. The new Asian intake was controversial (Blainey 1984) with critics and the media dubbing the area "Vietnamatta," highlighting the strong Vietnamese presence in the suburb and predicting that social conflict between Asians and others would result (Collins 1991, 66–69).

These concerns were as exaggerated as the estimates of the size of the Vietnamese population in the area. The Vietnamese were but one of more than one hundred different nationalities in the Fairfield Local Government Area. Census data for 2001[2] shows the ethnic diversity of Fairfield's population of 182,000 people. Just over half of Fairfield's total population were first-generation immigrants. Of these, those from Vietnam were the largest group, but this comprised only about one-eighth of the Fairfield population.

The census category "overseas born" does not include second and later generations, and birthplace does not always correlate with ethnicity. Many of the Vietnamese-born were ethnic Chinese, as shown by the ancestry data of the 2001 Census; 14 percent of the Fairfield population was ethnic Chinese and 13 percent was ethnic Vietnamese. These ancestry groups together comprise just over a quarter of the population of the Fairfield area, yet dominate the "enterprise-scape" of the Cabramatta shopping precinct. Along John Street (see figure 9.3), which runs down the western side of Cabramatta Railway Station, a vibrant ethnic precinct has emerged with over 820 ethnic businesses and institutions. Ian Burnley (2001, 252) gives a vivid description of the range of ethnic businesses in Cabramatta in 1988, featuring a wide range of goods and services:

> bakeries, butcheries (at least 20), cake shops, children's clothiers, confectioneries, arts and crafts, dress materials and fabrics, bridal wear shops, adult clothing retailers and manufactures, electrical goods suppliers, fish markets (6), general food stores, take-away foods (10 shops), fruit shops (12), many groceries, hair and beauty salons (10), herbalists (15), jewellers, laundries, newspaper proprietors, newspaper publishers, delicatessens and food importers and manufacturers. There were 30 medical practitioners, 15 dentists, several physiotherapists, over 20 accountants, several land agents, and . . . travel agencies.

Figure 9.3. Map of Cabramatta

The owners of these businesses were mainly Vietnamese (particularly ethnic Chinese Vietnamese) and other Chinese, with a few businesses owned by immigrants from Laos, Cambodia, Italy, Croatia, and Serbia.

As in the case of Chinatown, local and state policy makers have sought to redevelop the Cabramatta shopping precinct to attract more customers and visitors from outside the area. In the early 1980s, the Cabramatta Chamber of Commerce, which at that time had no Vietnamese entrepreneurs on it, received a grant of $20,000 from the Fairfield City Council to develop a plaza area along John Street. In the late 1980s, another campaign, "The Start-Up for Cabramatta Campaign," was organized to "change unfavourable images, to promote the acceptance of the Indo-Chinese community and foster multicultural activities such as the Fan Festival, the Dragon Boat Race, an International Cabaret and 'good eating'" (Burnley 2001, 248).

The unfavorable image was Cabramatta's growing reputation as unsafe—in 1988–89 there were fifteen murders in the area—and as one of Sydney's heroin centers (Burnley 2001). The NSW state government responded by increasing security in the area, including introducing closed circuit television cameras, doubling the number of police in Cabramatta Police Station, and introducing a 16-person foot-patrol of police along John Street and the Railway Station areas.

They also responded to local government authorities' initiatives to develop the area's tourist potential. The state government amended Section 89B of the *Factories, Shops and Industries Act 1962* to classify areas in Sydney "holiday resorts," so they could be open for trading on Sundays and public holidays. When the premier of NSW, Nick Greiner, opened the new Pailau Chinese gateway in Cabramatta's Freedom Plaza in February 1991, he stated: "Cabramatta, with its distinctive Asian culture has become a popular destination for visitors from outside the area" (qtd. in Burnley 2001, 250). Cabramatta is also the site of a number of festivals, particularly from the ethnic Chinese and ethnic Vietnamese calendar.

Increasingly, the tourism experience is linked to the cultural economy (Urry 2002), images of ethnicity (Halter 2000) and the experience of place (Suvantola 2002). Place marketing can be linked to cultural or ethnic diversity to promote ethnic or multiethnic precincts. The Fairfield City Council has continued in its endeavors to promote the tourist potential of Cabramatta by further developing and promoting the "Oriental" or Asian nature of the shopping precinct. A glossy brochure targeting visitors to the city and inviting tourists to visit Cabramatta was launched; it claims that "Cabramatta is a day trip to Asia. . . . Here, an hour from the center of Sydney, is an explosion of Asian colour—a bustling marketplace offering all the ingredients for a banquet for the senses." Local expert guides accompany visitors on a walk through Cabramatta to help them build an appreciation of the various types of Asian products sold there.

More recently, the Fairfield City Council launched a CD-guided driving tour of the ethnic sites and features of Cabramatta. According to the council, more than 350,000 visitors from Australia and overseas visit Cabramatta every year spending more than 83 million euros in local shops and on various services. Given Cabramatta's problems with crime and unemployment (Collins and Poynting 2000), the local and state authorities see this emergence of Cabramatta as an Asiatown as a way of promoting the region and creating new jobs.

CONCLUSION

With first- and second-generation immigrants comprising well over half of its inhabitants, Sydney's growth and character have been shaped fundamentally by immigrant entrepreneurs. They were the vanguard of changing cultural diversity that accompanied the postwar immigration program and changed the ethnic composition of the Sydney population. Before most Sydney-siders living in suburbia had experienced minority immigrant neighbors, they had a local immigrant entrepreneur selling them hamburgers, lettuce, and curried prawns and rice. While Sydney's ethnic economy has its roots in markets for ethnospecific products such as food and language-based services, immigrant entrepreneurs have quickly embraced the mainstream market, which has welcomed them as Sydney becomes cosmopolitan in taste and more ethnically diverse.

Immigrant entrepreneurs have played a critical role in the emergence, growth and feel of Sydney's ethnic precincts. In particular, ethnic precincts have a large concentration of ethnic restaurants that attracts both the mainstream and co-ethnic market as well as a set of immigrant entrepreneurs in the professions and services sector that caters predominantly to the co-ethnic community; ethnic food and eating can create an ethnic space in the city (Warde 1997; Warde and Martens 2000).

Regulation change has opened up opportunities for immigrant entrepreneurs while local government plays an important role in the emergence and development of a precinct's ethnic image, illustrating the institutional embeddedness of Sydney's ethnic precincts (Kloosterman and Rath 2001). In Chinatown, Little Italy, and Cabramatta, the "ethnic" atmosphere of the precinct derives as much from the patronage of co-ethnic customers who, along with the immigrant entrepreneurs who dominate the business-scape, give a general "ethnic" ambience to the precinct.

Ethnic entrepreneurs and the ethnic economy are a defining aspect of Sydney as a cosmopolitan global city. This chapter has attempted to address some aspects of this, particularly as they relate to place. Ethnic entrepreneurs, particularly those in precinct clusters, mark Sydney's downtown and suburban retail landscapes. They thus play an important economic function in creating jobs and providing goods and services. They and their customers also give ethnic precincts and most of Sydney's suburbs their cosmopolitan character and identity.

NOTES

1. The Australian census makes a distinction between employers (entrepreneurs who employ others) and the self-employed (entrepreneurs who do not employ anyone).
2. See Australian Bureau of Statistics (2003).

REFERENCES

Anderson, K. J. 1990. Chinatown re-oriented: A critical analysis of recent developments schemes in a Melbourne and Sydney enclave. *Australian Geographical Studies* 28 (2): 137–54.
———. 1991. *Vancouver's Chinatown: Racial discourse in Canada, 1875–1980*. Montreal: McGill-Queens University Press.
Australian Bureau of Statistics. 2002. *Sydney: A social atlas*. Canberra: Australian Bureau of Statistics.
———. 2003. 2001 Census basic community profiles and snapshots. www.ausstats.abs.gov.au/ (accessed 25 February 2006).
Blainey, G. 1984. *All for Australia*. North Ryde, Aus.: Methuen.
Burnley, I. 1988. Italian community life in Sydney. In *The Australian people: An encyclopaedia of the nation, its people and their origins*, ed. J. Jupp, 626–30. Sydney: Angus and Robertson.
———. 2001. *The impact of immigration on Australia: A demographic approach*. South Melbourne: Oxford University Press.
Chin, K. H. 1988. Chinese in modern Australia. In *The Australian people: An encyclopaedia of the nation, its people and their origins*, ed. J. Jupp, 317–23. Sydney: Angus and Robertson.
Choi, C. Y. 1975. *Chinese migration and settlement in Australia*. Sydney: University of Sydney Press.
Collins, J. 1991. *Migrant hands in a distant land: Australia's post-war immigration*. Sydney: Pluto Press.
———. 1992. Cappuccino capitalism: Italian immigrants and Australian business. In *Australia's Italians: Culture and community in a changing society*, ed. S. Castles, C. Alcorso, G. Rando, and E. Vasta, 73–84. Sydney: Allen and Unwin.
———. 2003. Australia: Cosmopolitan capitalists down under. In *Immigrant entrepreneurs: Venturing abroad in the age of globalisation*, ed. R. Kloosterman and J. Rath, 61–78. Oxford: New York University Press.
Collins, J., and A. Castillo. 1998. *Cosmopolitan Sydney: Exploring the world in one city*. Sydney: Pluto Press.
Collins, J., K. Gibson, C. Alcorso, D. Tait, and S. Castles. 1995. *A shop full of dreams: Ethnic small business in Australia*. Sydney: Pluto Press.
Collins, J., and S. Poynting, eds. 2000. *The other Sydney: Communities, identities and inequalities in western Sydney*. Melbourne: Common Ground Publishing.

Fitzgerald, S. 1997. *Red tape, gold scissors*. Sydney: State Library of NSW Press.

Fong, T. P. 2000. *The first suburban Chinatown: The remaking of Monterey Park, California*. Philadelphia: Temple University Press.

Halter, M. 2000. *Shopping for identity: The marketing of ethnicity*. New York: Schocken Books.

Kloosterman, R., and J. Rath, eds. 2001. Immigrant entrepreneurs in advanced economies: Mixed embeddedness further explored. Special issue, *Journal of Ethnic and Migration Studies* 27 (2): 189–202.

——, eds. 2003. *Immigrant entrepreneurs: Venturing abroad in the age of globalisation*. New York: New York University Press.

Light, I., and S. J. Gold. 2000. *Ethnic economies*. San Diego: Academic Press.

Li, W. 1998. Anatomy of a new ethnic settlement: The Chinese *ethnoburb* in Los Angeles. *Urban Studies* 35 (3): 479–501.

Lin, J. 1998. *Reconstructing Chinatown: Ethnic enclave, global change*. Minneapolis: University of Minnesota Press.

Organisation for Economic Co-operation and Development. 1998. *SOPEMI: Trends in international migration: 1998 edition*. Paris: OECD.

Pascoe, R. 1988. *Buongiorno Australia: Our Italian heritage*. Melbourne: Greenhouse Publications and the Vaccari Italian Historical Trust.

Suvantola, J. 2002. *Tourist's experience of place*. Hampshire, UK: Ashgate.

Urry, J. 2002. *The tourist gaze*. London: Sage Publications.

Viviani, N. 1984. *The long journey: Vietnamese migration and settlement in Australia*. Carlton: Melbourne University Press.

Waldinger, R., H. Aldrich, and R. Ward. 1990. *Ethnic entrepreneurs: Immigrant business in industrial societies*. Newbury Park, CA: Sage Publications.

Warde, A. 1997. *Consumption, food and taste*. London: Sage Publications.

Warde, A., and L. Martens. 2000. *Eating out: Social differentiation, consumption and pleasure*. Cambridge: Cambridge University Press.

Yuan, C. M. 1988. Chinese in White Australia, 1901–1950. In *The Australian people: An encyclopaedia of the nation, its people and their origins*, ed. J. Jupp, 304–7. Sydney: Angus and Robertson.

Zhou, M. 1992. *Chinatown: The socioeconomic potential of an urban enclave*. Philadelphia: Temple University Press.

Chapter Ten

Latino Business Landscapes and the Hispanic Ethnic Economy

Alex Oberle

In the Old West, general stores were the center of economic and social activity. They not only sold foodstuff, tools, clothing, and other necessary items, but they also were a point of social contact. Pioneers could meet with other local residents, send letters to family members in distant cities, and receive news from relatives who were still living overseas. In early America, the typical general store was an Anglo outpost on the wilderness frontier. Now, in contemporary America, Hispanic-oriented businesses[1] are increasingly Latino outposts on the Anglo suburban frontier. A profound increase in the Hispanic[2] population, coupled with Latino settlement patterns that are shifting away from the central city and toward the suburbs, has resulted in the proliferation of Hispanic-oriented businesses in Phoenix and many other cities (Davis 2000; Suro 1999). As a result, the Latino retail landscape serves as a proxy for understanding the evolving patterns of Hispanic settlement.

Of all Hispanic-oriented businesses, *carnicerías* are the most widespread and visible examples of Latino expansion into previously non-Hispanic areas. These establishments are a type of retail outlet that sells a variety of groceries, fresh meat, and commonly purchased products. Like general stores, *carnicerías* are also a center for diverse social activities. On a local level, *carnicerías* provide a place to meet, either as a chance encounter while waiting in line or through more formal interaction at an in-store lunch counter. Many *carnicerías* permit the displaying of flyers, pamphlets, advertisements, newspapers, or other information that connects local Latino residents with services and activities that occur outside of the local neighborhood, often in other parts of Phoenix or the surrounding metropolitan area. *Carnicerías* are also transnational conduits where Latino immigrants can purchase international phone cards, wire money to Latin America, and seek transportation to Mexico or other nations. In addition to their social function, *carnicerías* foster a

Figure 10.1.   Typical Carnicería *Exterior Illustrating Use of Nostalgic Names and Symbology along with Ubiquitous Advertising Techniques*

distinctive sense of place. The use of names, symbols, décor, and store layout invoke nostalgic images of Mexico and serve as a useful marketing device (figure 10.1). While mainstream supermarkets offer a wide selection and low prices, *carnicerías* strive for quality and freshness and cultivate an atmosphere that accentuates these virtues.

This chapter explores the dual significance of the *carnicería* landscape: first, as a "pioneer" business and an ethnic marker in previously non-Latino areas, and second, as an ethnic place that is shaped by its social significance and cultural atmosphere. While discussed separately, these are interrelated— *carnicerías*' success in previously non-Latino areas is the result of their function as ethnic places. Yet before exploring *carnicerías* in detail, this chapter will first describe the rationale for selecting Phoenix as the study area, briefly outline the history of Latinos in Phoenix, and detail the current characteristics of Phoenix's Latinos. Next, the chapter will provide a broader context, which includes the business-ownership patterns of Phoenix Latinos, and a brief discussion of the literature relating to Mexican ethnic economies.[3] The bulk of the chapter discusses the Latino retail landscape and then more specifically focuses on *carnicerías* as a proxy for Latino expansion into more peripheral, suburban areas of Phoenix and on the *carnicería* as a vibrant ethnic place.

Although the entire metropolitan area is affected by Latino immigration, this research limits the scope of the study to the city of Phoenix proper. Phoenix is a viable study site because it contains a large, but manageable, number of Hispanic-oriented businesses and a diversity of Latino neighborhoods and settlement patterns. The city exhibits both urban and suburban characteristics. The central and southern two-thirds of Phoenix is characteristically urban, but the northern one-third is more suburban as it includes many recent, low-density subdivisions that are continuously advancing into areas of newly annexed virgin desert. Several types of Hispanic neighborhoods also exist in Phoenix. South Phoenix is a long-standing Latino and African American community that includes some Mexican American barrios established since the first half of the twentieth century. A newer, vibrant Latino community has developed in east-central and west-central Phoenix during the past few decades. While the majority of the residents in the northern half of Phoenix are predominantly non-Hispanic, growing numbers of Latinos have settled in this area of the city, both in Hispanic "outlier" neighborhoods like Sunnyslope and Palominos and more generally in apartment complexes scattered across the urban expanse (Skop and Menjívar 2001).

CHARACTERISTICS OF THE PHOENIX LATINO POPULATION

Phoenix's history is quite different from that of many other Southwestern cities. Unlike Tucson, Albuquerque, or El Paso, the origins of Phoenix were largely Anglo rather than Spanish or Mexican. Some Mexican settlers arrived in Phoenix as early as the late 1800s, yet it was not until after the Great Depression and especially the Second World War that a small but steady stream of Latinos began to immigrate to the city. By 1980, Hispanics composed 13 percent of the population in Phoenix proper. This percentage increased to almost 20 percent in 1990 and skyrocketed to 34 percent in 2000, where now about one in three Phoenix residents is of Hispanic ancestry (U.S. Bureau of the Census 2000a; U.S. Bureau of the Census 1990). Today, among cities in the greater Southwest, only Los Angeles has a larger total Latino population.

Phoenix's dynamic Latino population is increasingly fast-growing, spatially dispersed, and heterogeneous. A recent study by the Brookings Institution incorporates data from the 1990 and 2000 Census to develop a typology that categorizes U.S. metropolitan areas into four categories based on the characteristics of their Latino population (Suro 2002). Phoenix is classified as a "fast-growing Latino hub" because it has a very large Hispanic base population that continues to increase at an extraordinary rate. Like Houston, Dallas, San Diego, and other cities in the same category, Phoenix has transcended its role as a secondary way station and it is now a major gateway for incoming Latino immigrants (Suro 2002; Skop and Menjívar 2001). Reflecting nationwide trends, Phoenix's Hispanics increasingly reside in suburban areas in

addition to traditionally Latino central-city neighborhoods. Of the eleven
"fast-growing Latino hub" cities, only Dallas and Houston surpassed Phoenix
in their rate of suburban Hispanic population growth from 1990 to 2000. According to the 2000 Census, about one out of three Phoenix area residents
lives in a suburban community, with Glendale and Mesa experiencing the
largest increases.

While Phoenix's Hispanic population seems somewhat homogeneous
when compared to New York, Miami, Los Angeles, or other large urban areas, the city's Latinos are actually a diverse group who often exhibit much internal heterogeneity: immigrant and second generation, resident and itinerant,
Mexican and non-Mexican. Nearly one-half of Phoenix's Latinos are foreign-
born immigrants, many of whom have resided in the United States for less
than five years. The other fifty percent are native-born citizens, likely a mixture of in-state migrants from rural areas; former residents of California, New
Mexico, and other states; and longtime Phoenix residents. However, only
about one in three Latinos has lived in Phoenix for longer than five years. The
majority of Phoenix Hispanics, regardless of their national origin, maintain
strong cultural ties as more than eighty percent speak Spanish at home. The
Mexican ancestry population still accounts for about 84 percent of the city's
Hispanics, although this majority has diminished since 1990 when 91.5 percent of Latinos claimed Mexican heritage. During this decade, the percentage
of most other Hispanic subgroups has increased, especially the Cuban and
Guatemalan populations.

THE MEXICAN ETHNIC ECONOMY

Although the work of Skop and Menjívar (2001) and Harner (2000) provide
a solid foundation, our understanding of the contemporary Mexican ancestry
population in Phoenix remains incomplete. This may be attributed to the
sheer size of the group and the complexity of the Mexican immigrant experience, as Waldinger and Lichter (2003, 275) suggest in their study of immigrant labor in Los Angeles. Likewise, the ethnic economy literature focuses
on Koreans, Cubans, Chinese, and other ethnic entrepreneurs, yet the burgeoning Mexican business sector remains understudied. Much of this lack of
research is the result of the comparatively limited success of the Mexican ethnic economy. Of the major ethnic groups, the Mexican ancestry population
outperformed only African Americans and Puerto Ricans in their participation
in the ethnic economy. Cubans, for example, exceeded the expected values
for involvement in the ethnic economy, while the Mexican ethnic economy
was only one-third of what would be predicted for its population size (Light

and Gold 2000). Villar (1994) suggests that low educational levels, a lack of skills, and the potentially divisive issue of hiring undocumented workers contributed to a small, economically isolated Mexican ethnic economy in Chicago. However, Hansen and Cardenas (1988) analyze Mexican-oriented businesses in south Texas and southern California and find that immigrant status does not affect the establishment of Mexican businesses, as owners generally possess a favorable impression of immigrant employees, especially among Mexican immigrant proprietors.

Spener and Bean (1999) argue that recent changes in the size of the Mexican ancestry population are concomitant with the increasing role of Mexican-origin self-employment. In his study of Mexican entrepreneurs in Los Angeles, Alvarez (1990) similarly asserts that sufficient Mexican business activity existed to justify the classification of the city's produce market as a vibrant immigrant enclave economy. Guarnizo (1998) dispels the common characterization of the Mexican labor force as manual laborers or sojourners. Despite the focus on Cuban ethnic economies, he notes that the Mexican ethnic economy is viable, particularly since there are 3.4 self-employed Mexican immigrants per every self-employed Cuban immigrant (Guarnizo 1998, 2). Guarnizo's research includes ethnographic and survey data that documents the social processes that contribute to the formation of Mexican ancestry entrepreneurship in Los Angeles.

Although the Mexican ethnic economy in Phoenix remains unstudied, the survey of minority-owned business enterprises provides for some comparative analysis of Hispanic-owned businesses (HOBs) (see table 10.1). While HOBs only account for a small percentage of all Phoenix-area businesses, their numbers have increased between 1992 and 1997. The percentage of Mexican-owned HOBs diminished during the same time period. Much of this is likely the result of changes in the survey, as the 1997 Survey of Minority-owned Business Enterprises included a new category called "Other Spanish/Hispanic/Latino." Involvement in the retail trade is also growing, with an additional increase from 1992 to 1997.

Table 10.1.   Characteristics of Hispanic-Owned Businesses in the Phoenix-Mesa MSA

Hispanic-Owned Businesses by %	1992	1997
Percentage of all businesses	5.6	7.3
Mexican-owned	75.2	60.6
Involved in retail trade	13.6	15.7
Involved in service sector	49.4	45.3

Source: U.S. Bureau of the Census 1992, 1997.

CARNICERÍAS: LATINO OUTPOSTS
ON THE ANGLO FRONTIER

Specific types of Hispanic businesses are indicative of varying ages of Mexican immigrant neighborhoods (Oberle 2004). While some establishments are largely confined to Phoenix's traditionally Latino core, others are ever more common on the suburban periphery. These businesses include *carnicerías* (meat markets/grocers), *panaderías* (bakeries), *yerberías* (small shops that sell medicinal herbs and religious items), *discotecas* (music stores), and *llanteras* (stores that sell tires and rims marketed to a specifically Spanish-speaking clientele). Some less prominent and widespread establishments include *dulcerías* (candy stores), *paleterías* or *neverías* (ice cream shops), beauty salons, and Western wear outlets. The distribution of these businesses coincides with areas of Latino settlement.

Of all of these retail establishments, *carnicerías* are the most likely to occur outside of the largely Latino central city in suburban areas with emerging Hispanic neighborhoods. Figure 10.2 illustrates a typology of census tracts in Phoenix and notes representative neighborhoods. Differing from the majority of Hispanic-oriented businesses, *carnicerías* locate in "Latino Fringe" neighborhoods, those that were less than ten percent Hispanic in 1990 but have seen their Latino population double by 2000. Nearly 80 percent of *carnicerías* exist adjacent to "Hispanic Edge/Satellite Barrios," neighborhoods that have increased the percentage of their Hispanic population from 10–25 percent in 1990 to 20–50 percent in 2000. Unlike other Hispanic-oriented businesses, only 43 percent of *carnicerías* exist in "Latino Dynamo" or "Hispanic Core" neighborhoods. "Latino Dynamo" neighborhoods are those that were 25 to 50 percent Hispanic in 1990 but have doubled their Latino population by 2000. "Hispanic Core" neighborhoods were already majority Hispanic in 1990 and have seen some additional Latino increase by 2000. With a few exceptions, the *carnicerías* in the fast-growing Hispanic neighborhoods only have been in operation since the mid-to-late 1990s or early 2000s. Table 10.2 details the relationship between Hispanic-oriented retail establishments and the Latino population within one mile of the various businesses. *Carnicerías* are more likely to occur in neighborhoods with a minority of Latino residents, while the other business types tend to locate where there are larger concentrations of Hispanics.[4]

Although *carnicerías* occupy a variety of retail spaces, the majority rent small or medium-sized units in strip malls. In older areas of the city, several establishments exist as freestanding structures, often in buildings that were once convenience stores or corner markets. In a few cases, *carnicerías* occupy new buildings that were constructed particularly for that purpose. For example, the *Plaza Del Sol* in largely Hispanic central Phoenix was completed in

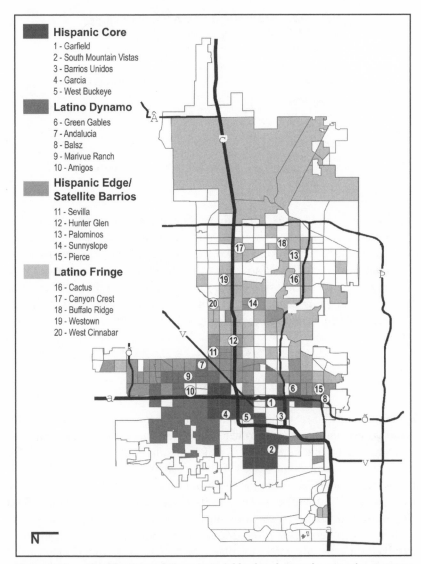

Figure 10.2.   Classifications of Phoenix Neighborhoods Based on Varying Patterns of Latino Growth between 1990 and 2000

mid-2003. This small shopping center is anchored by a Latino-oriented furniture store (*Mueblería del Sol*) that is surrounded by a new *joyería* (jewelry store), *discoteca*, and a combination *carnicería/panadería*. The *carnicerías* in many of the more suburban, previously non-Hispanic areas typically are generally not located proximate to other types of Hispanic-oriented businesses. Instead, they often occur adjacent to a range of non-Hispanic businesses. In

**Table 10.2. Relationship between Hispanic-Oriented
Retail Establishments and the Local Latino Population
in Phoenix**

Type of Hispanic-Oriented Establishment	% Latinos within a One-Mile Radius
Carnicerías	45.8
Discotecas	51.9
Yerberías	53.0
Panaderías	55.7
Llanteras	58.6

Source: U.S. Bureau of the Census 2000, SFI.

suburban far north Phoenix, for example, one of the *carnicerías* is located in a strip mall space next to a check-cashing outlet, skateboard shop, and chain Mexican restaurant. Some establishments outside of the majority Hispanic neighborhoods are adjacent to other non-Hispanic ethnic businesses like Vietnamese, Chinese, or Asian Indian grocers. In majority Hispanic areas of Phoenix, *carnicerías* tend to occur in conjunction with other types of Hispanic-oriented businesses and there is a definite pattern of spatial clustering.

CARNICERÍAS AS ETHNIC PLACES

While these spatial relationships indicate that *carnicerías* require a smaller threshold population than the other businesses, this only partially explains their success. In general, *carnicerías* are not simply the only alternative for purchasing Hispanic ethnic foods. This is particularly evident in comparing the location of *carnicerías* to the location of mainstream grocery stores like the Food City supermarkets. Despite its rather bland generic name, Food City is an Arizona-based chain of supermarkets that specifically caters to Latinos. The supermarket offers Mexican and other Latin American products including freshly made tortillas and breads, bulk foods, specialized produce, and an expanded selection of fresh meat. Food City engages in extensive advertising, especially in Spanish-language newspapers and radio, and is active in the community, sponsoring events such as youth soccer tournaments. Despite what would seem to be an overwhelming market advantage, Food City stores are commonly located in the same areas as *carnicerías*. In fact, more than half of *carnicerías* are found within a one-mile radius of Food City stores and 95 percent exist within a two-mile radius of a Food City supermarket. This demonstrates that patrons do not shop at *car-*

nicerías simply because they are the only alternative for acquiring Mexican or Latin American products.

While the name *carnicería* literally translates as "butcher shop," these stores offer much more. All stores have a meat counter that offers a variety of products, especially those that are not readily available in typical American supermarkets. These can include organ meats, tougher and less expensive cuts of meat, sausages like chorizo and longaniza, dried meat, and whole meat products like sides, ribs, and even intact heads. Many *carnicerías* offer seafood, often with an emphasis on shellfish such as oysters and shrimp. *Carnicerías* typically stock other items as well. There are prepackaged food products like dried pasta and beans, snacks, and canned food. Most are well supplied with beverages like soda, juice, and sometimes beer or liquor. Often, there is a modest collection of produce, including tomatoes, limes, onions, and other common fruits and vegetables. Some stores stock supplies and kitchen items like griddles, pots and pans, utensils, soap, garbage bags, and even cleaning supplies. Essentially, *carnicerías* are mini-markets, one-stop shopping for all sorts of commonly used products and supplies.

Carnicerías are also places to meet people in the local community and connect with others in distant places. While most are busy places with a constant flow of customers and industrious employees who diligently work to ensure that everything is stocked to the brim, the atmosphere remains friendly and laid-back with customers often engaging in small talk with each other and with the store employees. Many of these businesses provide take-out food services, and several have small lunch counters and provide a few tables, booths, or other places to gather, sit, and eat. Newspapers, fliers, handbills, want-ads, and other similar forms of advertisement are common.[5] These connect patrons with a variety of services, events, and cultural connections that are occurring in the local neighborhood, in other parts of the city, and in Mexico or other foreign countries. These can include newspapers from Mexican border cities or regional centers or advertisements for such things as *Norteño* concerts, job advertisements, cars for sale, van trips to Nogales or Hermosillo, legal services, urgent care clinics, and amateur boxing matches. *Carnicerías* are also transnational spaces where shoppers can purchase import products, wire money to Latin America, watch Mexican television, and purchase international phone cards.

In addition to their social function, *carnicerías* evoke a distinctive sense of place that attracts customers by accentuating nostalgia and enhancing cultural connections with Mexico and Latin America. A potent combination of atmosphere and product marketing allows these establishments to effectively compete with mainstream supermarkets. Store proprietors employ several methods for fostering a particular sense of place, both in the interior and exterior of their businesses. Outward appearances are important for drawing prospective clientele, and storeowners use symbols, colors, and names to attract shoppers (Miyares 2001; Manger 2002). Symbols typically occur either as a single logo or in the form of a mural, window etching, or other artwork. Among *carnicerías*, livestock symbols are the most common single logo, with cattle imagery like bullhorns, cow heads, or animal outlines predominating. Several *carnicerías* perpetuate this rural, bucolic imagery through mural or window paintings. Front windows, side walls, and even the back walls of some shops depict ranching scenes like cattle being roped and branded or livestock grazing in verdant fields.

Carnicería names also contribute to place-making. Table 10.3 groups the names of Phoenix *carnicerías* into five categories. Rural or agricultural names account for more than one-third of all establishments. Like logos and imagery, these names draw extensively from cattle ranching and related themes. Twenty-one percent of names are inspired by Mexican states, which likely serve a dual function. They entice customers by using the names of their home states and evoke regional ties that correspond to areas of livestock production. For example, Sinaloa and Michoacán are *carnicería* names that correlate to Mexican states that contribute large numbers of immigrants to Arizona (Harner 1995). Several *carnicería* names are also associated with states like Sonora and Chihuahua, states well known across Mexico for their beef production, cowboy culture, and expansive ranches. Some establishments use congenial designations or family names to elicit a degree of friendly informality, while others foster ethnic unity with names like *Hispana*, *Latina*, or *La Mexicana*.

Table 10.3.   Classification of Phoenix *Carnicería* Names

Carnicería Name	Number (n=42)	Percent	Examples
Rural/agricultural	15	36	*Puerto del Toro* (bull's horn), *El Rancho* (the ranch), *La Hereford* (the Hereford cow), *El Corral* (the corral)
Regional	9	21	*Sonora, Chihuahua, Michoacán, Hermosillo, Sinaloa*
Other	8	19	*Flash, El Rey* (the king), *Del Pueblo* (the people's), *El Camino* (the road)
Family name	5	12	*Dos Hermanos* (two brothers), *Murrietas, Sepulveda*
Ethnic	5	12	*Latino, Hispano, El Yaqui* (Yaqui Indian)

Carnicería interiors create an atmosphere that emphasizes familiarity, service, quality, and freshness. Nearly all advertising and transactions are completed in Spanish, which further contributes to the cultural sense of place. In many cases, employees speak only Spanish and have little or no proficiency in English. Store proprietors, however, are commonly bilingual, a skill which becomes necessary for effective interaction with food distributors, landlords, banks, and other external agencies. The Spanish-language emphasis of these establishments further suggests that *carnicerías* serve a largely Latino immigrant clientele rather than second- or third-generation Hispanics who may purchase Mexican food items but largely conduct their business in English.

Unlike larger supermarkets that are bright and spacious, most *carnicerías* have limited space and dim lighting. While these characteristics might frustrate or turn away the average American shopper, they foster a sense of closeness that appeals to many Hispanic customers, especially those who may be recent immigrants and unaccustomed to larger grocery chains.

Most family-owned establishments value service, and *carnicerías* are no exception. Despite their small size, nearly all stores have two or three employees working at one time. Typically, one employee operates the cash register and assists customers. One or even two employees are assigned to the butcher counter where they also answer questions and provide individualized service. Because meat products account for much of the business in most *carnicerías*, quality and freshness are extremely important. These attributes are extensively marketed through the use of conspicuous and carefully arranged displays. Meat products are always visible and displayed in such a manner that qualities such as leanness can easily be observed. Styrofoam and plastic are not used, and frozen meat is almost never part of a *carnicería* meat counter. While most mainstream supermarkets rely on refrigerated display cases, many *carnicerías* conspicuously use cubed ice that is constantly changed out and maintained in pristine condition.

Quality and freshness are a particular source of pride for many *carnicería* proprietors and employees. On a recent visit, a storeowner gave an extensive tour of his establishment. Like many *carnicerías*, this one was small yet thoroughly stocked with a variety of items. While an extensive selection of prepackaged foods occupied the majority of floor space, the store also included a small produce section and a refrigerated case that contained an assortment of soft drinks and juice. Most of the tour involved the butcher counter, which occupied a relatively small portion of the back of the store. This proprietor, like many others, articulated the importance of the meat counter both as a draw for customers and as the primary source of profits for the establishment. When asked about how his business could compete with large, Latino-oriented supermarkets, he emphatically stated that quality and freshness were far superior in *carnicerías*. While he admitted that his establishment had difficulty competing with their prices, he argued that freshness is very important to Latino shoppers; in Mexico and other countries, meat markets are far more common than supermarkets and have access to locally raised livestock rather than preprocessed meat shipped over great distances. Pointing to chorizo sausage, the owner said, "A supermarket mixes up maybe two hundred pounds of this in a day. How can they maintain quality? We do it here by hand with just the right mixture of ingredients—several times a day in small batches." This particular *carnicería* also had fresh salsa. The owner stated, "Like the chorizo, we make the salsa several times a day. The grocery store claims that theirs is fresh, but ours is completely homemade."

This combination of exterior symbolism and interior atmosphere shapes a distinctive sense of place that appeals to many Latinos, especially those whose lives are still deeply connected to Mexico or other Latin American countries. As Ricourt and Danta (2003, 47) state in their discussion of a *bodega* (Latino grocery) in a Latino neighborhood in New York City, "While the Latino panethnic array of products in Corona's *bodegas* was unlike anything in their customers' homelands, these stores nonetheless reproduced the social atmosphere and owner-customer relationships that Latin Americans were familiar with, whatever their country of origin." With the proliferation of *carnicerías* in neighborhoods with small, nascent, often immigrant Latino populations, these establishments serve as one of the few—or perhaps only—places where there is any local cultural connection and familiarity. The blend of bucolic symbolism, helpful customer service, and fresh quality products reminds customers of their origins and heritage. This is especially important in these areas that lack formal cultural institutions and present formidable new challenges that can include social marginalization and cultural estrangement.

CONCLUSION

Latinos have surpassed African Americans as the largest minority group in the United States (U.S. Bureau of the Census 2003). This is evident in many American metropolitan areas, both in traditionally Hispanic cities like Los Angeles and Miami and in areas without a history of Latino residents, including large cities, smaller urban centers, and rural communities across America. Furthermore, Latino populations are increasingly suburban and are no longer relegated to central city "barrios" (Arreola 2004; Suro 2002; Davis 2000; Suro 1999). This parallels research demonstrating that many groups of foreign-born immigrants exhibit heterolocal settlement patterns characterized by rapid dispersal to distant neighborhoods upon arrival, a lack of spatial propinquity, and widely separated living and working environments (Zelinsky 2001).[6] In addition to Latinos, heterolocalism is evident among such groups as Chinese in Los Angeles (Li 1998), Vietnamese in northern Virginia (Wood 1997), and Ethiopians in Washington, D.C. (Chacko 2003).

The proliferation of *carnicerías* and other Hispanic-oriented businesses provide an opportunity to document these evolving, heterolocal patterns of Latino settlement in Phoenix and other metropolitan areas. As pioneer establishments, *carnicerías* serve as a proxy and a visible landscape indicator of neighborhood change. While Arreola (1988) and Manger (2000) demonstrate how "housescapes" like fenced yards, religious shrines, and bright-colored homes mark Mexican American neighborhoods, Hispanic-oriented businesses are one of the few methods for indicating areas of Latino immigrant settlement in a new suburban environment. The proliferation of lower-income apartment complexes and trailer parks in Phoenix and other cities has provided reasonably affordable accommodations and a level of relative invisibility for Hispanic immigrants. As a result, businesses rather than homes are the most visible manifestation of Hispanic heritage and the "Latin Americanization" of cities and suburbs.

The relative isolation of these pioneer businesses promotes the development of *carnicerías* as ethnic places that foster social connections and cultivate a distinctive sense of place. This chapter discusses some of these place-making characteristics, yet there is still a great deal that is not known about the function of *carnicerías* and other Hispanic-oriented businesses. Additional research should explore how these types of establishments market culture and package their business as an ethnic destination. Further investigations should also assess how social connections establish *carnicerías* as a de facto cultural institution and as a transnational conduit and how this in turn might affect neighborhood dynamics.

NOTES

1. This study defines Hispanic-oriented businesses by their retail function rather than by the ethnicity of the proprietor. While many of these establishments are owned and operated by Mexican-ancestry proprietors, some storeowners are non-Mexican or even non-Hispanic. Thus, I have selected visible Spanish-language advertising as the primary criteria for differentiating Hispanic-oriented businesses—which specifically target the Latino immigrant population—from those that seek to attract a native-born Latino, non-Hispanic, or mixed ethnicity clientele.

2. The terms *Latino* and *Hispanic* are used synonymously and interchangeably in this chapter.

3. As previously mentioned, many—but not all—Hispanic-oriented businesses in Phoenix are owned by Mexican-ancestry proprietors and can be classified as part of the Mexican ethnic economy.

4. According to the Food Marketing Institute, convenience is very important to many Latino shoppers. Most carnicerías likely draw from local neighborhoods that are no more than one mile away. If this is the case, the threshold population for *carnicerías* is approximately 2,000–2,500 potential shoppers.

5. Recently, many shop owners have removed some of these advertisements in order to improve aesthetics.

6. *Heterolocalism* is a widely discussed term that, in reality, describes a rather nebulous geographic phenomenon. For example, Phoenix Hispanics became more residentially segregated between 1990 and 2000, indicating a spatial propinquity that runs counter to the heterolocal ideal. Yet, there has been an increasing suburbanization of Latinos and dispersion into previously non-Hispanic neighborhoods. In addition, identities and social connections are maintained through such venues as hometown associations that are not dependent on proximity. Similarly, there often remains a substantial distance between home and work as evidence in the day labor staging areas located across the metropolitan area.

REFERENCES

Alvarez, R. 1990. Mexican entrepreneurs and markets in the city of Los Angeles: A case of an immigrant enclave. *Urban Anthropology* 19:99–124.

Arreola, D. 1988. Mexican-American housescapes. *The Geographical Review* 78:299–315.

——, ed. 2004. *Hispanic spaces, Latino places*. Austin: University of Texas Press.

Chacko, E. 2003. Ethiopian ethos and the making of ethnic places in the Washington metropolitan area. *Journal of Cultural Geography* 20:21–42.

Davis, M. 2000. *Magical urbanism: Latinos reinvent the U.S. city*. New York: Verso.

Guarnizo, L. 1998. *The Mexican ethnic economy in Los Angeles: Capitalist accumulation, class restructuring, and the transnationalism of migration*. Davis: California Communities Program of the University of California.

Hansen, N., and G. Cardenas. 1988. Immigrant and native ethnic enterprises in Mexican-American neighborhoods: Differing perceptions of Mexican immigrant workers. *International Migration Review* 22:226–42.

Harner, J. 1995. Continuity amidst change: Undocumented Mexican migration to Arizona. *The Professional Geographer* 47:399–411.

——. 2000. The Mexican community in Scottsdale, Arizona. *Yearbook, Conference of Latin Americanist Geographers* 26:29–46.

Li, W. 1998. Anatomy of a new ethnic settlement: The Chinese ethnoburb in Los Angeles. *Urban Studies* 35 (3): 479–501.

Light, I., and S. Gold. 2000. *Ethnic economies*. San Diego: Academic Press.

Manger, W. 2000. The "idealized" Mexican American housescape. *Material Culture* 1:1–36.

———. 2002. Corporate colors and trademarked images in the Mexican retail landscape. PhD diss., Arizona State University.

Miyares, I. 2001. Changing landscapes and immigration: The "Mexicanization" of Sunset Park, Brooklyn migration. *Annals of Association of American Geographers* 97:101–7.

Oberle, A. 2004. Se venden aquí: The Latino commercial landscape in Phoenix, Arizona. In *Hispanic spaces, Latino places*, ed. D. Arreola, 239–54. Austin: University of Texas Press.

Ricourt, M., and R. Danta. 2003. *Hispanas de Queens: Latino panethnicity in a New York City neighborhood*. Ithaca, NY: Cornell University Press.

Skop, E., and C. Menjivar. 2001. Phoenix: The newest Latino immigrant gateway? *Yearbook of the Association of Pacific Coast Geographers* 63:63–76.

Spener, D., and F. Bean. 1999. Self-employment concentration and earnings among Mexican immigrants in the U.S. *Social Forces* 77:1021–47.

Suro, R. 1999. *Strangers among us: Latino lives in a changing America*. New York: Vintage Books.

———. 2002. *Latino growth in metropolitan America: Changing patterns, new locations*. Washington, DC: Brookings Institution.

U.S. Bureau of the Census. 1990. *Census of population, summary file 1*. Washington, DC: U.S. Bureau of the Census.

———. 1992. *Survey of minority-owned business enterprises*. Washington, DC: U.S. Bureau of the Census.

———. 1997. *Survey of minority-owned business enterprises*. Washington, DC: U.S. Bureau of the Census.

———. 2000a. *Census of population, summary file 1*. Washington, DC: U.S. Bureau of the Census.

———. 2000b. *Census of population, summary file 4*. Washington, DC: U.S. Bureau of the Census.

———. 2003. *Hispanic population reaches all-time high of 38.8 million*. www.census.gov/Press-Release/www/hispanic.html (accessed 20 July 2003).

Villar, M. 1994. Hindrances to the development of an ethnic economy among Mexican migrants. *Human Organization* 53:263–68.

Waldinger, R., and M. Lichter. 2003. *How the other half works*. Berkeley: University of California Press.

Wood, J. 1997. Vietnamese-American place making in northern Virginia. *Geographical Review* 87 (1): 58–72.

Zelinsky, W. 2001. *The enigma of ethnicity: Another American dilemma*. Iowa City: University of Iowa Press.

Chapter Eleven

The New Romans: Ethnic Economic Activities in Rome

Pierpaolo Mudu

In the 1970s, Italy experienced a historical transformation from an emigration to an immigration society (Ascoli 1985). In 1997, total official transfers of foreign immigrants from other countries for the first time exceeded total incoming transfers of Italians living abroad (Caritas 2002). In 2000, the proportion of foreign immigrants in the Italian population (about two percent) was lower than every EU country save Finland and Portugal (OECD 2003). Yet Italy exceeded every EU country in regard to non-EU immigrants. In the 1990s, the five largest groups of immigrants in Rome were from the Philippines, Poland, Egypt, Peru, and Bangladesh. From the mid-1970s onward, immigration remained negligible in quantitative terms[1] but played a significant role in establishing new spatial trends in Rome because of its distinct settlement patterns and territorial distribution. In this chapter, we address the emergence of ethnic minority business firms in the Esquilino and Pigneto–Tor Pignattara city districts and the social conflict associated with the emergence of multiethnic social spaces, especially in the Esquilino.[2]

THE ROMAN LABOR MARKET

There is no denying that the social networks put in place by the Catholic Church may explain some of the processes behind immigrants' settlement and ability to create, build, and access particular niches of the labor market (e.g., domestic work). The Catholic Church is strong in the Philippines and Poland, the former pope's country of origin—countries which supplied the two most important immigrant groups in Rome at the end of the twentieth century. The Church regulated the flow of migrants, and in many cases, the Roman parishes operated as job mediators to offer immigrants as domestic labor, electricians, or carpenters to Italians. However, issues associated with non-immigrant labor supply also need to be considered (Waldinger 1994). The Roman economy hinges on a huge public sector that employs about forty percent of the active population and a diversified universe of service sector firms carrying on activities ranging from restaurant catering, trade, transport, information technology, real property services, and tourist accommodations. Alongside these, there is a sizable grey underground economy with large numbers of irregular workers working mainly in the construction and property renovation industry.

In addition, Italians have only selectively withdrawn from so-called humble occupations. While jobs such as garbage collection, street-sweeping, or cab-driving are elsewhere typically taken up by first-generation immigrants, these are still perceived as protected domains, especially in Rome, and are not "surrendered" to immigrants. Immigrants from non-Western countries work mainly in low-level service and domestic occupations, and such jobs are carried out most exclusively by a "female component" that is significantly larger than elsewhere (ISMU 1997).

However, there is some scope both for people in search for qualified jobs and for self-employed activities such as trade, restaurant catering, building construction, and industrial cleaning. Self-employed activities include small firms set up by Polish and Rumanian immigrants in the construction sector, some two hundred Chinese restaurants scattered all over the city (Mudu and Li 2005), hundreds of shops and dozens of import-export businesses run by Bengalis and Chinese respectively, financial and communication services provided by Bengalis and Pakistanis, and street vending by Senegalese and Moroccans (Pugliese 1995). In this context, immigrants have attempted either to gain control of a market niche, as with Philippine or Latin American home helps, or they have created an ethnic brokerage environment, using ethnic relationships to build a customer reservoir that can be used as a resource to operate on the external market. A case in point is the practice known as *caporalato*: illegal work intermediaries who would find daily work for immigrants in exchange for a part of their salary. Immigrants from Eastern Europe adopted this strategy in order to control the hiring of illegal labor in construction (see Lazzaro 1998). A third ethnic strategy has created niches that excludes outsiders unfamiliar with the relevant customer base and/or the necessary knowledge to start businesses in the relevant field.

This third strategy will be analyzed in this chapter, focusing both on the social and economic activities of immigrants and on their visibility within public spaces. We will address the interrelations between immigrant activities and the surrounding space, as well as the extent to which the city is able to respond to demands from non-hegemonic groups. Two multiethnic enclaves—the Esquilino and Pigneto–Tor Pignattara districts, which today show the most important concentrations of immigrants in Rome—will anchor our discussion.

THE EMERGENCE OF IMMIGRANT BUSINESS IN ESQUILINO AND PIGNETO–TOR PIGNATTARA

The first immigrant-run businesses were set up in Rome within the last decade or so. Although immigrants are found throughout Rome, only two sites can be referred to as housing and business enclaves. We define *enclave* as a distinct area in which members of given ethnic and/or religious groups live close together with the aim of furthering their economic, social, and political growth (Marcuse 1997). These ethnic enclaves are mainly inhabited by Chinese and Bangladeshis but include commercial activities of at least twenty different ethnic groups. Figure 11.1 shows the location of the two areas, with Esquilino in the historical city center[3] and Pigneto–Tor Pignattara further east.

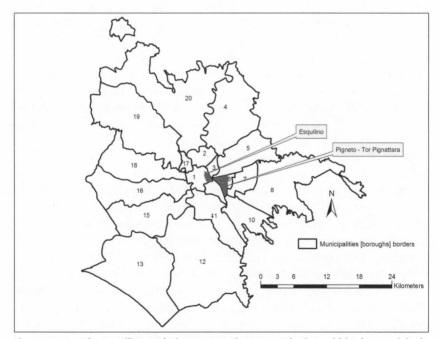

Figure 11.1.   The Esquilino and Pigneto–Tor Pignattara Districts within the Municipality of Rome

The 6,000 immigrants in the Esquilino and 4,000 immigrants in Pigneto–Tor Pignattara make up fifteen percent and six percent of their respective districts. The Esquilino is located in the neighborhood of the city's main railway station, Termini. It arose a century ago as a middle-class residential district but has gradually declined since the 1960s. In the late 1970s, it offered immigrants the opportunity to work in the large Piazza Vittorio street market and to live in low-cost boarding houses and cheap flats throughout the neighborhood. Just when the first immigrant businesses were being set up, the concentration of immigrants in the Esquilino and Pigneto suddenly increased. In the early months of 1991, squatters on the premises of an old pasta factory between the Esquilino and the Pigneto were evicted, among them 1,370 Bangladeshis. This resulted in a huge migration of people looking for some sort of accommodation in the Esquilino or in nearby Pigneto–Tor Pignattara. For decades, this latter neighborhood had been inhabited by migrants from southern Italy coming to Rome to work in nearby factories and building yard sites (Sirleto 2002). It contained several low-cost housing options and, due to the upsurge in rents even in the Esquilino, many Bengalis began to start up business firms there.

In no more than a decade, an ethnic commercial community carrying on trade at the local, nationwide, and transnational levels was established in these two districts. Overall, four hundred firms were set up in the Esquilino and some seventy firms in the Pigneto–Tor Pignattara district (see Mudu 2003).

A survey has been conducted to show the level of business activity throughout these two districts. The Esquilino is the more established area. As part of the city center, its pull on visitors and customers from all over the city is considerable. About four out of five firms owned or run by immigrants are currently operating in the Esquilino[4] were set up before 2000, mostly between 1992 and 1999. By contrast, three out of four businesses in the Pigneto–Tor Pignattara district were set up after 2000 and almost none were established prior to 1997.

The Esquilino's central position has caused a steep rise in property values, such that many immigrants cannot afford to live there. Pigneto–Tor Pignattara, on the other hand, offers cheaper rents for both business and residences. Only 46 percent of immigrant entrepreneurs in Esquilino live in Esquilino, while two-thirds of all immigrants who work in Pigneto–Tor Pignattara live there as well. Chinese and Bangladeshis are not monolithic groups; men and women have different possibilities within the community. Women are at a disadvantage within the comparatively richer economy of the Esquilino. Only eight percent of the women interviewed in the Esquilino own and run their activity, while this percentage rises to 19 percent in Pigneto–Tor Pignattara.

The large majority of all Chinese businesses in the Esquilino are either private limited companies or partnerships that trade in articles of clothing either as wholesalers or retailers. The rest are restaurants, foodstuffs shops, and a few tertiary businesses such as firms providing legal services and drug stores. In the Pigneto–Tor Pignattara district, this relationship is reversed. The twelve existing Chinese restaurants account for over fifty percent of all the Chinese firms set up in the area, though these include the very first Chinese-run hotel in Rome and a number of legal service firms.

Bangladeshis in the Esquilino mainly run, in decreasing order of frequency, costume jewelry and gift and fancy goods shops, foodstuffs shops, phone centers and money remittance agencies, jewelry shops, and video stores. Conversely, those in the Pigneto–Tor Pignattara district run eleven restaurants and grocery stores and ten service firms including call centers.

Commercial businesses run by immigrants are rather evenly distributed across the Esquilino (see figure 11.2), with a few exceptions such as the west side of Piazza Vittorio, where shops are run by Italian Jewish families, or the

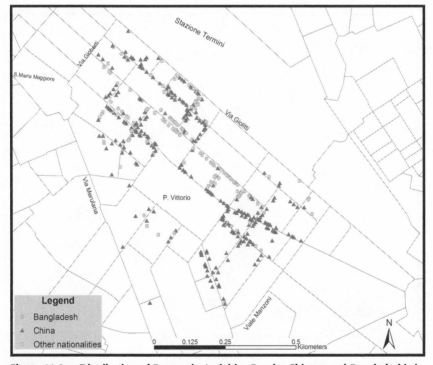

Figure 11.2. Distribution of Economic Activities Run by Chinese and Bangladeshis in the Esquilino

dilapidated Via Giolitti block between Via Cappellini and Via Rattazzi, where Nigerians and Senegalese run some shops (see Mudu 2003). By contrast, the Pigneto–Tor Pignattara district contains three distinct clusters: one spans part of Via Prenestina between Via Pigneto and Via Alberto da Giussano, another stretches over the area of the Maranella around Via Eratostene, and the third one extends along Via Tor Pignattara (see figure 11.3).

The concentration of immigrant businesses and residences across the Esquilino and Pigneto–Tor Pignattara districts co-exists with various social and political activities. The attraction of thousands of other immigrants during the day is particularly favored thanks to their central geographical position and the well-connected transport network. Thanks to its concentration in a multiethnic enclave, the immigrant population has been able to use the available space as a resource for handling money remittances and communications between the immigrant and his/her homeland, generally in the same business establishment (see figure 11.4).

Transnational income-generating activities are in part a response to discriminatory attitudes toward immigrants, especially in the banking sector.

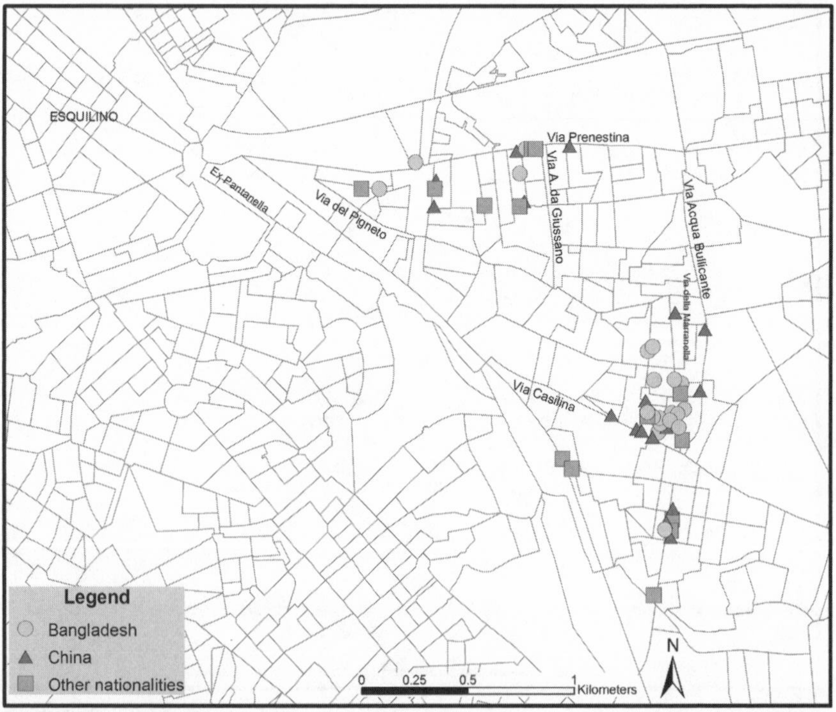

Figure 11.3. Distribution of Economic Activities Run by Chinese and Bangladeshis in the Pigneto–Tor Pignattara City Districts

Figure 11.4.   Call Center in the Esquilino

Credit institutions scrutinize immigrants more thoroughly than Italian citizens so that an immigrant waits an average of six months before obtaining an ATM debit card. What is more, few banks print leaflets in languages other than Italian, loan applications are usually denied, remittance charges are excessive, and no banks have immigrants among their staff (Mazzonis and Naletto 2001). Such a banking system is out of tune with the needs of most immigrants, who are generally net savers. Bankers' neglect of immigrant concerns dampens immigrant demand for the official banking system (Casacchia and Strozza 2001). Even though remittances are increasing, non-bank financial institutions such as Finint (which runs Western Union) has registered a boost in commission income from two to eight million euros between 1996 and 1998 (Mazzonis and Naletto 2001).

IMMIGRANT SPACE-RELATED CONFLICT

Discriminatory attitudes are also reflected in the conflict over how native and immigrant Italians use space. From the 1980s onward, the increase of immigrants and the shortage of private or semipublic spaces led many to increase their use of public areas to meet their friends and fellow countrymen. On Thursday afternoons, many public squares were thronged with immigrant women meeting on their half-day off from their jobs as maids and nannies. In many respects, the concentration of immigrants in central districts such as the Esquilino, and to a lesser degree the Pigneto–Tor Pignattara, reflects the importance of public spaces. Compared to Italians, immigrants spend more time in parks and gardens, churches, and squares. For more than twelve hours every day, the streets of the Esquilino and Pigneto are crowded with immigrants working, meeting, walking, and chatting. The traditional Piazza Vittorio street market, which has recently been moved away from the square to a nearby covered structure, survives because immigrants run 34 percent of the activities and work 42 percent of the stalls in the food area.[5] The situation is further complicated by the fact that the social support structures put in place by the Catholic Church—soup kitchens for the poor, flophouses, etc.—are particularly numerous around the Esquilino city district.

There is widespread agreement that the Esquilino is an area with an identity separate from the rest of Rome's historical center. Its urban landscape has undergone a remarkable change. A recent study counted over 1,500 signboards, including shop signs and menus posted outside restaurants, in languages other than Italian (Senatore 2004). The immigrants who have opened shops there have transformed almost fifty percent of the buildings' street-level façades into an endless sequence of signboards with special symbols and communication codes. Some of these shop signs are intended for immigrants only (e.g., with painted ideograms on the wall), some are bilingual, and others still are only in Italian in accordance with the laws. Within these representations, there are forms of resistance, integration, and domination. The mechanisms whereby ethnic identity is built and asserted become evident in an environment simmering with conflict and power disparities. In the Esquilino, discriminatory practices started as soon as the area became attractive to speculators, and conflict broke out abruptly when immigrants' use of space came under attack. On the pretext that "shop signs must be in harmony with the identity of the city district involved," the left-wing municipal government is planning to enforce regulations that will outlaw shop signs only written in Chinese or any language other than Italian (Di Frischia 2003).

The growth of the Esquilino as an enclave—and especially the greater usage of its space by immigrants—has been accompanied by conflict at different scales. There have been confrontations during condominium owners' meetings in single apartment buildings. People have demonstrated on the streets. Committees have been activated at the neighborhood level. Finally, this activity has brought in both local and national political parties. The attention drawn to the neighborhood has meant that, in only a few years, Esquilino has been visited in person by the Minister of the Interior, the Questore [Chief of Police], the Prefetto, and the leaders of the most important national political parties. Shopkeepers have invariably been at the forefront of this movement, advocating policies to restrict the free use of public spaces, while the majority has used straightforward discriminatory actions and well-known forms of exoticization to restrict immigrant spaces (see Anderson 1991).

The dominant perception of the Esquilino is that of a once middle-class district turned into a blighted area by the influx of immigrants—a picture based on a biased historical reconstruction of a multiethnic district's origins (see Mudu 2003). Chinatown, Bronx, kasbah, souk, and other comparable terms that recur in newspaper articles clearly point to a conflation of immigration with dilapidation, reflecting the resolve to describe the Esquilino as a case of "alien space" (see, among others, Bisso 1998, 2002; Lombardi and Picchi 1999; Vuolo 1999). The conflict over space also betrays a desire to expel immigrants from the area. Some propaganda describes the Esquilino as a once-beautiful district now shed of its "exquisitely Roman traits" as typical local products are threatened by the bric-a-brac imported by hundreds of illegal immigrants.

The spatial dimensions in this conflict are indeed strong. Frequent street demonstrations denounce and oppose the loss of Roman identity and the birth of "a new Chinatown." All political parties from both the center-left and the right endorse stricter ethnic-based police controls within the area (Mudu 2003). All of them have welcomed the transfer of the Piazza Vittorio market from the open square to a covered structure. The construction of a luxury hotel, the opening of premises for university faculty, the ethnic-based controls by state, and municipal police forces in the area are likely to lead to a sort of filtering process where the population of the Esquilino will move to the Pigneto–Tor Pignattara enclave (see Di Frischia 2003), where the rents are lower and there are fewer protests. While the Esquilino is compared to the Bronx in New York City, Pigneto is associated with Greenwich Village (*Repubblica* 2005).

CONCLUSION

Workplaces and the use of public spaces for social purposes have a greater impact on the relations between Italians and immigrants than their residential concentrations because interactions between immigrants and other citizens happen during work-time. Immigrants also tend to reproduce and reuse those social spaces that have fallen into disuse as a result of contemporary living patterns and reappropriate them for purposes of work, communication, prayer, and leisure.

Neoliberalist urban planning policies in the 1990s have promoted the idea that the Rome city center be reserved for political and economic elites (Berdini 2000). Tourism-related activities have gradually but forcefully made headway and now dominate much of Rome's historical city center. The only exception is the Esquilino, where property speculators have found it more profitable to let flats out to foreign immigrants. Bent on redoubling their incomes in the short run, these dominant Italian groups failed to account for the long-term emergence of a multiethnic district. The growth experienced by the Pigneto–Tor Pignattara enclave in the past ten years has instead involved the implementation of a network of immigrant-run local services within a typical working-class neighborhood.

Although these two enclaves were settled in different manners, they aptly illustrate the strategy adopted by ethnic minority business firms to turn spatial constraints to their advantage (Kaplan 1998). In the 1990s, ethnic entrepreneurs emerged who obtained two significant results. First, by setting up shops, firms, restaurants, drugstores, and other businesses, they disproved the view that immigrants are suitable only for domestic or other humble occupations. Second, by reappropriating the territory, they proved that local and transnational business enterprises can prove successful even in the face of economic globalization. In fact, while the firms and signs of globalization have grown throughout the tourist part of the city in the last few years, they are completely missing in Esquilino.

Immigrants have played an active role in the urban transformation processes. Immigrant business activities create neighborhoods that in appearance and character are far different from those the majority groups might prefer. The extent to which immigrants will create their own social space is determined not only by the characteristics of personal and group networks, but also by forms of social oppression or government policies. Frequently, when immigrants settle in an enclave, conflict is likely to arise because ethnic identity formation occurs within an environment of unequal power relations. The local context of practices, transformation, and discourses over the production of ethnic economies can determine the presence and possible scale of political conflict. Ultimately, territory becomes a means of renegotiating ethnic boundaries. Rome was not built in one day, but its most recent multiethnic neighborhoods have developed in less than one decade and the new Romans are questioning the old space with quick and challenging requests.

NOTES

1. In 2001, Rome had about 2,440,000 inhabitants, 100,000 of whom lived in the historical city center. Based on municipal population register figures, the 186,481 immigrants (including expatriates from the European Union and the United States) living in Rome in 2002 accounted for about 6.6 percent of the city's total population.

2. This study is based on a survey conducted in the Esquilino and Pigneto–Tor Pignattara city districts for several months between 2001 and 2003. A field survey was carried out in October–November 2003 in the part of the Esquilino district delimited by via Gioberti, via Giolitti, via Manzoni, and via Merulana, as well in the Pigneto–Tor Pignattara area delimited by the Prenestina and Casilina thoroughfares, via dell'Acqua Bulicante, via di Tor Pignattara, and the railway track running parallel to the Mandrione. Additional sources used include articles on the situation of immigrants published in major Italian dailies (*Corriere della Sera*, *Giornale*, *Manifesto*, *Messaggero*, *Repubblica*, and *Tempo*) between 1997 and 2003. A sample of interviews concerning immigrants running "ethnic" commercial firms in the Esquilino (24 interviews) and the Pigneto–Tor Pignattara (42 interviews) city districts was conducted in November 2003. I wish to thank Marta Leopardo for her help in conducting the interviews.

3. Rome is divided into nineteen boroughs or municipal divisions. The Esquilino district is part of the first municipal division, which also includes the greater part of the historical city center. The Pigneto–Tor Pignattara district is part of the sixth municipal division.

4. About 400 immigrant business firms have been set up in the Esquilino (65 percent Chinese, 17 percent Bengali, 3 percent Nigerian, and 14 percent by immigrants from several other countries, mainly Asian and African) and about 70 in the Pigneto–Tor Pignattara district (31 percent Chinese, 24 percent Bengali, and the rest by immigrants from Pakistan, Senegal, Egypt, Nigeria, Ecuador, the Philippines, Lebanon, and Peru).

5. Data drawn from a survey dated 2 November 2002.

REFERENCES

Anderson, K. 1991. *Vancouver's Chinatown: Racist discourse in Canada, 1875–1980*. Montreal: McGill-Queens University Press.

Ascoli, U. 1985. Migration of workers and the labor market: Is Italy becoming a country of immigration? In *Guests come to stay*, ed. R. Rosemarie, 51–68. Boulder, CO: Westview Press.

Berdini, P. 2000. *Il Giubileo senza città: L'urbanistica negli anni del liberismo*. Rome: Editori Riuniti.

Bisso, M. 1998. Via le lanterne rosse Chinatown fa paura. *Repubblica*, 6 December.

———. 2002. Esquilino, porto mondiale del "made in China." *Repubblica*, 24 January.

Caritas di Roma. 2002. *Il risparmio degli immigrati e i paesi di origine: Il caso italiano*. Rome: Caritas.

Casacchia, O., and S. Strozza. 2001. Le rimesse degli immigrati in Italia: Dimensioni, determinanti e loro impiego. In *Componenti demografiche ed economiche nell'integrazione Euro-mediterranea*, ed. M. C. Pellicani, 151–79. Bari: Cacucci Editore.

Di Frischia, F. 2003. No alle insegne selvagge. *Corriere della Sera*, 12 September.

ISMU. 1997. *Secondo rapporto sulle migrazioni 1996*. Milan: Franco Angeli.

Kaplan, D. 1998. The spatial structure of urban ethnic economies. *Urban Geography* 19:489–501.

Lazzaro, C. 1998. I nouvi schiavi. *Corriere della Sera*, 22 February.

Lombardi, M., and Picchi, B. 1999. Esquilino, il giorno della rabbia. *Messaggero*, 26 September.

Marcuse, P. 1997. The enclave, the citadel, and the ghetto: What has changed in the post-Fordist city. *Urban Affairs Review* 33 (2): 228–64.

Mazzonis, M., and G. Naletto. 2001. *Migrants and banks in Italy and in Europe*. Rome: Lunaria.

Mudu, P. 2003. Gli Esquilini: Contributi al dibattito sulle trasformazioni nel rione Esquilino di Roma dagli anni Settanta al Duemila. In *I territori di Roma,* ed. R. Morelli, E. Sonnino, and C. M. Travaglini, 641–80. Rome: University of Rome.

Mudu, P., and W. Li. 2005. A comparative evaluation of recent Chinese immigration in USA and Italy: Settlement patterns and local resistance. In *Crossing over: Comparing recent migration in Europe and the United States*, ed. H. Henke and C. Özdemir, 277–302. Lanham, MD: Lexington Books.

Organisation for Economic Co-operation and Development. 2003. *Trends in international migration: 2002 edition*. Paris: OECD.

Pugliese, E. 1995. Gli immigrati nell'economia italiana. In *Per una società multiculturale*, ed. M. I. Macioti, 45–76. Naples: Liguori Editore.

Repubblica. 2005. Pigneto, aria di village. 16 April.

Senatore, G. 2004. Un centro di eccellenza a caccia di idiomi. *Manifesto*, 2 December.

Sirleto, F. 2002. *La storia e le memorie*. Rome: Associazione Culturale Viavai.

Vuolo, P. 1999. Massacrato a coltellate nel suk dell'Esquilino. *Messaggero*, 7 September.

Waldinger, R. 1994. The making of an immigrant niche. *International Migration Review* 28 (1): 3–30.

Chapter Twelve

Spatial and Identity Transformations of the Japanese American Ethnic Economy in Globalizing Los Angeles

James M. Smith

Ethnic groups are a form of social organization whose members identify themselves as part of a community that maintains social boundaries when interacting with other ethnic groups (Barth 1998). This emphasis on maintaining boundaries explains ethnic persistence better than studies based on traits, some of which change over time with shifts in historical, ecological, and social conditions (Barth 1998). In-group self-definitions are situationally varied and contested (Marston 2002), but ethnic identities persist as a crucial form of human bonding. These identities, whether based on territories or social networks (Mitchell 2000; M. P. Smith 2001), are even more vital in an era of transnational corporations (TNCs) and powerful governments (Castells 1996; Harvey 2000).

Because these sociocultural groups tend to spatially cluster, they also shape material lifeways and cultural landscapes. Ethnic economies are recognized as crucial factors in place making and consumption patterns and play an important role in the maintenance of ethnic identities (Barth 1998; Brass 1991). Likewise, the commodification of culture is especially apparent in urban areas that have witnessed intense capital flight and uneven development (Harvey 2001). The interplay of these processes at various scales, together with the sociocultural practices of ethnic agents, shapes the urban morphology of places at the scale of the district and neighborhood (Kaplan 1997, 1998; Peet 1997).

To a tremendous degree, the landscape of Little Tokyo in Los Angeles, California, has changed with politicoeconomic shifts at various scales from southern California agriculture to geopolitical turbulence, patterns of foreign direct investment, and the urban spaces of late capitalism (Castells 1996, 1997; Harvey 1989). The Little Tokyo district is less than a mile east-southeast of the Los Angeles central business district (CBD), about one mile due south of Chinatown and less than two miles south of Dodger Stadium. It covers roughly thirteen square blocks, bounded by Los Angeles Street to the north with its southern edge formed by Alameda Avenue. Third Street and Temple Street form the western and eastern edges, respectively. In contrast to Chinatown, Little Tokyo historic district occupies the same urban space since its inception in the first decade of the twentieth century. The heart of the traditional ethnic enclave economy is East First Street, which is now recognized as a historic district by the city of Los Angeles (see figures 12.1 and 12.2).

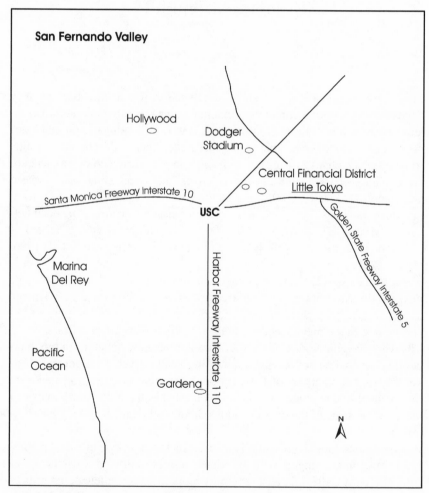

Figure 12.1.　Greater Los Angeles Region (not to scale)

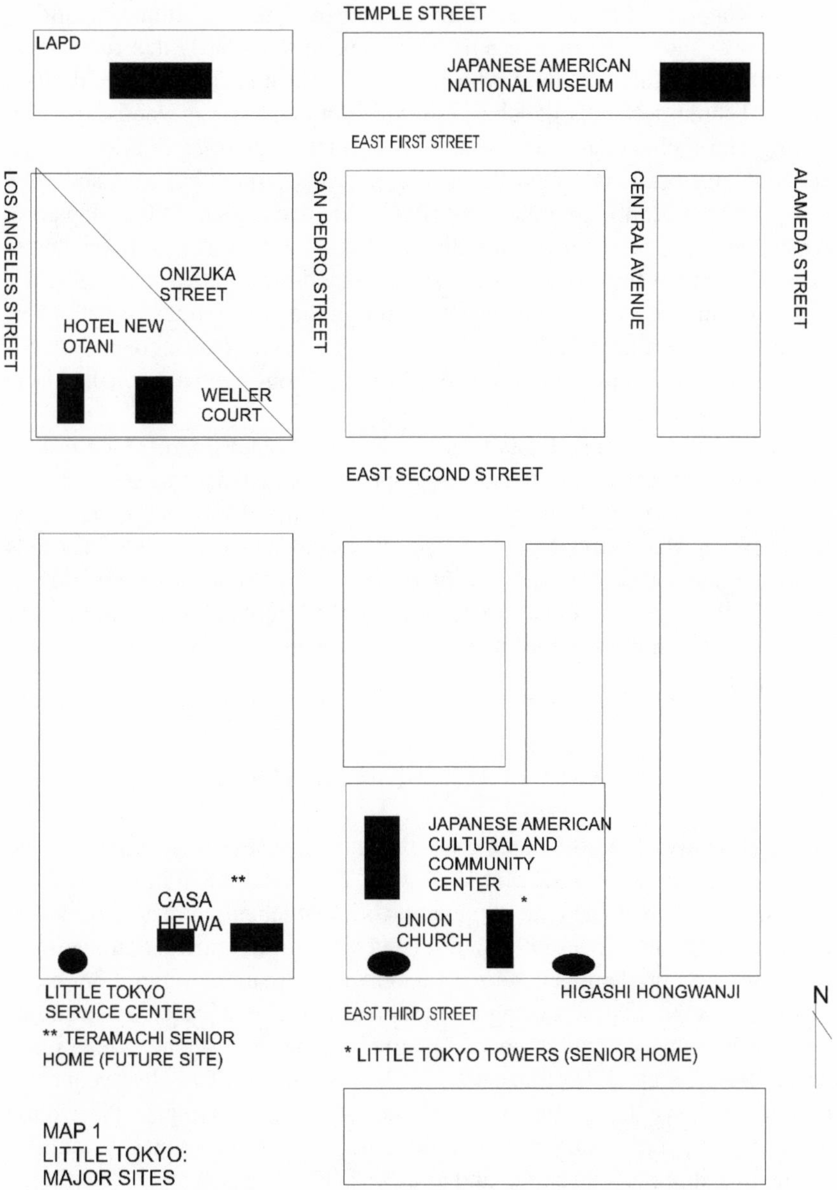

TEMPLE STREET

LAPD

JAPANESE AMERICAN
NATIONAL MUSEUM

EAST FIRST STREET

LOS ANGELES STREET

SAN PEDRO STREET

CENTRAL AVENUE

ALAMEDA STREET

ONIZUKA
STREET

HOTEL NEW
OTANI

WELLER
COURT

EAST SECOND STREET

CASA
HEIWA **

JAPANESE AMERICAN
CULTURAL AND
COMMUNITY
CENTER

UNION
CHURCH *

HIGASHI HONGWANJI

N

LITTLE TOKYO
SERVICE CENTER

** TERAMACHI SENIOR
HOME (FUTURE SITE)

EAST THIRD STREET

* LITTLE TOKYO TOWERS (SENIOR HOME)

MAP 1
LITTLE TOKYO:
MAJOR SITES

Figure 12.2. Little Tokyo

This chapter investigates the intermeshed processes of ethnic identities, economies, and landscapes. Ethnic actors create landscapes that reflect and impact the identities of those who live and work in such culturally defined places. Ethnic networks of labor, cultural preferences (e.g., landscape gardening and architecture), and contested political memories (e.g., museums and war memorials) are mediated and expressed through business activities into localized landscape outcomes (Berry and Henderson 2002). Japanese Americans have persevered and maintained their cultural signature on the urban landscape of the district. Their resilience and fortitude has enabled Little Tokyo to survive as an ethnic enclave through the jarring transformations of the last century. Likewise, the creation of a particular ethnic economic landscape within this small urban place has had profound impacts on Japanese American identities.

In this context, archival data from the period of redevelopment are important, as are the accounts of those who opposed such changes by participating in protest movements. Most empirical and qualitative data was acquired from fieldwork in March and August 2002 and January 2004. Archival materials and qualitative methods such as interviews and participant observation at sites of cultural production and consumption shed light on the role of place in ethnic identity reinforcement and in current changes in the economic landscape of Little Tokyo.

EARLY JAPANESE MIGRATION

Approximately 275,000 Japanese—primarily young men—entered the United States between 1861 and 1924, with 245,000 of them migrating from 1900 to 1924. Given the type of manual work that labor contractors sought to fill and conditions in peasant villages, most were rural farmers. Southwestern Japan was the predominant source region for international migration, especially productive rice-producing areas such as Hiroshima prefecture in southwestern Honshu, where the peasants suffered from heavy land taxes (Takahashi 1997; Takaki 1989; Hane 1990). Most of the Issei had clear economic motives to leave Japan, but many did not anticipate staying in the United States. They were young men who dreamed of earning money to build a home, to acquire an education, and to establish businesses.

Why was California so important in the geographies of Japanese American stories and experiences? Coastal California's moderate Mediterranean climate was the perfect setting for the production of winter fruits and vegetables. Also, transcontinental freight rail and refrigerated rail cars established economic complementarities with cities in the Midwest and Eastern seaboard, where the demand for fresh produce was great during the long winter. Also important were the skills of Japanese farmers in intensive wet-rice agriculture and vegetable gardening, both of which demanded heavy labor, attention to detail, and a strong work ethic. Together, this combination of factors made the trans-Pacific labor migration from Japan very profitable for white-owned agricultural operations (Takahashi 1997).

The exploitation of culturally isolated migrant workers has been a feature of plantation and food crop agriculture in global and regional peripheries (Walker 1997; Ong, Bonacich, and Cheng 1994). In California, the first-generation Japanese immigrants were forbidden to own land. But the Alien Land Laws designed to keep them in migrant work did not succeed in preventing the Japanese immigrants from starting productive small farms growing flowers, strawberries, lettuce, and other crops with a high demand. Migrant workers became green grocers with their own businesses, and the Issei proved to be very resourceful and creative in outflanking the restrictions placed on them. To a large degree, Little Tokyo was formed as a cluster of wholesale and retail businesses meant to service this predominantly agricultural community.

CREATION OF AN ETHNIC ENCLAVE

Little Tokyo does not have a single founding date. The term was coined by white "native" Californians in the early twentieth century as a way to give a racial label to space set aside for those deemed unassimilable and alien (Anderson 1987). As with other communities from Asia such as the Chinese, Japanese immigrants were severely restricted in where they could work and live. Laws on the ownership and use of land and on where land could be leased for farming or commerce created geographies of social restrictions (Takahashi 1997; Takaki 1989).

Nevertheless, by 1903, a recognizable area of shops provided Japanese Americans with specialized food, drink, and clothing, as well as more generic goods and services. Little Tokyo's core was established in the area of San Pedro and First Street (figure 12.2). Because Japanese immigrants were often refused service by local businesses, this new immigrant enclave developed a very complete ethnic economy. Medical offices, legal and accountant services, and religious (Buddhist and Christian) and funerary institutions were all established and vital to meet the material and spiritual needs of the ethnic community (Breton 1964; Fugita and O'Brien 1991).

By 1924, about 10,000 Japanese Americans resided in Little Tokyo. The community's numbers had increased through secondary migration from other urban centers such as San Francisco, where the 1906 earthquake had laid waste to the housing and financial resources of Japantown and where anti-Asian sentiment had become more strident. Moreover, discrimination had even prevented the Nisei, native-born second-generation Japanese Americans, from acquiring jobs outside the community except in menial unskilled positions. The educated Nisei employed as "carrot washers" and house cleaners were frustrated with their social and economic status, but the ethnic economy became vertically integrated and institutionally complete out of necessity. Both wholesale and retail services were present in Little Tokyo, giving a strength and depth to the ethnic economy that was also sustained by an intense ethnic awareness (Bonacich and Modell 1980; Yokota 1996).

The effects of the Great Depression, though severe, were less apparent in Little Tokyo than in Los Angeles at large. The personal loyalties and social ties fostered by the ethnic economy resulted in employers retaining employees and workers accepting wage decreases. Likewise, by 1930, Japanese agriculturalists controlled about half of the total profits of the produce market in southern California, which combined with the institutional richness of the Japanese American community, helped to lessen the harsh effects of the Depression (Takahashi 1997; Kurashige 2002; Fugita and O'Brien 1991).

However, the legal and de facto restrictions on Japanese Americans worsened with the increasing geopolitical tensions of the 1930s. Enforced spatial isolation and accusations of Japanese insularity reinforced suspicions of disloyalty and treachery. In addition, the success of Japanese American farms and businesses in the produce industry motivated local racists and jealous competitors who wished to acquire the well-kept and productive lands of people they labeled as subversive.

INCARCERATION AND ENCLAVE RECONSTITUTION

The outbreak of war in December 1941 gave persons hostile to the Japanese American community an opportunity to tarnish the entire group as a threat to national security, in concert with both military and civilian regional and national authorities (Ichioka 1988; Takaki 1989; Weglyn 1976). The result was devastating for the Japanese Americans, as the subsequent incarceration effectively deprived the community of all basic constitutionally guaranteed freedoms and property rights. From mid-1942 to early 1945, Japanese Americans from the West Coast were incarcerated in camps surrounded by barbed wire and armed guards. The entire community was dispersed throughout the intermountain West, the Southwest, and Arkansas, and Little Tokyo was extinguished as a Japanese American ethnic enclave (Yokota 1996; Takaki 1989; Weglyn 1976).

In December 1944, a Supreme Court ruling declared the removal of Japanese Americans from the West Coast a violation of constitutional rights, and by the end of 1946, over 25,000 Nikkei had settled in Los Angeles (Yokota 1996). Faced with harsh housing and employment discrimination and fearful of dealing with the outside community, many former residents of Little Tokyo clustered together, often forced to find shelter in hostels that were set up in Buddhist temples and Christian churches. Gradually, some businesses managed to reopen, and other returnees were able to find work in the informal economy, especially gardening, landscaping, and domestic work, with many establishing sole proprietorships.

However, by the late 1950s, the relaxation of housing discrimination enabled more Japanese Americans to move to suburban communities such as Gardena, fifteen miles southwest of the original enclave. As the population base of Little Tokyo declined, the district was targeted by the city of Los Angeles as a prime location to establish a new police headquarters. The subsequent appropriation of land and construction of the Los Angeles Police Department (LAPD) headquarters building, or Parker Center, wiped out much of the traditional core area north of First Street (figure 12.2).

Not surprisingly, these activities provoked struggles by community activists and residents. During the late 1960s, activist politics increased in the Asian American communities, much of it led by students, in the context of the peace marches against U.S. involvement in the Vietnam War. These activists in the Asian American movement were also crucial in efforts to resist redevelopment in Little Tokyo, which would force the removal of elderly and poor Japanese Americans from their homes in condemned buildings. During the early 1970s, plans of the Los Angeles Community Redevelopment Agency (CRA) to award a contract to the Kajima Company, a Japanese construction transnational, provoked strong resistance. The project initiated construction of the New Otani Hotel and Weller Court shopping mall, which were planned and built to facilitate tourism from Japan (figure 12.2).

This struggle had crucial symbolic significance because traditional Japanese American ethnic businesses and associations such as the Japanese American Chamber of Commerce, a local chapter of the Japanese American Citizen's League (JACL), and other local organizations maintained offices in the Sun Building. Even more emotive, the buildings provided long-term low-income housing for working class and senior residents (Keil 1998). According to one community leader familiar with these conflicts, the feeling in the community was that the CRA was making sweetheart deals with big corporations from Japan. The Japanese TNCs were seen as not having any connection with the local economy, community, or small businesses. To create a certain level of accountability, the Little Tokyo People's Rights Organization

(LTPRO) pushed the CRA to build low-cost senior housing, which resulted in the construction of Little Tokyo Towers. Likewise, a hotel for low-income residents was completed not long thereafter.[1]

These events highlight the conflict between redevelopment supported by the municipal government of Los Angeles and powerful Japanese companies and the resistance of various ethnic community organizations and movements. Redevelopment and gentrification in Little Tokyo has generated conflict and cooperation between different groups representing a wide range of interests, such as powerful global companies that seek opportunities to make a profit and community and ethnic networks that seek to secure the interests of people outside of the large corporate or governmental organizations. These conflicts have intensified with the increase in globalization pressures in the late twentieth century. These groups can operate at varied geographical scales, as when a community group seeks attention from global media (M. P. Smith 2001).

GLOBALIZATION AND THE TRANSFORMATION OF THE LANDSCAPE AND ECONOMIES OF LITTLE TOKYO

In cities, governments, TNCs, and local businesses build spaces in areas labeled "blighted" in an attempt to make them profitable. These policies reflect patterns of capital circulation and accumulation (Harvey 1989, 2001). By the 1980s, patterns of gentrification and creating spaces of pleasured consumption were supported by government and business in Los Angeles. This was seen as a positive strategy in a city that always excelled in the production of fantasy and indeed typified the Disneyfication of urban space.

In Little Tokyo, redevelopment was supported by a regional alliance that included the city of Los Angeles, real estate companies, and construction companies from the local area and Japan. By prioritizing the creation of geographies of profit, this urban entrepreneurial alliance in Los Angeles was typical of redevelopment in other cities. Specific low-income neighborhoods were labeled "blighted," which then led to attempts to expel residents. Banks, hotels, and malls were then constructed to benefit the most powerful municipal and global actors (N. Smith 1990, 1996).

Problems arose because this form of development comes at the expense of affordable housing and local community empowerment. By encouraging corporate investment, municipal governments used public funds to encourage private profit. In Little Tokyo, this was expressed bluntly in the construction of the New Otani Hotel and more subtly in the creation of what Keil (1998) termed "postmodern images of spectacle and consumption."

Moreover, the redevelopment of Little Tokyo was accompanied by enhanced security as both the LAPD and private security companies were mobilized (Keil 1998, 223–26). Little Tokyo is adjacent to some of the poorest neighborhoods in Los Angeles, where surplus value is extracted from Central American migrants working in the garment industry's "Fashion District." Extreme wealth is juxtaposed with urban conditions similar to those found in less developed metropolises such as Rio de Janeiro (Soja 1996, Dear 1996), and Little Tokyo was to be protected as an upscale safe haven for the consumption patterns of tourists and office workers.

JAPANESE AMERICAN BUSINESS IN LITTLE TOKYO: LOCAL AND TRANSNATIONAL PATTERNS

Scholars of immigration and ethnic identity have long stressed the importance of institutions in the maintenance of an ethnic community (Breton 1964). More specifically, ethnic business activity that is aimed at co-ethnic consumption, employs members of the community, and is spatially clustered can be a self-reinforcing system that is perpetuated through generations. Geographers have analyzed ethnic economies and concluded that spatial concentration can actually enhance profitability through an "incubator effect" that also fosters business linkages to co-ethnic companies outside of an enclave and with non-ethnic firms (Kaplan 1997, 1998).

With the intensification of globalization processes since the 1980s, urban ethnic enclaves market historical qualities to enhance their role in the larger processes of making culture profitable (Castells 1996; Harvey 2001; Keil 1998). Japanese American civil society associations and individual businesses forge market links at various scales through personal interaction and increasingly through the Internet.

Local ethnic business publications—in print and on the Internet—such as *Sushi and Tofu* provide a wealth of information on commercial activities and contacts, emphasizing temporal, festival-oriented (*matsuri*) events based on traditional observances of Japanese Americans and overseas Japanese (or Nikkei). These events give flavor to the unique character of Little Tokyo as a place, which territorially grounds the experiences and tastes of Japanese Americans. Japanese cuisine is touted as "the main selling point of Little Tokyo," with its unique flavors and superior health benefits (Sushi and Sake 2003). Where best to consume Japanese food than in a place recognized by toponym as "genuinely" Japanese? With this emphasis on Little Tokyo as a place of ethnic production, exchange, and consumption (noting especially the consumption practices of non–Japanese

Americans), ethnic news and advertising outlets suggest the transformation of mixed residential and commercial spaces into areas now devoted primarily to business, cultural presentation, and performance (Harvey 1989, 2001; Sayer 1997).

Local institutions such as the Little Tokyo Business Association forge links with commercial interests at the larger municipal and transnational corporate levels. Strategies are formulated "where Little Tokyo's interests are made known to the 'big players' in and around downtown LA" (Sushi and Sake 2003). The values of business and its imperatives are manifested in statements such as "To get anywhere in life, it's not *what* you know, but *who* you know." The Little Tokyo Area Business Counselor used this phrase for the Little Tokyo Service Center Community Development Corporation, a representative of civil society that assists in marketing, raising capital for local businesses, and interacting with government agencies. The counselor also conducts seminars on taxation, health issues, and accessing capital.

Nikkei ethnic business networks have also been expanded to the broader Asian American Pacific Islander (AAPI) community, as evidenced by participation in the Annual Asian Pacific Islander Small Business Expo. Specifically oriented to the Asian small business community, this event plays a key mediating role in facilitating communication between ethnic business and sources for capital and insurance, office suppliers, and various small scale producer services. These patterns of cooperation lead to interesting linkages that begin to transcend divisions based upon different ancestries and suggest that a pan–Asian American identity framework is practical and desirable in certain situations (Sushi and Sake 2003).

The ethnic press also highlights the achievements of individual businesses to foreground the unique elements of the urban landscape and situate commodities within the larger discourse of food cultures. The Fugetsu-Do shop on East First Street has been operated within the same family since 1903. Today, the shop's products are available for purchase on a website for a Japanese grocery associated with a transnational corporate air carrier. Thus, a confectionary that once typified an enclave business at the turn of the last century is now globally linked to consumers through technology that merges scales in the global economy. Such practices are now typical of ethnic businesses.

SHIFTING STRUCTURES AND THE RESURGENCE OF LOCAL AGENCY: 1990s TO THE PRESENT

During the 1990s, new economic patterns at the trans-Pacific, national, state, and local scales had a profound impact on the Greater Los Angeles area. The relative decline in transnational corporate Japanese investment in choice U.S. real estate properties corresponded with the bursting of the stock market bubble and the exposure of the weaknesses of Japanese corporate organization. In Japan itself, the implosion of the financial and real estate bubble resulted in a massive retreat of investment from North American urban markets, in particular from choice, high-end acquisitions which had caused so much anxiety among politicians in the United States (Katz 2001). Within the context of Little Tokyo, this resulted in the abandonment of mega-projects for malls and hotels that had been planned during the apogee of Japanese power in the late 1980s (Takehara 1990).

For the city of Los Angeles, the decline in TNC investment from Japan certainly had negative effects. But these developments in global finance capitalism, coupled with the end of the cold war, shriveled investment from the national defense and aerospace industries that had employed so many highly-skilled engineers and researchers in the Los Angeles basin. Thus, two powerful sources of capital and employment in Southern California were fundamentally undermined by events in the global geopolitical economy (Walker 1997).

Then, on 17 January 1994, the effects of the powerful Northridge earthquake spread structural, material damage throughout the region. The costs associated with infrastructural repair to roads, buildings, and bridges added to the sense of economic and fiscal crisis. This combination of economic, geopolitical, and geologic events cast a pall over city leadership that had looked to tourism and commodification as a way out of its decline. Not surprisingly, at the most localized of scales, Little Tokyo businesses experienced a decline in capital, customer base, and the sense of confidence about the future that had characterized the area in the 1980s.[2] For example, the large white stone tower of City Hall had to be abandoned for years due to the need to retrofit the structure for future earthquake events. Many City Hall workers had taken their lunch breaks in the nearby ethnic neighborhoods, and restaurant businesses suffered acutely.

As buildings were retrofitted in the late 1990s, City Hall workers began to return to the downtown site damaged by the Northridge earthquake, thus partially reviving the customer base for the Little Tokyo and Chinatown restaurant businesses vital to those ethnic economies. In addition, projects jointly supported by local actors such as the Little Tokyo Service Center and the municipal state resulted in the construction of low-cost, high-rise housing for seniors. This contributed to the viability of such voluntary ethnic associations as Christian churches and Buddhist temples, with the latter in particular having mostly senior congregants. By increasing the population of residents in spaces formerly given over to parking lots, these projects assured the continued pattern of an influx of people such as younger relatives of senior residents.

But the revival of ethnic businesses cannot be separated from the importance of Little Tokyo as a place of central importance to the wider Japanese American ethnic consciousness. Although Japanese investment and the overall economy fluctuated, ethnic community organizations, the municipal state, and even some federally based funds has led to the construction of several institutions crucial to Little Tokyo's revival. Given the importance of voluntary ethnic associations to ethnic identity and community persistence, the Japanese American Cultural and Community Center (JACCC) has become a focal point for efforts to provide a central place for cultural performances, language instruction, and outreach to other Asian American Pacific Islander (AAPI) communities.

Finally, from the standpoint of the cultural symbolism and identity persistence of Japanese Americans on a national scale, the most important project is the Japanese American National Museum, which first opened in 1992 in the old Nishi Hongwanji Buddhist Temple Building on East First Street and Central Avenue. By 1999, a stunning new 84,000 square foot museum structure was completed, and this area has since been expanded to over 100,000 feet (Japanese American National Museum 2003). Traditional Japanese aesthetics and building materials such as cedar and stone with Mediterranean biota such as palm trees, cacti, and flowers symbolically mark the museum as a unique repository of Japanese American experiences. From an economic point of view, the building of a national museum dedicated to the Nikkei experience assures the primacy of Little Tokyo as a symbolic field of care for decades to come (Tuan 1974). Within a short walking distance are memorials to the Nisei soldiers who fought in the Second World War and the Union Center for the Arts, which houses the East-West Players, the oldest Asian American fine arts organization in Southern California.

CONCLUSION

Native-born Japanese Americans, more recent shin-Issei migrants, and business actors at all scales have made, and continue to remake, Little Tokyo in a number of ways. First, successive historical shifts in socioeconomic and political relationships between Japanese Americans, the political economies of southern California, and trans–Pacific Rim flows of people and money have shaped the ethnic economic landscape of the enclave. Foreign direct investment associated with globalization combined with urban entrepreneurialism has transformed the sociospatial and built environments in many districts of Los Angeles, including Little Tokyo. The linkages between local business interests, municipal government, and Japanese TNCs also set in motion controversial gentrification processes with landscape outcomes in the district. The simultaneous destruction and recreation of places through globalization processes have intensified Japanese American local, regional, and transnational ethnic networks and identities (Castells 1996; Ciccolella and Mignaqui 2002; M. P. Smith 2001).

Second, the Japanese American ethnic economy is now focusing on this sense of "Nikkei" identity as a business strategy (Kaplan 1998). As a result, declining investment from Japan has not had a significant impact on Little Tokyo as a symbolic place for Japanese American identities. In fact, since the collapse of the "bubble economy" in Japan, Japanese American cultural, community, and religious organizations have played crucial roles in Little Tokyo's recovery from the effects of economic recession and the 1994 Northridge earthquake. This pattern contrasts with the emerging ethnoburbs of the San Gabriel Valley east of downtown Los Angeles, where mainly Taiwanese networks of overseas investors and highly skilled immigrants have been the main players in the transformation of local business and residential geographies (Li 1998).

Third, the shin-Issei, or new first-generation Japanese migrants, are bringing transnational ties into the enclave and sharpening its identity as a place materially and socially linked to Japanese cultural forms. These migrants are having an impact on businesses by increasing demand for more recently popular products from Japan such as films and music and flavoring Little Tokyo's social space with more current Japanese popular culture. In addition, the shin-Issei have created a much greater demand for Japanese language services in health care provision, law, accountancy, entertainment, and religious institutions.

Fourth, the influx of shin-Issei has also led to the increasing landscape presence of residential high rises for seniors, as evidenced by the construction of four major housing centers and the current construction of another, Teramachi senior condominiums on Third Street and San Pedro (figure 12.2). This trend will reinforce the Japanese character of the district by insuring the presence of ethnic residency, which has cumulative effects for local business.

Case studies in the geographies of ethnic economies reveal the importance of spatial clustering and place context in the persistence of ethnic social patterns, commercial activities, and identities. By engaging in historically informed research in place, geographers can reveal how landscapes of ethnic economies have been shaped by spatial processes and flows at varied scales.

NOTES

1. For information on the struggles of LTPRO with the CRA and the extensive redevelopment projects in the mid to late 1970s, I am indebted to Bill Watanabe, current director of the Little Tokyo Service Center and a participant in some of these events as an LTPRO member.

2. I am indebted to Don Nakanishi, PhD, director of the Asian American Studies Program at UCLA, for these insights. In particular, he provided important information on more recent social and economic trends and vital perspectives on the Japanese American community generally.

REFERENCES

Anderson, K. J. 1987. The idea of Chinatown: The power of place and institutional practice in the making of a racial category. *Annals of the Association of American Geographers* 77 (4): 580–98.

Barth, F. 1998. Introduction. In *Ethnic groups and boundaries: The social organization of culture difference*, ed. F. Barth, 9–38. Prospect Heights, IL: Waveland Press.

Berry, K. A., and M. L. Henderson. 2002. Envisioning the nexus between geography and ethnic and racial identity. In *Geographical identities of ethnic America: Race, space, and place*, ed. K. A. Berry and M. L. Henderson, 1–14. Reno: University of Nevada Press.

Bonacich, E., and J. Modell. 1980. *The economic basis of ethnic solidarity: Small business in the Japanese American community*. Berkeley: University of California Press.

Brass, P. 1991. *Ethnicity and nationalism*. New Delhi: Sage Publications.

Breton, R. 1964. Institutional completeness of ethnic communities and the personal relations of immigrants. *American Journal of Sociology* 1 (1): 193–205.

Castells, M. 1996. *The rise of the network society*. Oxford: Blackwell.

———. 1997. *The power of identity*. Oxford: Blackwell.

Ciccolella, P., and I. Mignaqui. 2002. Buenos Aires: Sociospatial impacts of the development of global city functions. In *Global networks, linked cities*, ed. S. Sassen, 309–26. New York: Routledge.

Dear, M. J. 1996. In the city, time becomes visible: Intentionality and urbanism in Los Angeles, 1781–1991. In *The city: Los Angeles and urban theory at the end of the twentieth century*, ed. A. J. Scott and E. W. Soja, 76–105. Berkeley: University of California Press.

Fugita, S. S., and D. J. O'Brien. 1991. *Japanese American ethnicity: The persistence of community*. Seattle: University of Washington Press.

Hane, M. 1990. *Modern Japan: A historical survey*. Boulder, CO: Westview Press.

Harvey, D. 1989. *The condition of postmodernity*. Cambridge, MA: Blackwell.

———. 2000. *Spaces of hope*. Berkeley: University of California Press.

———. 2001. *Spaces of capital: Towards a critical geography*. New York: Routledge.

Ichioka, Y. 1988. *The Issei: The world of the first generation Japanese immigrants, 1885–1924*. New York: Free Press.

Japanese American National Museum. 2003. *Little Tokyo resource guide*. Los Angeles: Japanese American National Museum.

Kaplan, D. H. 1997. The creation of an ethnic economy: Indochinese business expansion in Saint Paul. *Economic Geography* 73 (2): 214–33.

———. 1998. The spatial structure of urban ethnic economies. *Urban Geography* 19 (6): 489–501.

Katz, R. 2001. *Japan: The system that soured*. London: M. E. Sharpe.

Keil, R. 1998. *Los Angeles: Globalization, urbanization and social struggles*. New York: John Wiley.

Kurashige, L. 2002. *Japanese American celebration and conflict: A history of ethnic identity and festival, 1934–1990*. Berkeley: University of California Press.

Li, W. 1998. Anatomy of a new ethnic settlement: The Chinese ethnoburb in Los Angeles. *Urban Studies* 35 (3): 479–501.

Marston, S. A. 2002. Making difference: Conflict over Irish identity in the New York City St. Patrick's Day parade. *Political Geography* 21 (3): 373–92.

Mitchell, K. 2000. Networks of ethnicity. In *A companion to economic geography*, ed. E. Sheppard and T. J. Barnes, 392–408. Oxford: Blackwell.

Ong, P., E. Bonacich, and L. Cheng. 1994. The political economy of capitalist restructuring and the new Asian immigration. In *The new Asian immigration in Los Angeles and global restructuring*, ed. P. Ong, E. Bonacich, and L. Cheng, 3–35. Philadelphia: Temple University Press.

Peet, R. 1997. The cultural production of economic forms. In *Geographies of economies*, ed. R. Lee and J. Willis, 37–46. London: Arnold.

Sayer, A. 1997. The dialectic of culture and economy. In *Geographies of economies*, ed. R. Lee and J. Willis, 16–26. London: Arnold.

Smith, M. P. 2001. *Transnational urbanism: Locating globalization*. Oxford: Blackwell.

Smith, N. 1990. *Uneven development: Nature, capital, and the production of space*. Oxford: Blackwell.

———. 1996. *The new urban frontier: Gentrification and the revanchist city*. London: Routledge.

Soja, E. 1996. *Thirdspace: Journeys to Los Angeles and other real-and-imagined places*. Cambridge, MA: Blackwell.

Sushi and sake (formerly Sushi and tofu). www.sushiandtofu.com (accessed 25 November 2003).

Takahashi, J. 1997. *Nisei/Sansei: Shifting Japanese American identities and politics*. Philadelphia: Temple University Press.

Takaki, R. 1989. *Strangers from a different shore: A history of Asian Americans*. Boston: Little, Brown.

Takehara, D. 1990. CRA listens to Li'L Tokyo residents' concerns. *Rafu Shimpo*, July 28.

Tuan, Y-F. 1974. Space and place: Humanistic perspective. *Progress in Human Geography* 6:233–46.

Walker, R. 1997. California rages: Regional capitalism and the politics of renewal. In *Geographies of economies*, ed. R. Lee and J. Willis, 345–55. London: Arnold.

Weglyn, M. 1976. *Years of infamy: The untold story of America's concentration camps.* New York: William Morrow.

Yokota, K. A. 1996. From Little Tokyo to Bronzeville and back: Ethnic communities in transition. Master's thesis, University of California, Los Angeles.

Chapter Thirteen

The Evolution of Manchester's Curry Mile: From Suburban Shopping Street to Ethnic Destination

Giles A. Barrett and David McEvoy

Cities change, but as Conzen (1960) told us long ago, not all elements of cities change at the same rate. Street patterns persist longer than building plots, and building plots long outlast the individual structures which successively occupy them. The uses to which land and buildings are put are still more changeable, and these in turn can lead to structural adaptations and modifications in appearance (Brand 1994). Such differential aging may often mean that function has to be accommodated in a built form originally intended for other purposes. Changes in national and urban economies simply occur too frequently for new buildings to be provided for every new urban activity.

Therefore, immigrant groups, who typically move into the lower economic and social niches of a city, often find themselves living, working, and praying in properties constructed for quite different predecessors and purposes. This chapter examines an urban retail district during its ethnic and functional transformation into an exotic restaurant quarter. It begins with a description of the change that has occurred and then considers why it has happened. These developments are next related to public policy on the economic regeneration of Manchester as a whole. Finally, the case study is considered as a possible model for the revival of other British urban areas.

This study draws on field observations made over several decades in Rusholme, a nineteenth-century suburb of Manchester, in the north of England. In common with many other British cities, Manchester experienced significant immigration from the Caribbean and South Asia during the 1950s and 1960s. Although British immigration laws have since been tightened, substantial ethnic minority communities have now emerged as a result of family reunification and natural growth. The metropolitan area of Greater Manchester now has over 140,000 ethnically South Asian residents, over half of them

Pakistani, in an overall population of just under 2,500,000. Rusholme has emerged as the principal retail and consumer service center for this South Asian population, although it is also more than this.

THE EMERGENCE OF THE CURRY MILE

Until the 1960s, Rusholme was an ordinary suburban shopping district. It occupied an obscure niche in the lower rungs of Greater Manchester's retail hierarchy (McEvoy 1968). West of it was the high-density working-class terraced housing of Moss Side. To the east of it was the lower density of Victoria Park, a decaying nineteenth-century gated community increasingly subject to multiple occupation (figure 13.1). Most shops occupied the ground floor of the late nineteenth- and early twentieth-century buildings lining Wilmslow Road, a busy thoroughfare between the residential suburbs to the south and the jobs and retailing of the city center about two miles to the north.

Today many of the retail premises of the 1960s, through an evolutionary process of adaptive reuse, have been converted into "Indian" restaurants (figure 13.2). They form a ribbon along both sides of Wilmslow Road, known

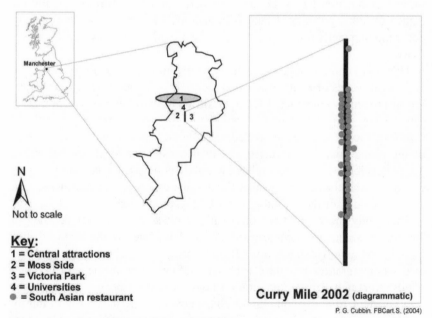

Figure 13.1.   Manchester and the Curry Mile

Figure 13.2.   Restaurants in Converted Victorian Premises

popularly as the Curry Mile. The Curry Half-mile or Curry Kilometre would be more accurate, but the image potential of the mile, reminiscent of the "Golden Miles" in British seaside resorts, such as Blackpool and Southend, is too great to stand in the way of pedantry. The majority of "Indian" restaurants in the United Kingdom are actually run by Bangladeshis, but in Rusholme, most restaurants are owned and operated by members of the Pakistani community.[1]

This transition from retail to restaurants is captured in the business counts shown in table 13.1. The aggregate number of businesses has remained relatively stable over the study period, but the make-up of that total has altered markedly in response to changing transport and consumption patterns, the pressures of competition, and government (de)regulation.

Between 1961 and 2001, Britain's automobiles per capita increased fourfold (McGoldrick 1990; Office of National Statistics 2003). This allows British consumers to travel much further to stores and services than was the case in 1966. Large supermarkets with wide catchments have grabbed market share from smaller food stores, whether general grocery shops or specialists such as butchers, greengrocers, and bread shops. A major catalyst for the growth of supermarkets and of chains in other retail sectors was the national government's 1964 abolition of Resale Price Maintenance, a practice

Table 13.1. Rusholme Business Counts, 1966–2002

	South Asians				Whites and Others				Total			
	1966	1976	1992	2002	1966	1976	1992	2002	1966	1976	1992	2002
Food stores	4	7	14	11	26	14	4	3	30	21	18	14
CTNs*	0	1	1	5	7	5	5	1	7	6	6	6
Clothing stores	0	4	6	10	19	15	1	0	19	19	7	10
Other retail	0	8	18	14	27	19	5	4	27	27	23	18
Restaurants/take-away foods	2	5	29	43	5	5	6	9	7	10	35	52
Public houses	0	0	0	0	5	5	4	4	5	5	4	4
Other consumer services	0	4	5	8	28	16	11	11	28	20	16	19
Total	**6**	**29**	**73**	**91**	**117**	**79**	**36**	**32**	**123**	**108**	**109**	**123**

*Confectioners, tobacconists, and newsagents

whereby manufacturers set the retail price of their products. In 1966 the competitive consequences were just emerging, but they rampaged through subsequent decades. Competition was sharpened further by the 1994 relaxation of most controls on retail opening hours. Supermarkets have successfully colonized the evening hours in which many small food stores formerly took advantage of lax enforcement of restrictions on opening hours. In Rusholme the number of food stores declined from thirty in 1966 to only fourteen in 2002. The four butchers became two; the four greengrocers became one; the four wine and spirit vendors fell to two; and the four bread and cake shops, the single fishmonger, and the health food store just disappeared. General food stores did a bit better, only falling from thirteen to eight. Rusholme may be doing better than other localities in this particular regard, at least partly because six of the eight are operated by South Asians, a group willing to struggle against competition by opening long hours in exchange for modest profits (Jones, McEvoy, and Barrett 1994).

Non-food retailing also experienced the effects of competition and deregulation. In 1966 Rusholme had nineteen clothing shops, but this fell to ten in 2002. Meanwhile, "other retail," a heterogeneous group including furniture and electrical goods retailers, hardware stores, pharmacies, and booksellers, saw its numbers fall from twenty-seven to eighteen. As with food stores, a major cause of decline is competition from major chains. Furniture, electrical goods, and hardware chains were assisted by the relaxation of town planning restrictions on retail location by Margaret Thatcher's administration during the 1980s. Formerly restricted to traditional shopping quarters, these activities were freed to open new "big box" outlets in off-center locations, easily accessible mainly by automobile rather than public transport (Thomas and Bromley 1993).

More automobile ownership also allows the rising popularity of eating out, itself an outcome of improving incomes, to be exercised at greater distances from home. Preference rather than proximity becomes the major influence on where to dine. As the global phenomenon of Chinatown shows us, clustering is often an effective strategy for attracting customers to restaurants. Patrons from a wide hinterland are confident that the number of establishments more or less guarantees a table, even on busy nights. The congregation of restaurants also gives an exotic ambience to the consumer experience. Rusholme resembles Chinatown in this regard, with restaurant numbers increasing from seven to fifty-two between 1966 and 2002, of which forty-three are now South Asian. Since the others comprise one Chinese establishment and eight Middle Eastern restaurants, there is no reminder that you are dining in Britain. As the local newspaper expressed it, "Who needs abroad when you live in Manchester?" (Macdonald 1989).

WHY THE CURRY MILE GREW

Clearly the decline of traditional retailing left a gap in the property market that South Asian restaurants have been able to fill. But why did it happen in Rusholme? Manchester contains many other declining retail centers, with surplus properties abounding. Aldrich et al. (1989) showed that the normal pattern of South Asian business development in Britain is one of ecological succession, whereby an ethnic transition in the population of a neighborhood is accompanied by an ethnic transition in business ownership. As Rusholme's ethnic business transition began, however, it was not a South Asian residential area. The main population concentrations were in Longsight, a mile to the east; Whalley Range, two miles to the west; and Cheetham Hill, four miles north, on the other side of the city center.

Local Pakistani community sources suggest that South Asian business came to Rusholme as a result of the survival struggle of two local cinemas. In the 1960s, television was destroying the customer base of Britain's scattered suburban cinemas. In Rusholme the owners sought solvency by renting out their facilities on Sundays for the showing of South Asian "Bollywood" movies. In the late 1970s, the coming of the VCR put an end to this market, but in the meantime, South Asian moviegoers had been attracted to Rusholme in large numbers. This concentration of customers attracted entrepreneurs seeking to provide other culturally specific goods and services. Grocers selling spices, Asian vegetables, and other foodstuffs not yet available in mainstream retailers began to arrive; stores specializing in South Asian fashions and jewelry were established; the music of the subcontinent became available on disc and tape; and consumer services, such as travel agents specializing in flights to Asia, emerged. Restaurants too began to multiply to serve the flows of South Asian consumers. Pakistani entrepreneurs predominated simply because they were from the largest local South Asian community.

Once Rusholme's South Asian business cluster was established, it grew by processes of circular and cumulative causation. Every extra business made the area more attractive to potential patrons from a wider region beyond Manchester itself, especially the mill towns to the north and east of the city. In these places, sizeable South Asian communities had been recruited in the 1950s and 1960s by a cotton textile manufacturing industry struggling against overseas competition. These immigrants provided a workforce willing to work night shifts and accept wages that the native population started to see as unacceptable (Kalra 2000). When these potential patrons actually came to Rusholme, they made the locale more attractive to more South Asian enterprises.

This explanation of Rusholme's evolution is satisfactory for most of the South Asian firms present today, but it does not account for the number of restaurants. This is apparent when one strolls through Rusholme observing the ethnic mix of the clientele. The jewelry and clothing stores attract mainly South Asian customers, while most other retailers also mainly serve this group. Although some larger restaurants benefit from the South Asian wedding market and South Asian patronage generally increases at weekends, the majority of restaurant patrons are white. These observations confirm earlier business interviews (Annabel Jackson Associates 1994). Not a single restaurant was discovered where over forty percent of customers were Asian.[2] In retailing and other activities, many businesses served a clientele which was over ninety percent Asian (table 13.2).

A white customer base is not characteristic only of Rusholme. All large urban areas in Britain, most small towns, and many villages now have their Indian restaurants. Even in regions with few members of any ethnic minority, there is usually a pioneering South Asian business presence in the form of a restaurant (Barrett, Jones, and McEvoy 2001). During Rusholme's transformation, the British palate has changed: from being a nation of conservative diners, devoted to traditional dishes with an often-bland taste, the British have become devotees of culinary experiences marketed as exotic. "'Curry and chips' is said to have displaced 'fish and chips' as the nation's favourite dish" (Cook, Crang, and Thorpe 2000, 109). The most popular curry dish, chicken tikka masala, is an adaptation of Punjabi food for the British market rather than an importation of an authentic recipe (Cook, Crang, and Thorpe 2000, 129), but even this modified cuisine does not appeal to everyone. Gender, age, and other social variables mark differences in the propensity to try and adopt culinary innovations. Age is particularly important, with young adults experimenting with new foods earlier than older consumers. The young also eat South Asian and other imported menus more frequently than their elders (Jamal 1996).

Table 13.2.   Number of Businesses by Customer Ethnicity

	Asian Proportion of Customers					
	<10	10–20	20–40	40–60	60–80	>90
Restaurants	2	2	2	—	—	—
Retailers	—	2	3	1	6	5
Others	—	—	2	1	1	3
Total	2	4	7	2	7	8

Source: Annabel Jackson Associates (1994)

The younger market emerges as a key element of Rusholme's restaurant clientele. The area is very close to two large universities,[3] with a combined total of over 60,000 students, and to a major teaching hospital. The main campuses are alongside Wilmslow Road in the mile and a half north of Rusholme. Other academic buildings and student residences are scattered along the same axis to both north and south. Even in the 1960s, Manchester University and nearby colleges had over 10,000 students. The students and staff of these institutions provided a group of customers willing at first to try, and then to enthuse over, a cuisine which was both cheap and exotic. Today their successors continue to sustain the Curry Mile: trade falls markedly during vacation periods, for some restaurants by half. Even at the beginning of the study period in 1966, before the serious multiplication of South Asian restaurants began, Rusholme had more eating places than similar retail locations in Manchester.

Most of the foregoing could easily be taken for a success story, and on one level it is. A growing group of restaurants, more numerous than those in Manchester's celebrated Chinatown, cater to an average of 65,000 customers each week and employ about 850 people. So many restaurants in one location create considerable competitive pressure, and most businesses have to price their meals economically in order to retain their market share. This in turn makes it difficult to afford the rents charged by the six or seven major landlords, themselves members of the Pakistani community. Few restaurants own their own premises.

Competition, high rents, and limited profits exert heavy downward pressure on rates of pay to employees. The election of Tony Blair's "new" Labour government in 1997 led to the introduction of a national minimum hourly wage, which, unlike the equivalent U.S. legislation, applies to all restaurant work as fully as to other forms of employment. It is nevertheless believed locally that many kitchen and waiting staff in Rusholme are paid well below the legal minimum. This situation is possible because a number of the workers have no legal right to work in Britain. Some of these are in the country officially as students or as asylum seekers. Others have overstayed tourist visas, or they may simply have evaded immigration controls. In each case, employers are able to exploit their vulnerability with low pay, which puts pressure on the rates wholly legitimate workers and employers are able to negotiate.

THE CURRY MILE AND MANCHESTER'S URBAN RENAISSANCE

Peter Dicken (2002) has described Manchester's change from a global city in the nineteenth century to being a globalized city now. From being the "shock city" of the industrial revolution (Briggs 1963, 56) and "the first industrial city" (Hall 1998, 310–47), it has, in the second half of the twentieth century, endured deindustrialization and depopulation. In the last twenty years, there have been strenuous efforts to reverse these trends. A coalition of local government, a self-styled business "Manchester Mafia," and central government agencies has engaged in an often-successful program of grant applications, capital raising, and building regeneration, especially in and around the central business district. Setbacks have been taken as learning experiences. Thus an unsuccessful bid for the Olympic Games led to the holding of the 2002 Commonwealth Games, the world's second largest multisport event. Even the disaster of a very large Irish Republican Army bomb taking out the core of the city center's retailing in 1996 has been turned into a triumph of renewal (Cochrane, Peck, and Tickell 1996; Holden 2002; Mellor 1997; Quilley 2000; Williams 2003).

As a result of these endeavors, a whole range of recognized and newly imagined quarters is now vigorously promoted: Chinatown, the Gay Village, the Northern Quarter, Castlefield, the Millennium Quarter, Salford Quays, Sportcity, and Ancoats Urban Village/Little Italy. They comprise an east-west belt though the city center (figure 13.1) and fill brochures aimed at business and tourist visitors. Some of these quarters, especially the Gay Village, have received attention in a burgeoning academic literature. They figure prominently in the intellectual dissection of the local growth machine's "Manchester Script" (Brown, O'Connor, and Cohen 2000; Hughes 2002; Law 2000; Quilley 1997; Taylor 2000).

The Curry Mile has, in contrast, largely escaped both programmed investment and academic analysis, which leads to considerable local resentment at the perceived neglect of Rusholme. One source argued that the Curry Mile had grown in spite of the city council and in the virtual absence of enterprise support. On the other hand, one might argue that the incremental conversion of retail premises to restaurants over a thirty-year period is too slow and too small scale a process to attract public and private investment of the magnitude which has gone into prestige developments such as the Bridgewater (symphony) Hall, the City of Manchester Stadium, and the museums of the Castlefield area. It can also be argued that there has been some positive city council action in Rusholme, particularly in the areas of distinctive local street signs and traffic management along a busy main road. In addition, the city's planning department has, over the years, readily allowed "change of use" permission for the conversion of shops into eating places.

Moreover, the city council now recognizes that the Curry Mile stands alongside Chinatown, the Gay Village, and other city center cultural quarters as an important element in the city's tourist attractions. This was perhaps first signaled by the commissioning of the report on marketing and economic strategy for Wilmslow Road, Rusholme from Annabel Jackson Associates (1994). Now official websites and brochures trumpet the locality to visitors in language that leaves little room for doubt about Rusholme's virtues: "Journey through the flavours of the East along the Rusholme highway of gastronomic delights, direct from the Asian sub-continent and the Middle East. Savour the very best in cuisine bought to you by award winning, highly skilled chefs" (Manchester City Council 2003). If this is thought too modest, we are told that the Curry Mile is "thought to be the best spot in Britain and possibly even the world for an Indian meal" (Northwest Regional Development Agency 2002).

CONCLUSION

If Manchester now capitalizes upon its ethnic culinary resources, can other British cities do likewise? Henry, McEwan, and Pollard (2002) have already described how Birmingham is experiencing "globalization from below." Part of this process has been the emergence of the Balti Quarter, an inner city zone with many South Asian restaurants and which plausibly lays claim to the invention of an entirely new South Asian cuisine (Ram et al. 2002). Meanwhile Glasgow celebrates its victory in a competition to identify the "Curry Capital of Britain," much to the dismay of Bradford, a city with a much larger South Asian population (Hebden 2003). None of these rival cities matches Rusholme's geographical form, however. Restaurants elsewhere are scattered over wider areas rather than linearly concentrated in the manner of the Curry Mile. Other notable ribbons of South Asian business, such as Southall Broadway in west London and Belgrave Road in Leicester, have a stronger retail character than Rusholme, so the night time ambience of incorporation in an environment of otherness is weakened. Just as in the world's Chinatowns, the very close proximity of many restaurants is the distinctive character of the Rusholme model. Perhaps only Brick Lane, with over forty Bangladeshi restaurants adjacent to the City of London financial district, closely resembles the Curry Mile in both form and function (Carey 2004; Shaw, Bagwell, and Karmowski 2004).

Other communities are well aware of Rusholme's apparent success and may seek to emulate it. In Blackburn, a former textile town twenty-five miles north of Manchester, with over twenty percent of its population of South Asian origin, there are plans to develop an "Asian Gateway" modeled on the Curry Mile to attract visitors from across the county of Lancashire and further afield (Gill 2002). In seeking to emulate Rusholme, Blackburn may find that its Achilles' heel is the absence of a large student population. The historically fortuitous juxtaposition of a declining shopping district, a large student market, and a cluster of South Asian entrepreneurs may be difficult, not just for Blackburn but for most British cities, to replicate.

There are four possible market spaces open to South Asian businesses in Britain: local ethnic space, local non-ethnic space, ethnic non-local space, and non-local non-ethnic space (Barrett, Jones, and McEvoy 1996). The most common types of enterprise occupy the first two spaces. Local ethnic spaces include enterprises supported by neighborhood concentrations of co-ethnic clientele. In local non-ethnic space, South Asians perform the classic middleman minority role in catering to the needs of the majority population. Both these spaces are problematic, involving high personal labor inputs in return for unsatisfactory financial returns. In the ethnic case, limitations are imposed by the finite nature of markets, communities sharing poverty as well as culture, and by the ready supply of co-ethnic competition. In the non-ethnic case, the problems arise from the corporate threat to the characteristic endeavor, corner shop convenience retailing.

There are fewer difficulties for businesses operating in non-local space, whether ethnic or non-ethnic. Owners' hours of work are lower, and incomes and profits are better. "Breakout" from spatially and ethnically restricted markets has been achieved, together with a mental transition from a culturally constrained entrepreneurial mindset to a rational business outlook (Ram and Hillin 1994). In Rusholme, the two market spaces served seem to be these two more promising environments. On the one hand, clothing and jewelry retailers and specialist consumer services target a regional ethnic market. On the other hand, restaurants serve a predominantly non-ethnic market, which includes both whites and South Asians from beyond the locality. It nevertheless remains moot whether this constitutes a complete mental and business transition. The main products on offer rely for their authenticity on close connection to South Asian culture; the labor force is mainly co-ethnic and poorly paid; and relationships with lawyers, landlords, and other business actors often remain within the community. Perhaps a truly progressive breakout requires changes in these areas as well as in the acquisition of wider markets.

Despite occupying one of the favored niches in the theoretical framework of market spaces, the South Asian restaurants of Rusholme have not been depicted as constituting an unalloyed success. This may in part be a consequence of the competitive pressures in a growing agglomeration of similar businesses. Even in an expanding market, an overabundance of suppliers is likely to create survival difficulties for some, as the experience of nineteenth-century British railway companies and late twentieth-century U.S. information technology enterprises shows. As in most developed economies, restaurant meals have become a growing element of consumer expenditure in Britain, but much of this growth depends on keen pricing and therefore on restricted profitability. In both Rusholme and the Balti Quarter, customer expectation of low prices is a key problem for restaurateurs (Annabel Jackson Associates 1994; Ram et al. 2002).

In research on the ecological succession of businesses (Aldrich et al. 1989), new immigrant groups were depicted as occupying the rungs of the opportunity ladder that are no longer attractive to the indigenous population. The South Asian presence in low-order retailing in Britain fitted this explanation well. Just as immigrants had been recruited in the 1950s and 1960s to fill the unwanted jobs of the white British economy, so in the 1970s and 1980s South Asians occupied a residual entrepreneurial niche.

These earlier studies were based on relatively short-term change, over the period 1978 to 1984, in which it is possible to conceive of a relatively stable economic structure. This chapter has considered a much longer period over which a country thinking of itself as an economy based on the export of manufactured goods has had to recognize its postindustrial status. The multiplication of South Asian restaurants is a manifestation of this changing economy. Despite this innovative adaptation to changing circumstances, the ethnic restaurant sector in Rusholme and elsewhere is no permanent solution to the economic challenges facing South Asian communities. The skill levels it uses and the rewards it provides may be appropriate for immigrants with few qualifications, for the undocumented, or for students working their way through university. But the long-term aspirations of Britain's South Asians, especially of those born and educated in Britain, are unlikely be met by enterprises such as those on the Curry Mile (Barrett and McEvoy 2005).

NOTES

1. The table uses the general category "South Asian" rather than "Pakistani" because the data from earlier years was collected for other purposes and does not have sufficient specificity to do otherwise.

2. This source, in line with a common British practice, uses *Asian* to mean "South Asian." This custom derives from the numerical dominance of South Asian populations over other Asian groups in most British cities with a significant Asian population.

3. This remark treats the University of Manchester Institute of Science and Technology as part of Manchester University, although it was a totally independent institution from the late 1960s until a merger in progress at the time of writing.

REFERENCES

Aldrich, H., C. Zimmer, and D. McEvoy. 1989. Continuities in the study of ecological succession: Asian businesses in three English cities. *Social Forces* 67 (4): 920–44.

Annabel Jackson Associates. 1994. Marketing and economic development strategy for Wilmslow Road area of Rusholme. Report to Manchester City Council, Manchester.

Barrett, G. A., T. P. Jones, and D. McEvoy. 1996. Ethnic minority business: Theoretical discourse in Britain and North America. *Urban Studies* 33 (4–5): 783–809.

———. 2001. Socio-economic and policy dimensions of the mixed embeddedness of ethnic minority business in Britain. *Journal of Ethnic and Migration Studies* 27 (2): 241–58.

Barrett, G. A., and D. McEvoy. 2005. Not all can win prizes: Asians in the British labour market. In *Asian immigrants in European labour markets*, ed. T. van Naerssen, E. Spaan, and F. Hillman, 21-41. London: Routledge.

Brand, S. 1994. *How buildings learn: What happens after they're built.* New York: Viking.

Briggs, A. 1963. *Victorian cities.* London: Odhams Press.

Brown, A., J. O'Connor, and S. Cohen. 2000. Local music policies within a global music industry: Cultural quarters in Manchester and Sheffield. *Geoforum* 31 (4): 437–51.

Carey, S. 2004. *Curry capital: The restaurant sector in London's Brick Lane.* London: Institute of Community Studies.

Cochrane, A., J. Peck, and A. Tickell. 1996. Manchester plays games: Exploring the local politics of globalisation. *Urban Studies* 33 (8): 1319–36.

Conzen, M. R. G. 1960. *Alnwick, Northumberland: A study in town-plan analysis.* Publication no. 27. London: Institute of British Geographers.

Cook, I., P. Crang, and M. Thorpe. 2000. Regions to be cheerful: Culinary authenticity and its geographies. In *Cultural turns/geographical turns: Perspectives on cultural geography*, ed. I. Cook, D. Crouch, S. Naylor, and J. Ryan, 109–39. Harlow, England: Prentice-Hall.

Dicken, P. 2002. Global Manchester: From globaliser to globalised. In *City of revolution: Restructuring Manchester*, ed. J. Peck and K. Ward, 18–33. Manchester: Manchester University Press.

Gill, S. 2002. Blackburn ready to taste success: Multi-million pound curry quick fix. *Eastern Eye*, 20 September.

Hall, P. 1998. *Cities in civilization: Culture, innovation and social order.* London: Weidenfeld and Nicolson.

Hebden, A. 2003. Council let curry award go cold. *Telegraph & Argus*, 18 June. www.thisisbradford.co.uk/bradford_district/archive/2003/06/18/brad_news01.int .html (accessed 9 September 2003).

Henry, N., C. McEwan, and J. S. Pollard. 2002. Globalization from below: Birmingham—postcolonial workshop of the world? *Area* 34 (2): 117–27.

Holden, A. 2002. Bomb sites: The politics of opportunity. In *City of revolution: Restructuring Manchester*, ed. J. Peck and K. Ward, 133–54. Manchester: Manchester University Press.

Hughes, H. L. 2002. Marketing gay tourism in Manchester: New market for urban tourism or destruction of "gay space"? *Journal of Vacation Marketing* 9 (2): 152–63.

Jamal, A. 1996. Acculturation: The symbolism of ethnic eating among contemporary British consumers. *British Food Journal* 98 (10): 12–26.

Jones, T. P., D. McEvoy, and G. A. Barrett. 1994. Labour intensive practices in the ethnic minority firm. In *Employment, the small firm and the labour market*, ed. J. Atkinson and D. Storey, 172–205. London: Routledge.

Kalra, V. S. 2000. *From textile mills to taxi ranks: Experiences of migration, labour and social change*. Aldershot: Ashgate.

Law, C. M. 2000. Regenerating the city centre through leisure and tourism. *Built Environment* 26 (2): 117–29.

Macdonald, K. 1989. Into the melting pot. *Manchester Evening News*, 9 January.

Manchester City Council. 2003. Unique areas of the city. www.manchester.gov.uk/visitorcentre/areas.htm (accessed 7 July 2003).

McEvoy, D. 1968. Alternative methods of ranking shopping centres: A study from the Manchester conurbation. *Tijdschrift voor Economische en Sociale Geografie* 59 (4): 211–17.

McGoldrick, P. J. 1990. *Retail marketing*. London: McGraw-Hill.

Mellor, R. 1997. Cool times for a changing city. In *Transforming cities: Contested governance and new spatial divisions*, ed. N. Jewson and S. McGregor, 56–69. London: Routledge.

Northwest Regional Development Agency. 2002. *A guide to Manchester and England's Northwest*. London: Rough Guides.

Office of National Statistics. 2003. Motor cars currently licensed and new registrations, Department for Transport and Department of the Environment, Northern Ireland. www.statistics.gov.uk/Expodata/Spreadsheets/D6033.xls (accessed 20 November 2003).

Quilley, S.1997. Constructing Manchester's "new urban village": Gay space in the entrepreneurial city. In *Queers in space: Communities/public places/sites of resistance*, ed. G. B. Ingram, A. Bouthillette, and Y. Ritter, 275–92. Seattle: Bay Press.

———. 2000. Manchester first: From municipal socialism to the entrepreneurial city. *International Journal of Urban and Regional Research* 24 (3): 601–15.

Ram, M., and G. Hillin. 1994. Achieving "break-out": Developing mainstream ethnic minority business. *Small Business Enterprise and Development* 1 (1): 15–21.

Ram, M., T. Jones, T. Abbas, and B. Sanghera. 2002. Ethnic minority enterprise in its urban context: South Asian restaurants in Birmingham. *International Journal of Urban and Regional Research* 26 (1): 24–40.

Shaw, S., S. Bagwell, and J. Karmowski. 2004. Reimaging multicultural districts for leisure and tourism consumption. *Urban Studies* 41 (10): 1983–2000.

Taylor, I. 2000. European ethnoscapes and urban redevelopment: The return of Little Italy in 21st century Manchester. *City* 4 (1): 27–42.

Thomas, C. J., and R. D. F. Bromley. 1993. The impact of out-of-centre retailing. In *Retail change: Contemporary issues*, ed. R. D. F. Bromley and C. J. Thomas, 126–52. London: UCL Press.

Williams, G. 2003. *The enterprising city centre: Manchester's development challenge*. London: Spon Press.

Index

AAPI. *See* Asian American Pacific
  Islanders
African American neighborhoods, 69,
  71, 73, 79, 151
African American owned businesses,
  23, 67–79, 113; banks, 123;
  characteristics of, 70–71; and
  institutional racism, 68, 76, 79;
  neighborhood characteristics of, 67,
  73–74, 79; police protection of,
  76–77; racial dynamics of, 68. *See
  also* Black owned businesses
African Americans, 20, 67–79; and
  access to capital, 67; as customers,
  27; entrepreneurship of, 67–79, 152
  (*see also* Black owned businesses);
  rates of business ownership of, 67,
  79; unemployment of, 69
agglomeration of ethnic businesses, 8,
  28–29, 93, 156, 185, 198, 203. *See
  also* spatial concentration
Alien Land Laws, 119, 181
"alien space," 173
Annabel Jackson Associates, 202
API. *See* Asian and Pacific Islanders
apparel, retail, 23, 88, 89, 137, 141,
  143, 154, 169, 197, 199, 203
Asian American business ownership:
  characteristics of, 90–91, 113;

lending circles and, 113, 119; and
  reliance on formal financial
  institutions, 113. *See also under
  specific ethnic groups*
Asian American Pacific Islanders
  (AAPI), 186
Asian American political movements,
  183
Asian and Pacific Islanders (API), 113,
  114
Asian immigration: to Australia,
  135–36, 143; to Canada, 85–86, 88;
  to Italy, 165; to the United Kingdom,
  193–94, 198; to United States, 17,
  20, 113, 120–21, 123, 180–81. *See
  also specific ethnic groups*
Asiatown, Sydney, 135, 142–45; crime
  in, 145; local government promotion
  of, 144–45; multiethnic nature of,
  143–44; as tourist destination,
  145
ATI, as successful immigrant
  manufacturing business, 92
Auburn, as Arab suburb, 138
Australia, immigration to. *See* Sydney
automobile traffic: as crime deterrent,
  69; as factor in ethnic business
  success, 7, 27, 29, 195, 197
Azores, Portugal, 51, 57

209

About the Contributors

Hyeon-Hyo (Harry) Ahn is currently assistant professor at the Department of Social Studies, Daegu University, Daegu, South Korea. He has published several articles on the dynamics of capitalist economies and the financial aspects of modern capitalism.

Christopher Airriess is professor of geography at Ball State University, Muncie, Indiana. Dr. Airriess earned a Ph.D. from the University of Kentucky in 1989. His research interests include cultural landscapes, ethnicity, development, and maritime ports in East and Southeast Asia. His research articles have appeared in *Journal of Historical Geography*, *Geoforum*, *Tijdschrift voor Economische en Sociale Geografie*, and *Geographical Review*. Dr. Airriess is the recipient of two Fulbright awards that allowed year-long research stays in Indonesia in 1987 and Hong Kong in 2000, and he is currently working on National Science Foundation funded research on the impact of Hurricane Katrina.

Heike Alberts is assistant professor of geography at the University of Wisconsin-Oshkosh. Her research interests focus on international migration and the adaptation of immigrants to their host societies, in particular the United States and Western Europe. Dr. Alberts's recent projects include a study of the Cuban enclave economy in Miami and the migration patterns of international students and scholars to the United States.

Carolyn Aldana is professor of economics and assistant dean of the College of Social and Behavioral Sciences at California State University, San Bernardino. Her current research interests include examinations of the contributions of ethnic banks to local community and economic development, and issues related to wealth creation for people of color.

Giles A. Barrett is senior lecturer in human geography at Liverpool John Moores University. Dr. Barrett was the British partner in the EU Fourth Framework Targeted Socio-economic Research network *"Working on the Fringes,"* and he is the founder of the Base Line research consultancy at Liverpool John Moores University. His publications include papers in *Urban Studies, Journal of Ethnic and Migration Studies, International Journal of Entrepreneurial Behaviour and Research,* and several edited volumes.

Maria W. L. Chee is currently a member of the administrative faculty in the Office of the Provost at the University of Virginia. She received her doctorate in sociocultural anthropology from the University of California, Riverside, in 2003 and was awarded a Fulbright grant for her dissertation fieldwork. Her research interests lie in migration, transnationalism, political economy, Asian diaspora, and the Pacific Rim. Dr. Chee is the author of *Taiwanese American Transnational Families: Women and Kin Work.*

Jock Collins is professor of economics at the University of Technology, Sydney (UTS). He has been researching and writing about Australian immigration and cultural diversity for thirty years and is the author or co-author of nine books and numerous journal articles and book chapters. His latest book, *Bin Laden in the Suburbs: The Criminalisation of the Arabic Other* (with Scott Poynting, Greg Nobel, and Paul Tabar), was published in 2004. Dr. Collins's work has been translated into French, Japanese, Italian, Chinese, and Arabic.

Gary Dymski is director of the University of California Center Sacramento and on leave as professor of economics at the University of California, Riverside. He is the author of *The Bank Merger Wave* and four co-edited volumes. He has published many articles and chapters on banking, financial fragility, urban development, credit-market discrimination, the Latin American and Asian financial crises, economic exploitation, and housing finance.

Felicitas Hillmann is senior lecturer *(Privatdozent)* at the Free University, Berlin. Her academic interests are in the fields of social geography and development research. For some years her research has focused on migration and gender, ethnic economies, and the labor market insertion of immigrants.

Bessie House-Soremekun is associate professor of political science at Kent State University. Dr. House-Soremekun serves as executive director and founder of the Center for the Study and Development of Minority Businesses at Kent State University and director of the Entrepreneurial Academy in the Empowerment Zone of the city of Cleveland. Dr. House-Soremekun has written four books, numerous scholarly articles, and book chapters. She is the author of *Confronting the Odds: African American Entrepreneurship in Cleveland, Ohio*, which received the Henry Howe Book Award.

David H. Kaplan is professor of geography at Kent State University. He received his Ph.D. from the University of Wisconsin at Madison, and his B.A. from The Johns Hopkins University. Dr. Kaplan has published articles in a wide variety of academic journals and has five books out: *Segregation in Cities*, *Nested Identities*, *Boundaries and Place*, *Urban Geography*, and *Perthes World Atlas*. Dr. Kaplan's urban-related research interests include ethnic and racial segregation, urban and regional development, and housing and transportation.

Wei Li is associate professor in the Asian Pacific American Studies Program and the Department of Geography at Arizona State University. She received her Ph.D. in geography at the University of Southern California in 1997. Her research foci are urban ethnicity and ethnic geography, immigration and integration, and financial sector and minority community development. Her scholarly articles have appeared in *Annals of the Association of American Geographers*, *Environment and Planning A*, *Geographical Review*, *Urban Studies*, *Urban Geography*, *Social Science Research*, and *Journal of Asian American Studies*. She has three books forthcoming on suburban Asian communities and ethnic economy. Dr. Li has served as a member of the U.S. Census Bureau's Race and Ethnic Advisory Committees (Asian Population) since 2003.

Lucia Lo received her B.A. and M.A. from McMaster University, and her Ph.D. from the University of Toronto. She is currently associate professor of geography at York University and leader of the Economics Domain of the Joint Toronto Centre of Excellence for Research on Immigration and Settlement (CERIS). Dr. Lo's research spans several areas, including transportation modeling, consumer behavior, migration, and immigrants. She has researched extensively on the social and economic particulars of Chinese immigrants in Toronto, covering residential patterns, labor market performance, businesses and entrepreneurship, and consumer behavior.

David McEvoy is visiting professor of ethnic entrepreneurship at the School of Management at the University of Bradford. From 1991 to 1998 he was director of the School of Social Science at Liverpool John Moores University, where he has since been emeritus professor of urban geography. Dr. McEvoy's research on ethnic minority business in Britain and Canada stretches over thirty years and has been funded by numerous agencies. Dr. McEvoy has published extensively in books and academic journals.

Pierpaolo Mudu received his Ph.D. in geography at the University La Sapienza of Rome Italy in 2000. He collaborates with the "Interdepartmental Centre for Studies on the Population and Society of Rome" of the University of Rome. He has been lecturing at the University of Reading (UK). Dr. Mudu's research interests include ethnic geography, immigration, focusing on the Chinese and other Asian groups in Italy and Rome, social movements, and social networks. His scholarly articles have appeared in *Antipode*, *GeoJournal,* and *Urban Geography.*

Alex Oberle received his Ph.D. in geography from Arizona State University in 2005 and is currently assistant professor in the Department of Geography at the University of Northern Iowa. His research interests include ethnic geography, Latino urban settlement, and Hispanic entrepreneurship. While much of his research has focused on Phoenix, he is embarking on studies in metropolitan areas in the Midwest. Dr. Oberle's scholarly articles have appeared in such journals as *The Professional Geographer* and *Journal of Geography.*

James M. Smith received his Ph.D. from Kent State University and is currently assistant professor at Towson University in Maryland. A native of Baltimore, Dr. Smith has interests in urban social geography, globalization, and identities. His dissertation focused on Japanese American identities in Los Angeles, and he is currently conducting research on Asian migration to the Mid-Atlantic region, using both qualitative and statistical analysis.

Carlos Teixeira is assistant professor at the University of British Columbia Okanagan, Canada. He received his B.Sc and M.Sc at the Université du Quebec and his Ph.D. in geography at York University. Dr. Teixeira's research interests include urban and social geography, with an emphasis on migration processes, community formation, housing and neighborhood change, ethnic entrepreneurship, and the social structure of Canadian and American cities. Dr. Teixeira has authored two books, numerous book chapters, and articles in journals such as *Urban Studies*, *Urban Geography*, and *The Professional Geographer*. He recently received the Order of Portugal for his work on the Portuguese communities of the diaspora.

Yu Zhou is associate professor in the Department of Geology and Geography, Vassar College. She has done research in the areas of ethnic business, gender and ethnic communities, and transnational business networks. Her recent research is on globalization, firm networks, and competition in the high-tech sectors in China.